WRITING IN THE CLOUDS

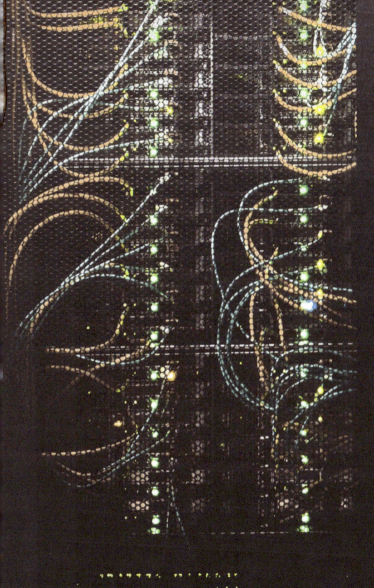

Lauer Series in Rhetoric and Composition
Editors: Thomas Rickert and Jennifer Bay

The Lauer Series in Rhetoric and Composition honors the contributions Janice Lauer has made to the emergence of Rhetoric and Composition as a disciplinary study. It publishes scholarship that carries on Professor Lauer's varied work in the history of written rhetoric, disciplinarity in composition studies, contemporary pedagogical theory, and written literacy theory and research.

Selected Books in the Series

Feminist Circulations: Rhetorical Explorations across Space and Time (Enoch, Griffin, & Nelson, 2021)

Creole Composition: Academic Writing and Rhetoric in the Anglophone Caribbean (Milson-Whyte, Oenbring, & Jaquette, 2019). MLA Mina P. Shaughnessy Prize 2019-2020, CCCC Best Book Award 2021.

Retellings: Opportunities for Feminist Research in Rhetoric and Composition Studies (Enoch & Jack, 2019)

Facing the Sky: Composing through Trauma in Word and Image (Fox, 2016)

First-Year Composition: From Theory to Practice (Coxwell-Teague & Lunsford, 2014)

Contingency, Immanence, and the Subject of Rhetoric (Richardson, 2013)

Rewriting Success in Rhetoric & Composition Careers (Goodburn, et al., 2012)

Writing a Progressive Past: Women Teaching and Writing in the Progressive Era (Mastrangelo, 2012)

Greek Rhetoric Before Aristotle, 2e, Rev. and Exp. Ed. (Enos, 2012)

Rhetoric's Earthly Realm: Heidegger, Sophistry, and the Gorgian Kairos (Miller) *Winner of the Olson Award for Best Book in Rhetorical Theory 2011

Techne, from Neoclassicism to Postmodernism: Understanding Writing as a Useful, Teachable Art (Pender, 2011)

Walking and Talking Feminist Rhetorics: Landmark Essays and Controversies (Buchanan & Ryan, 2010)

Transforming English Studies: New Voices in an Emerging Genre (Ostergaard, Ludwig, & Nugent, 2009)

Ancient Non-Greek Rhetorics (Lipson & Binkley, 2009)

Roman Rhetoric: Revolution and the Greek Influence, Rev. and Exp Ed. (Enos, 2008)

Stories of Mentoring: Theory and Praxis (Eble & Gaillet, 2008)

Networked Process: Dissolving Boundaries of Process and Post-Process (Foster, 2007)

Composing a Community: A History of Writing Across the Curriculum (McLeod & Soven, 2006)

Historical Studies of Writing Program Administration: Individuals, Communities, and the Formation of a Discipline (L'Eplattenier & Mastrangelo, 2004). Winner of the WPA Best Book Award for 2004–2005

Rhetorics, Poetics, and Cultures: Refiguring College English Studies Exp. Ed. (Berlin, 2003)

WRITING IN THE CLOUDS

INVENTING AND COMPOSING IN INTERNETWORKED WRITING SPACES

John Logie

Parlor Press
Anderson, South Carolina
www.parlorpress.com

Parlor Press LLC, Anderson, South Carolina, USA
© 2022 by Parlor Press
Printed in the United States of America on acid-free paper.

SAN: 254-8879

Library of Congress Cataloging-in-Publication Data on File

978-1-64317-293-4 (paperback)
978-1-64317-294-1 (pdf)
978-1-64317-295-8 (epub)

1 2 3 4 5

Cover image:
Book Design: David Blakesley
Copyediting by Jared Jameson

Parlor Press, LLC is an independent publisher of scholarly and trade titles in print
and multimedia formats. This book is available in paper and ebook formats from
Parlor Press on the World Wide Web at https://parlorpress.com or through online
and brick-and-mortar bookstores. For submission information or to find out
about Parlor Press publications, write to Parlor Press, 3015 Brackenberry Drive,
Anderson, South Carolina, 29621, or email editor@parlorpress.com.

Contents

List of Illustrations

Additional images appearing throughout the book

Dedicated with love to my dear daughters, Nora and Shane, who have challenged me to keep up with their own understandings of the world I describe in these pages and who have made me laugh as they did so.

Acknowledgments

First, I must acknowledge Janice Lauer Rice, a scholar, leader, and exemplar for scholars of rhetoric and its cognate fields. Professor Lauer is rightly celebrated for her work as a founding member of the Rhetoric Society of America, her founding of the English, Rhetoric, and Composition program at Purdue university, and—of special significance to me—as a scholar who delighted in questions of rhetorical invention. When she died in April, 2021, I was deep in revisions for this project, knowing it was scheduled for the Janice Lauer series in Rhetoric and Composition. I am so proud that this book will, in its small way, contribute to Professor Lauer's reverberating legacy.

My thanks are also due to the scholars who have contributed to the reviewing, editing, and preparation of this book. I am appreciative to my reviewers, who contributed greatly to helping this project find its final form. Beyond the helpful advice that necessarily arrived from behind the veil of anonymity, reviewers included my Lauer Series editors, Jennifer Bay and Thomas Rickert—whose constructive comments were insightful, helpful, and sometimes hilarious—and Parlor Press publisher David Blakesley. I wish to underscore that Parlor Press remains the most flexible and adventurous space I have ever found for my academic writing. I often approach publishers with requests for images, color, unusual typefaces, non-traditional licenses . . . in short, my work has made some of my projects *complicated*. I have learned, over time, that Parlor is ready to take on these kinds of challenges for me and for others working in rhetoric and its partner fields. I am so grateful for Parlor's presence within my scholarly community.

I also received strong support while developing this project from my colleagues at the University of Minnesota. My Chair, Lee-Ann Breuch has offered insightful and helpful advice throughout my development of this project. Professor Emerita Mary Lay Schuster deserves special thanks for her advice, support, and for her tremendous example as a scholar and colleague. The University of Minnesota's College of Liberal Arts offered substantial support in the form of an Imagine Fund grant which allowed me to get hands-on with two different smartphone platforms simultaneously, and also a Fall, 2020 sabbatical that proved incredibly timely when COVID-19 pushed this project back from its intended completion date of spring of that year. Additionally, this project took its first steps under the auspices of the Rhetoric Society of America's Career Retreat for Associate Professors, led by Cheryl Geisler. I exchanged early drafts with Charlotte Hogg and Marsha

Lee Baker and our esteemed mentor, Patricia Roberts-Miller. I am grateful for their critiques and support.

I now conclude this project with renewed gratitude for all the family members who have modeled delight in words and wordplay for so many years. From my mother, Susan, and her Duerr family members, I have absorbed a fascination with words, books, and the multifarious pathways of linguistic play. I witnessed my grandfather composing fiendish acrostic crossword puzzles and facing off in a never-ending game of Boggle with my grandmother, who was every bit his match. My Duerr aunts and uncles include a now-retired bookstore owner, an uncrowned pun champion, and the four siblings together are all among the greatest correspondents I could hope to know. My father, who died from the consequences of Alzheimer's in the fall of 2021, lived most of his life taking joy from the power of words in his roles as an attorney and mayor. *His* mother, Queenie, who I never knew, was a formidable book collector who ran ahead of the crowd in her preferences. I am grateful to my Aunt Shane for offering a window into my grandmother's appreciation for the writers of her moment. I also appreciate the ways sisters, Susannah and Maggie, and their children, carry forward the family's knack for startling and delightful turns of phrase.

Finally, I wish to offer grateful acknowledgement to the members of my immediate family. In my experience, even under the best of circumstances, book-length projects depend on the patience and forbearance of family members. The final stages of this project unfolded in what were, emphatically, *not* the best of circumstances, owing to the COVID-19 pandemic of 2020–2021. My wife, Carol, and my daughters, Nora and Shane, were called upon in many ways as we adapted ourselves to a collectively shared home/writing space. Notably, this involved family members serially helping me haul my cherished writing desk — decoupaged by Carol with John Tenniel's gorgeous illustrated pages from *Alice in Wonderland* — to each of the three floors of our home as our collective needs for space and solitude changed. I thank them for literally and figuratively lifting me up throughout these challenging months. I also wish to express my appreciation to our pandemic puppy, Daisy Mae Potato, for being, all things considered, a very good dog and for *eventually* taking long enough naps to allow me to gather myself for the final push.

Introduction: The More Things Change . . .

This project has been a part of my life for the better part of a decade. For years now, I have been weighing the impact of internetworked digital tools on processes and perceptions of writing. I was born in 1965, making me (barely) older than the Internet and older than computers that remotely resemble the tools that have become central to the act of writing in the twenty-first century. And while *Writing in the Clouds* is directed at understanding many of the observable shifts in the invention and composition of written texts over the past dozen years, this project will often argue (spoiler alert) for the remarkable persistence of print-based practices in our current communication ecologies.

My purpose in these arguments was never to suggest that these practices would endure for all time. Rather, it was to contribute to a body of scholarship that points out the degree to which shifts in writing practices tend to *supplement* existing practices rather than *supplant* them. The transformations within my lifetime have been profound, but the shifts in any given decade of my life have often *felt* incremental. With the possible exception of browser-based access to the World Wide Web, none of the shifts in writing and writing-related technologies that arrived with attendant claims that a revolution was at hand could withstand strict scrutiny. Thus, this project, has endeavored to make measured assessments about our technological, cultural, and communicative ecologies and, further, to offer reasonable conclusions about where we might find ourselves in the coming years.

That said, the project as initially conceived did not take into account the possibility and implications of the COVID-19-driven global pandemic that has dominated every element of daily life in 2020 and 2021. While much of this project was composed prior to the pandemic, the deep work of determining the final shape of the project unfolded throughout 2020, and elements of the ways these chapters were revised for final submission respond to the experience of that awful year.

As I finalize this introduction, the world is still taking stock of dramatic cultural changes developed in response to the threat presented by COVID-19. Two of these changes feel especially significant for the arguments that follow. First, in a United States context, many more people are now working from home than ever before. Second, education in many locales has moved more online than ever before. In both cases, we can infer that these practical changes in the physical circumstances of work and schooling have prompted significant investments (where people can still afford to make them) in both the hardware and the bandwidth needed to facilitate these activities. I suspect this investment in hardware and bandwidth has accelerated the adoption of internetworked digital tools—tools based in the clouds that give this book its title—and not merely for the Zoom meetings that increasingly fill the days of knowledge workers and students.

At root, *everything* that happens within an internetworked computer can be reasonably understood as a form of writing. If, as we are routinely reminded, the core of the computer's activities is encoding and decoding of data into binary code, those zeros and ones represent texts that are Banks written and read . . . just not by humans. To this foundational layer of heavily automated code writing, we can add all the writing that found a home within internetworked digital tools and also the novel genres of writing facilitated by these tools, like SMS text messaging and tweets.

The accelerated investment in hardware and bandwidth, initially driven by a desire to hold meetings of various kinds, has the potential to significantly expand the pool of people who are now able to experience collective and collaborative writing in real time. Indeed, many children will now learn how to write in spaces where the possibility of composing collaboratively across distance is a baseline feature of the tools on which they learn the basics of writing. This, I suspect, will be a difference that will make a difference in what it means to write going forward.

As I argue throughout this text, one of the most significant characteristics of the technologies of this moment is the degree to which they facilitate collaborative writing. While much of this writing might be considered ephemeral or low stakes, the habits and practices that are implicitly taught by way of these interactions are likely to have a profound impact on how we understand writing, invention, composing, and authorship.

In the following pages, I offer a series of thematically-linked essays reflecting my understanding of the cloud-based writing practices of this moment and the ways these practices build upon and break with the writing practices of our shared pasts. I'll offer brief guides to the goals of each chapter here.

Chapter 1, "We Are Not Alone," is directed at surfacing the point at which changes in writing technology began to illuminate the degree to which the figure of the solitary author represents individual preferences and choices, rather than a baseline account of "what it takes" to be a "real author." This chapter positions the typewriter as representing a technology-driven interruption of a larger history of socially connected modes of writing.

Chapter 2, "What We Wrote About When We Wrote About Writing in the 1990s," honors the achievements of some of the "big books about writing" that worked to address how writing worked and how writing felt in the immediate wake of the widespread adoption of digital writing tools. Especially notable among these were Jay Bolter's *Writing Space: The Computer, Hypertext, and the History of Writing*, Christina Haas's *Writing Technology: Studies in the Materiality of Literacy*, and James E. Porter's *Rhetorical Ethics and Internetworked Writing*. Each of these books function as a sometimes-prescient time capsule, and I'll risk acknowledging that my aspirations for this project include that it might someday be thought of in a similar way.

Chapter 3, "Clouds, Composers, and Collaboration," begins by tracing the history of the spaces we now know, collectively, as "the cloud." It resituates cloud spaces as very physical spaces constructed of cables and servers that nevertheless facilitate very virtual modes of writing. The chapter closes with a discussion of meme compositions as an emblematic genre of writing in cloud-based spaces.

Chapter 4, "Arranging Invention: The Rise of the Second Rhetorical Canon in Internetworked Writing," is my contribution to a collective acknowledgment by scholars of rrhetoric and writing that the traditional understanding of the canons of rhetoric must be adapted to respond to the specifics of internetworked digital writing. This chapter offers remix composition strategies as a way of illustrating the canon of arrangement occupying spaces and roles historically assigned to the canon of invention.

Chapter 5, "Looking Back at PureText: The 'Black and White' Writing of Our Past," addresses the degree to which the presence or absence of color within pages reflects larger cultural understandings about the appropriate look and feel for "serious" writing. Cloud-based composing spaces routinely use color to orient composers to their interfaces and offer composers robust choices with respect to how and whether to use color as an element in their compositions. This will inevitably distinguish the look and feel of twenty-first-century writing from its print predecessors.

Chapter 6, "The Android and 'i': The Politics of Twenty-First-Century Writing Interfaces," traces the historical development of smartphone and tablet interfaces with an eye towards understanding what internetworked composing spaces might look and feel like after the desktop iteration of the graphical user interface recedes from view. This chapter also addresses two cultural phenomena informing interface design: *dealphabetization* and *iconification*.

Chapter 7, "On 'Surrender to the Digital Revolution': Nostalgic Rhetorics and *The New York Times*," addresses the apparent bias of the *New York Times* against ebooks and internetworked media within its editorial and news pages. The recurring dismissal of cloud-based technologies within the *Times* is notable because the *Times* has a special role as arbiter of cultural value with respect to books and literary culture. Additionally, the *Times*'s bias is at odds with it own standing as a leader in sophisticated multimedia journalism. This chapter works to understand how the *Times* simultaneously occupies suffocatingly traditionalist *and* leading-edge roles in relation to internetworked media.

Chapter 8, "Keywords for Writing in the Clouds," offers a visual and textual guide to ten especially significant words, and their associated concepts, that circulate throughout *Writing in the Clouds*. Taken together, these keywords function as a shortlist for those who wish to compose effectively in internetworked writing spaces.

My conclusion, "Clouds, From Both Sides Now," offers an alternative to the evolution/revolution framing that has sometimes misrepresented the practical realities and lived experiences of writers as they respond to times of substantial technological change. My afterword, "The End of 'Viral' Writing" speaks to my hope that we are ready to turn away from the "viral" as a descriptor for the kinds of highly connective writing we compose and consume within cloud spaces. Taken together, these chapters and subsections speak to the experience of working to understand writing in a moment of profound change, one which for me recalls the initial turn from the digital (and sometimes networked) writing spaces of the 1990s to the internetworked writing spaces that pointed us toward the clouds.

When, in the Spring of 1993, the Mosaic browser barreled through the then overwhelmingly academic Internet, it was immediately clear to those who used it that the browser was about to transform the experience of the Internet in ways that would open it to a much broader public. To the degree that 2020's challenges prompted a massive investment in technologies that facilitate collective communication and writing, it may yet prove to be similarly transformative. This is not to minimize the pain of living through these times, or to suggest that the possibilities now opening in any way counterbalance the profound losses of the pandemic. Rather, it is to encourage readers and composers to embrace the possibilities of the moment, and to explore these possibilities with a renewed sense of the value and importance of communication. When communities and cultures face profound challenges, finding a productive path forward usually depends on people using communicative tools to connect, to work together, and, ultimately, to draw closer together.

It is in this spirit that I offer *Writing in the Clouds*, in the profound hope that the tools and techniques I explore in these pages will eventually be understood as part of what connected us, reinforced our humanity, and helped us meet the challenges of this moment.

1 We Are Not Alone (or Why We Turned Toward the Clouds)

Writing is a lonely job. Even if a writer socializes regularly, when he gets down to the real business of his life, it is he and his typewriter or word processor. No one else is or can be involved in the matter.

—Isaac Asimov, *I. Asimov: A Memoir*
(written circa 1990)

With Google Drive, you can now access your files from wherever you are . . . even the big ones. Whichever program you're using, just drag and drop, and there are all your files ready to be opened by you, and shared with anyone you want. Forget files being too big to e-mail. Just share them with Drive and everyone has the same file, automatically, that they can edit together, from anywhere. Now all your stuff, work or play is in one place, easy to find, and easy to share. **Google Drive: Keep Everything. Share Anything.**

—Go Google: Google Drive (Google)
(uploaded to YouTube April 24, 2012)

In July of 2012, something strange happened that—I now realize—transformed how I understood my relationship with computers as writing tools. In that month, Apple Computer released its latest iteration of its operating system for desktop and laptop computers, formally known by the clumsy name "OS X 10.8," but more generally known by its marketing name: "Mountain Lion." While this update incorporated many changes large and small to my day-to-day interactions with my Apple devices, the one that surprised me most was the presence of a new Notes application in the dock housing all my favorite applications at the bottom of my MacBook's screen.

The icon for this application looked very much like the icon for the Notes app that I had grown fond of on my iPhone. My grocery lists ended up there, as did to-do lists that were not organized enough for my calendar applications. Occasionally, I would use my smartphone to take notes at talks by fellow academics, thereby earning furrowed brows from others in the audience who assumed I was texting or—worse—playing *Words with Friends*. Having become habituated to using the Notes app on my phone, I was intrigued to see a parallel application on my laptop, though I wondered why this would function any better than a word processor document or a brief e-mail to myself.

Then I opened the application.

All the notes I had taken on multiple iPhones over about the past three years were there, waiting for me: the grocery lists, the to-do lists (some unfinished), and the notes from the talks I had attended. For the moment I had typed these messages, they had been stored in a "cloud." Apple had pre-emptively stored and saved these messages not only on my hardware, but on *their* servers.

This, of course, is no longer a novel experience. Some readers may now be impatiently wondering whether I was also surprised (or could yet be surprised) to learn that my Gmail account also produces information stored on servers that we colloquially refer to as "the cloud." So, yes, I have been aware for years, that some portion of my work was stored not only locally, but also elsewhere in the areas formerly known as cyberspace. That wasn't what surprised me about the Notes app.

What surprised me was that I was—by default—writing in the clouds *without* ever formally having made the decision to do so. The iPhone app announced itself as little more than a tidy little onboard repository for information, calibrated to the space of the smartphone as a piece of hardware. Indeed, the app's look and feel were carefully managed to visually suggest a standard small yellow ruled "legal pad."

Figure 1.1: The skeumorphic design aesthetic of Apple's virtual and cloud-based Notes apps, Apple Computer, 2012.

The default typeface for the app was "Marker Felt," which—as its name suggests—looks like human handwriting executed with a Sharpie. Indeed, the degree to which Apple's skeumorphic design ethic prompted them to—for example—mimic the specifics of a legal pad right down to "torn" pages at the top of the pad prompted ridicule from design experts, including this outburst from information architect Oliver Reichenstein:

> What sells is sentimentalism, nostalgia, solemnity—what sells is kitsch. That's why kitsch can be so cheap. Because it sells so well. That is true for any kind of design. And this is why iCal has this f**king leather surface that makes any user interface designer puke wet feverish dogs. (qtd. in Hachman)

But no matter how hard Apple tried to visually persuade its users that they were just writing on a legal pad much as they always had, something else altogether was occurring.

The "pad" lived in the cloud.

With other cloud-based applications, I had always felt a moment of decision. Do I wish to have access to my whole music library via iTunes in iCloud? Do I wish to store some of my files on DropBox's servers? Do I see benefit in the potential to share work and comments via Google Docs or Google Drive? All these decisions involved me taking formal steps to establish presence in cloud-based server spaces.

But with Apple's Notes application, I had been quietly writing in the cloud all along. Increasingly, this is the "default setting" for most of the digital tools used to compose texts. The Notes application surprised me by throwing a spotlight on just how much of the work within my digital tools no longer resided only on my hard drives and flash drives. Most of what I write now lives both within and outside my hardware, by default. And, by and large, I am content with the benefits I receive from working both within and outside my digital tools.

But this is more than a matter of convenience. This is a shift in many practices of writing and in what it means to write. "The Cloud" has been an increasingly present metaphoric descriptor for the aggregation of wires and wifi that allow writers to experience what feels like real-time composition on a device's screen while actually composing in an array of servers residing far from the site of composition. Public consciousness of this metaphor on a reasonably broad scale can be traced back to 2007, with one especially notable marker being a pair of articles titled "Why Can't We Compute in the Cloud" by John Markoff in the Bits section of *The New York Times*. In the first of the two articles, Markoff concludes, "[n]obody seems to be ready to gamble on computing on the Web." In the second, in the immediate wake of a catastrophic hard drive crash, Markoff is left to patch together what's possible with a compromised computer and hotel wi-fi. This turns out better than Markoff expected:

What I discovered was that—with the caveat of a necessary network connection—life is just fine without a disk. Between the Firefox Web browser, Google's Gmail and and [sic] the search engine company's Docs Web-based word processor, it was possible to carry on quite nicely without local data during my trip.

Markoff then observes: "it made me wonder why there aren't more wireless, Web-connected ultralight portables for business travelers. Somebody, it would appear, is missing an obvious market opportunity." Markoff was writing as a technology expert in 2007 about how distant cloud computing felt as a practical reality. Nevertheless, only a year later, the cloud's footprint was becoming apparent.

This project is my sustained examination of these shifts. It is about the increased distance between our keyboards and the spaces where our words reside. It is about the compressed distance between our thoughts and the thoughts of others. It is about how these changes are influencing and will influence our composing processes as we continue to engage with one another through writing.

For centuries (but, notably, *not* for millennia) the act of writing has been understood as a process in which a composer applies dark marks to white or light-colored paper. The means of applying those marks has varied. For most of the centuries since paper was invented in China, those marks were applied with a stylus-shaped writing instrument of some sort, a pen or, much later, a pencil (the first record of something resembling the modern pencil dates back only to 1565). In the more recent past, these styli were complemented by writing machines designed to apply marks to paper. William Austin Burt patented an ancestor to the typewriter — the "typographer" in 1829. The first commercially successful typing machine, the Sholes and Glidden Type-Writer was first sold in 1873.

Fig. 1.2: The lavishly decorated 1874 Remington No. 1 Sholes & Glidden Typewriter, courtesy Daderot via Wikimedia Commons

I have fond memories of firmly pushing the keys on my mother's portable Olympia typewriter whose keys struck the paper with a resounding and satisfying mechanical slap. In 1961, the IBM Selectric substituted a golf-ball sized "type element" for the keys that would inevitably jam when high-speed typists approached their top speeds. By 1991, IBM was out of the typewriter business altogether. A generation of legal secretaries mourned as their Selectrics were carted away in favor of personal computers. For me, at least, many of these dates feel surprisingly close. The pencil, in particular, seems a shockingly recent innovation. *Pens* are indeed ancient, as are paper's predecessors, papyrus and parchment. But the economies and ecologies of papyrus and parchment are well removed from the experience of composing on and for paper. In early literate cultures, composers wrote on scrolls or on skins. The materials they wrote on were expensive and labor-intensive. Every element of their writing process was costly, including the location and maintenance of adequate light. The phenomenon of the palimpsest underscores these costs. Parchment was *so* valuable that it made economic sense to scrape off existing writing from parchment pages to have a *somewhat* blank page for a new composition. All of this underscores that every time we retro-project a contemporary notion of "writing" back through time, we are likely dramatically misunderstanding what it meant for our ancestors to set out to produce written compositions. Contemporary readers of my words will have likely thrown tens of thousands of sheets of paper into wastebaskets, never having experienced their writing space as a precious commodity. We now live in an era informed—if not transformed—by the ready availability of disposable writing surfaces.

Yet, writing *happened* before pencils and paper. People scraped and struggled to create clean work surfaces for writing and painstakingly scratched or embedded their chosen characters onto these surfaces. The whole of Plato's writings predate paper. So, too, the Upanishads and the I Ching. The holy texts of the Jewish, Christian, and Muslim faiths were all composed prior to their respective cultures adopting the use of paper.

Invented in China in the second century BCE, paper spread to the Islamic world about a millennium later, but it did not reach Europe until *the eleventh century*. All texts from the Roman Empire up through the night Nero fiddled—in spite of the flames—predate the adoption of paper in the West. This history underscores an important fact: the filling of white rectangles with black alphanumeric characters is a small portion of what writing has been, is, and of what writing can be. Even my chosen title's invocation of writing in the clouds calls to mind two forms of writing that might strike many Western readers as falling outside the scope of writing *qua* writing: smoke signals and skywriting. Smoke signalling, practiced by an array of peoples stretching from Chinese soldiers along the Great Wall, to the indigenous peoples of what is now the United States is generally not thought of as writing because—for the most part—it is used to transmit messages rather than alphanumeric characters. Skywriting by planes expelling smoke counters this by delivering alphanumeric characters, but it might be distinguished from the writing that is celebrated, especially in Western contexts, on the grounds that it is brief, ephemeral, and typically commercial in character. All these characteristics are also common within Twitter, a cloud-facilitated writing space. This, obviously, leads us to the overarching questions of what kinds of writing count, when, and why.

Michél Foucualt famously zeroes in on these questions in the initial steps of his 1969 lecture, now presented as an essay, "What Is an Author?":

> The author's name manifests the appearance of a certain discursive set and indicates the status of this discourse within a society and culture. It has no legal status, nor is it located in the fiction of the work; rather it is founded in the break that founds a certain discursive construct and a very particular mode of being. As a result, we would say that *in a civilization like our own* there are a certain number of discourses endowed with the "author function" while others are deprived of it. A private letter may well have a signer—it does not have an author; a contract may well have a guarantor—it does not have an author. An anonymous text posted on a wall probably has en editor —but not an author. The author function is therefore characteristic of the mode of existence, circulation, and functioning of certain discourses within a society. (211, emphasis added)

My work as a scholar of authorship and textual ownership has prompted me to engage with Foucault's lecture many times, but on my most recent reading, Foucault's narrowing of his claims to "civilizations like our own" resonated in new ways. Elsewhere, Foucault links the author function introduced here to the advent of copyright laws, and this sheds light on the dividing line between "civilizations like our own" and others. Some cultures have invested heavily in the figure of the author as owner and seller of texts. Not all civilizations have chosen this path, and many have functioned quite well as literate cultures in the author's relative absence.

Human impulses to compose and record have, for most of history, occurred in defiance of the considerable technological challenges involved in simply securing an adequate medium for the recording of text. Clearly, writing *will happen* after pencils, pens, and paper take their positions alongside papyrus, parchment, quill pens, and typewriters as "vintage" writing technologies. After more than three decades of observing composers gravitating toward digital tools for written composition, we can confidently project that as long as the power grid stays up, most people will choose to compose in internetworked, digitally-enabled writing spaces more often than not.

This project is directed, in part, at assuaging the concerns reverberating throughout our culture because of the ongoing shift to internetworked digital composing spaces—colloquially known as "cloud" spaces—as the default for most writing work. At nearly every academic conference addressing writing and composition I have attended, I have heard at least a few of my fellow scholars of writing and rhetoric grumbling that we are hurtling off a precipice, bewitched by our glowing LCD screens until—like Wile E. Coyote—we will all make the mistake of looking down.

These arguments shortchange both human creativity and human adaptability. The notion that the capacity for serious intellectual engagement with one another's written compositions is in precipitous decline (as Sven Birkerts, for example, famously claimed in his 1994 book *The Gutenberg Elegies*) is at odds with any empirical examination of what people are actually doing in the midst of our shift to digital media. Somehow reading has endured. In 2019, the Pew Research Center reported that in the United States, eighteen-to-twenty-nine-year-olds were the demographic group most likely to have read a book in any format (eighty-one percent) and most likely to have read print books and ebooks (seventy-four percent and thirty-four percent, respectively). In all these categories, eighteen-to-twenty-nine-year-olds were six to nine percent more likely to have read a book than any other demographic. The only category where eighteen-to-twenty-nine-year-olds lagged behind any other demographic was audiobooks, and there eighteen-to-twenty-nine-year-olds trailed thirty-to-forty-nine-year-olds by four percent (twenty-seven versus twenty-three percent). Simply put, young adults now read more books than their elders and nimbly mix and match media to fit their reading goals (Perrin). If we observe people's behavior, it is clear that the United States will almost certainly remain a substantially literate culture even as composing on and for paper becomes an increasingly "old-fashioned" mode of composition. Indeed, for all our reliance on screen-based reading and writing, we still have yet to move away from the cultures and ecologies prompted by print literacy.

Tellingly, contemporary discussions of writing routinely speak of "pages" even in cases where no paper page ever existed. It is, for example, by no means uncommon for contemporary college students to compose and complete, submit, and receive graded assignments without a single tree falling. (This is not necessarily a net gain, environmentally, as considerable energy is needed to illuminate all the screens involved in these processes.) Even so, in my own experience as a college-level instructor, many students still request page "equivalents" for major projects even when the projects (e.g., a Prezi or a pechakucha presentation) bear only a limited relationship to traditional paper-based compositions.

We now live amid a paper "hangover," constructing virtual facsimiles of paper in our minds and on our machines to facilitate familiar composing processes. In this, we are responding to shifts in literacy technology much as people always have. In her 1980 book, *The Printing Press as an Agent of Change*, Elizabeth Eisenstein argues that during the "age of incunabula" the practices of scribal culture remained so entrenched that print texts were largely indistinguishable from handwritten texts prepared by scribes. Eisenstein asserts: "[t]he more closely one observes the age of incunabula the less likely one is to be impressed by the changes wrought by print" (26). To cruelly compress Eisenstein's argument, the first generations of printers couldn't quite *see* print as capable of delivering anything more than multiple copies of texts that—in their appearance and structure—mimicked handwritten texts. It was only over time that people were able to conceptually free themselves from the conventions that had grown up around script literacy. It was only over decades that people would come to favor the machined precision of refined typography—of letter shapes that were clearly *not* executed by human hands. Over centuries, this preference has become entrenched. Unsurprisingly, digital writing spaces have been developed to reflect these preferences.

In the present moment, we tend to compose pages in ways that mimic familiar practices that we have projected forward from the typewriter and the writing ecologies it prompted. The QWERTY keyboard is only the most obvious artifact of the typewriter era. Key placements designed to minimize the likelihood of frequently struck keys jamming into one another persist despite the half-century that has passed since the invention of the IBM Selectric's "type ball"—which eliminated the possibility of keys jamming. But the cultural attachment to typewriter ecologies extends far beyond the keyboard.

What undergirded Apple's marketing claim that the 1984 Macintosh might be "the computer for the rest of us" was that machine's specific implementation of the graphic user interface (GUI) to mimic typewriter ecologies. Unlike its near peers, the Macintosh offered a visual representation of a *white* page. Keystrokes produced images of *black* characters on that white "page." Indeed, the entire Macintosh interface was grounded in the specifics of a paper-based office culture, with file folders, paperwork, and a trash can all underscoring the notion that the virtual "desktop" offered up by the interface was really a close parallel to the real-world desktops in the "cubes" that had—by the mid 1980s—come to epitomize contemporary intellectual work spaces. Because the Mac could display *and print* pages that looked roughly the same on screen and off, it was dramatically more accessible to novice computer users who had been frustrated by the crude approximations of page spaces within programs like WordStar and WordPerfect on the amber and green monochrome monitors of the era. Indeed "WYSIWYG" printing, short for "what you see is what you get," was arguably the central selling point of the Macintosh's companion printer, the ImageWriter.

One could easily be drawn into lionizing the Macintosh OS and, later, the Windows operating systems for their ability to successfully mimic familiar features of workplace environments in ways that seemed at least somewhat intuitive to their users. But it is also important to acknowledge that we have always had "operating systems." In the typewriter era the operating system—that is, the writing interface and associated systems of composition—involved metallic typebars striking an ink-soaked ribbon to impress characters onto paper before being brought to a sudden stop by the platen. This system also encompassed an array of materials placed *into* the typewriter ranging from the various types and sizes of paper (e.g., 20 lb. cotton, onionskin, carbon paper, A4 paper) to envelopes, to various methods of correcting mistakes (Wite-Out, Liquid Paper, correction tape). Taken together, all these elements of the typewriter ecology add up to a sharply defined and *sharply circumscribed* landscape of possibility.

With respect to positioning alphabetic characters on pages, the typewriter performed very well, allowing even amateurs to—with practice— deliver "professional" appearing documents with clean surfaces and high readability. But the typewriter offered no real opportunities for the incorporation of images into compositions. One could certainly remove a sheet of paper and affix an image to the page with rubber cement or glue, but this would then make it difficult (if not impossible) to type on or around the resulting layered page.

While it is tempting to argue that it would never have occurred to typewriter-using composers in, say, the 1940s to envision pages with sophisticated mixtures of text and image, in the United States, these same composers were likely reading *Life* and *Look* magazines, and their children were almost certainly reading comic books or the graphically intensive Little Golden books or the early books of Dr. Seuss. These then-contemporary examples were fairly straight-line descendants of illuminated manuscripts, which had then existed for more than a millennium. Certainly, the notion of texts and images coordinated with one another was by no means unusual in the first half of the twentieth century. But the tools for producing such texts were comparatively rare and required professional skillsets.

My argument here echoes those made by others in other contexts. Don Norman's 1988 book *The Design of Everyday Things* (originally published as *The Psychology of Everyday Things*) popularized the notion of *affordances*, building upon work by psychologist James J. Gibson (Norman 12). Central to Norman's conception of affordances is the notion that any environment offers a limited pool of specific options with some options being significantly more available or apparent than others. Norman's work applied this concept to designed objects, shining a spotlight on the degree to which the design of any technological object both offers opportunities for interaction and circumscribes possible alternatives. This circumscription can be the product of the design itself or cultural constraints, or—in many cases—the by-product of convention.

When we view the 1940s typewriter as an operating system—as a *system* of *operations* developed to produce composed texts—these affordances and constraints are thrown into sharp relief. The typewriter of the 1940s offered its users a single typeface, in a single size. Scaling letters for emphasis or to draw readers' attention is flatly impossible. The primary method of emphasizing text was through use of bicolor (red and black) typewriter ribbons, invented by Charles Underwood in 1909.

Fig. 1.3: A typewriter using a bicolor (red/black) typewriter ribbon, courtesy Tejyng via Pixabay

While professionally published scholarly texts have long reflected the development of robust systems for footnotes, the typewriter had no specific capacity for distinguishing between the main text and annotations. And, as mentioned, the possibilities for images being coordinated with texts bordered on non-existent. Taken together, the aggregation of limitations makes it clear that the typewriter was not understood as a tool for producing *finished* texts. Rather, it was seen as a means of producing *manuscripts*. The typewriter offered its users the opportunity to produce relatively polished texts that stood in a space between handwritten texts and fully composed print texts. The typewriter allowed "regular" people to prepare the texts that editors, designers, and typesetters could transform into the sleek and clean print texts of the first half of the twentieth century.

Nevertheless, the look and feel of pages composed on typewriters has achieved a certain nostalgic "charm." Almost every contemporary computer operating system offers at least one typeface that recalls the particular aesthetics of typewriter text, this being Apple's "American Typewriter." Further, font designers routinely challenge themselves to precisely reproduce the array of imperfections that accumulated as ribbons faded and fingers struck keys imperfectly, as in Draconian Typewriter by Nicolas Coranado. As the preceding sentences illustrate, contemporary operating systems offer composers *so many options*. But these options are *not* limitless. The typewriter's century-long heyday allows us to see with clarity that it was introduced with fanfare as the replacement for the pen. But the *manus*—the hand—embedded in the concept of the manuscript remained present throughout the life cycle of the typewriter. What the hand lost in proximity to the written page, it gained in speed and visual clarity. For decades, the tasks of the typewriter were understood as those of streamlining and regularizing the production of what had formerly been handwritten texts. This was all that was asked of it. This constrained sense of the machine's purpose sharply circumscribed the types of innovation that might have otherwise occurred.

So too, we see today's tools for written composition sharply constrained by the accumulated array of conventions that solidified during the typewriter era. Microsoft Word slavishly reproduces most of the conventional patterns of composition established in the typewriter era, including margins, tabs, and restrictions on how and whether columns can be used. Images are an afterthought. Word's developers' decisions were clearly driven by the compartmentalization of words and images that bracketed off "tables" and "figures" as floating elements that might or might not appear on the specific page where their contents were being discussed. The notion that

An image *might* be simply an embedded element in an argument.

is one that clearly was beyond the reach of the initial designers of Microsoft Word, and it is only just now finding purchase in the latest generations of what remains, for many, the "default" software for written composition in the United States.

This is not to minimize the importance of the more general democratization of access to profoundly sophisticated tools for textual composition. We are, at present, witness to an extraordinary explosion of creativity driven by composers' access to opportunities for textual production and manipulation that used to be available only to highly trained professionals with prohibitively expensive tools. This is an unalloyed positive, and to the extent that Moore's Law and economies of scale make the initial cost of access to these technologies increasingly available to broader swaths of composers, we can expect even more inventive approaches to textual composition in the coming years.

But in the almost thirty years of widely accessible digital tools for textual composition we have only begun to break free from the conventions of the tool that the computer was supposed to supersede every bit as much as the typewriter was supposed to supersede the pen. We still are in the thrall of the vertically oriented rectangular page. And in the US, we still spend countless hours producing *manuscripts* even though it is now not only possible but easier than it has ever been for composers to produce finished texts. It was only after more decades of built-in access to italics on computers that the arbiters of the APA and MLA citation systems allowed *italics*—rather than underlines—in their prescribed textual treatments for endnotes (APA in 2001 and MLA in 2009). This does not necessarily imply that the APA has entirely reconsidered its role as a facilitator of *manuscripts* rather than of finished texts. As of the sixth edition (2009) of the APA style manual, Times New Roman was the *only* font allowed in APA-style texts. Thus, the array of scientific and associated fields that adhere to the APA's manual have pre-determined that the benefit of allowing composers a measure of precise visual expression is outweighed by the benefits of having no significant variation among those texts submitted for publication. Thus, we await acknowledgment that composers of scholarly texts might *not* be producing work that would be handed off to others for editorial and design refinement. We await full recognition that composers might be using digital composing tools to produce complete and finished works *themselves.*

At present, the spaces in which many composers are learning that they have both the tools and skills they need to produce finished works are cloud-based spaces. For many digitally literate people who were at least teenaged by the turn of the twenty-first century, the question was not *whether* to blog, but where and how. While many people in my demographic are deeply embarrassed by photographs of the haircuts (and in some cases beards) that marked their efforts to settle into adulthood, it is clear to me that many of those younger than me will look to their initial forays into public writing on sites like MySpace as recording too much of their own all-too-awkward paths to adulthood. Though not commonly described as such at the time, early social networks and blog spaces were "cloud" spaces in the sense that the writing that appeared on these sites was prepared within browsers, housed on external servers, and delivered to audiences within browsers. Thus, the writing on MySpace (as well as the engineering of decorative "bling" to personalize individual sites within MySpace) was largely external to an individual MySpace user's computer.

We can now see MySpace as ancestral to the always external and by-default collaborative space of a browser-based app like Google Docs. While the menu bar at the top of a Google Docs page superficially resembles Microsoft Word's, the degree to which Google Docs participates in inter-networked digital composition is readily announced by the array of colorful icons that pop up and *even overlap the menus* when collaborators join in the development of a particular composition. Google Docs *presumes* and *prioritizes* collaboration. It is the "value added" that Google Docs initially offered relative to its competitors. But more fundamentally, it is a signal that writing is, for the foreseeable future, no longer as lonely as it once was widely understood to be.

The writer of the first epigraph for this introduction, Isaac Asimov, believed writing to be lonely in 1990 because he was acculturated to tools that isolated him from others. Asimov—who wrote more than 470 books across a range of genres but is best known for his science fiction writing—no doubt speaks for a broad swath of writers who composed their texts in the half millennium prior to his characterization of writing as necessarily isolating. For centuries, writers sought out rooms of their own, for contemplation, for gathering thoughts, and for the act of writing itself. This loneliness was exacerbated by the mechanization of personal written composition over the course of the twentieth century. The clatter of typewriter keys—especially when struck by a driven composer—was often deafening. Few could hope to sustain a conversation in a room where another person was typing.

When Asimov wrote "Even if a writer socializes regularly, when he gets down to the real business of his life, it is he and his typewriter or word processor. No one else is or can be involved in the matter," he is speaking to not only his own narrow experience, which was informed by the available writing technologies of his lifetime. He is also speaking to his own sense of assuredness with respect to defining what it is that writers, or perhaps "real" or "serious" writers do. While Asimov was an exemplar of a thin strip of writerly culture, he was by no means speaking for the experiences of most of the people who were writing for a living within his own lifetime. While one might wish to overlook Asimov's historically conventional sexism ("when *he* gets down to the real business") this exclusionary language is especially disappointing coming, as it does, from a writer associated with genres (science fiction, mystery, fantasy) that tend to fall outside the most celebrated spaces of literate life. Whatever Asimov meant to achieve by constructing the lonely, implicitly male writer of these sentences, we must turn towards a broader and more inclusive understanding of who writers might be, the variability of their composition strategies, and the degrees to which writing technologies that facilitate sharing productively expand opportunities for participation in writing as a practice and as a profession.

During Asimov's lifetime (1920 –1992) the "typewriter" and the "word processor" were the obvious tools of the trade for writers. As a product of his time, Asimov—despite having the ability to conceive "Three Laws of Robotics" that have been widely adopted by subsequent science fiction writers—had difficulty viewing computers as serious tools for written composition. In his memoir, Asimov recalls:

> I was once asked to say what I wanted for Christmas in the way of computers. I was urged to describe anything I could imagine, whether it was feasible or not. I answered briefly and truthfully that I had an antediluvian electric typewriter and a medieval word processor and both worked properly. They were all I needed, and I really didn't want, for Christmas or for any other time, anything beyond what I really needed. (230)

Later in the memoir, Asimov recounts a story where, in the spring of 1981, he is "asked [by a computer magazine] to do an article on my experiences with my word processer" (472). He responds that he does not have one and cannot write the essay. This prompts the magazine to deliver what Asimov refers to as his "word processor." It is in fact a "Radio Shack TRS-80 Micro-Computer with a daisy-wheel printer and a Scripsit [word processing] program" (472). This particular computer is fondly remembered for its easy-to-understand BASIC programming language. But for Asimov, this "word processor" served a single purpose:

> I use it for only one job and no more—the preparation of manuscripts. I had the Radio Shack people adjust it so that it gave me the margins I wanted and the double spacing I wanted, and everything else that I wanted. I haven't the faintest idea of how any of these things can be changed. I couldn't make it single space, or adjust the margins, for instance, so I don't use it for anything *but* manuscripts. (473)

Asimov had limited what was—for its time—a remarkably powerful personal computer to a single function. His choices recast the TRS-80 *computer* as a dedicated word processor.

In fairness to Asimov, the true dedicated word processors of this era represented only incremental steps beyond the typewriter. Dedicated word processors were—at best—relatively portable and relatively quiet tools for written composition. In 1990, The Smith Corona company, best known for its typewriters, was selling a "laptop personal word processor" that cleverly separated the task of composition from the task of character generation. This six hundred dollar machine allowed a composer to type quietly and briefly (given the limited battery charge) and then select an appropriate time for the mechanized printout of the composed text. As a former owner of this product, I have a clear memory of the chattering sound of the daisy wheel printer furiously typing out the pages I had composed. I could never, in good conscience, print any documents while others might be sleeping under the same roof.

Figure 1.4. The Smith-Corona PWP 7000 LT "Personal Word Processor," screenshot from YouTube video by offensive_jerk

Thus, for most of the twentieth century, for reasons that have little to do with artistic temperaments or inclinations toward strong drink, writers were not pleasant to be around. The machines they used were simply *too damn loud* for polite company. Simply put, current technologies for writing do not have the assaultive sonic qualities that, for much of the twentieth century, assured that writers would necessarily remove themselves from their families, friends, and communities. The keys on contemporary laptops are unobtrusive. The virtual keyboards on the touchscreens on contemporary tablets are all-but silent. For centuries, writers have written in cafes and coffee shops, but it is only in the past two decades that they have been able to comfortably and quietly do so with their preferred composing machines. This has become so much part of contemporary writing, that the use of a typewriter in public spaces has become especially disfavored. I am not at liberty to share the specific image, but a sighting of a young man typing on his portable typewriter inside a local coffee shop prompted my academic peers to deliver a memorable auto-da-fé via Facebook, in which his apparent hipster ethos was unfavorably associated with certain strands of vinyl LP purism, leading briefly to a #hipster/douche hashtag. In short, this man's choice to write loudly when it was, in the eyes of these viewers, *so easy* to write quietly in public rendered his motivations suspect.

For these, and other reasons, writing is no longer as lonely as it was throughout Asimov's lifetime. In addition to the cloud-based Notes application, Apple's 2012 Mountain Lion operating system incorporated a feature called "Notification Center." By default, Notification Center places small badges in the upper-right-hand corner of a computer screen notifying the computer user—for example—that an email has arrived, or that a friend has commented on a Facebook posting, or a shared calendar has been updated, or a Twitter tweet has been retweeted. Many Apple users found this feature annoying, and the Web is now awash in mini-tutorials helping users turn off the notifications. But Apple's decision to pursue this feature illustrates how very different composing in internetworked digital spaces is from *all* prior writing circumstances.

In a sense, Apple's OS was only making explicit what has always been true about internetworked writing spaces. To borrow the tagline from Steven Spielberg's *Close Encounters of The Third Kind*, when we compose in these spaces "we are not alone." The personal computers of the 1980s were the last to offer their users an approximation of the sense of isolation that Asimov encapsulates in this chapter's first epigraph.

For what we can now understand as a brief window of time, between the eras of mainframe computers with so-called "dumb" terminals (from the 1950s through the mid 1980s) and the widespread adoption of the World Wide Web (from 1993 forward), personal computers were not necessarily attached to anything more than the power grid. But from at least the 1990s forward, computers have been built with connectivity to the Internet as a foundational design element. As a practical consequence of this connectivity, twenty-first century writers are now far closer to others—and others' texts—than at any point in human history (with the possible exception of those writers who routinely composed within major libraries).

Not only are twenty-first century composers habituated to the link as a rhetorical strategy, they compose using software that often recognizes URLs and e-mail addresses and makes them active by default. The distance between written ideas is collapsing, with the overly long term of copyright being one of the few marginally effective firewalls separating texts from one another. Over and above the steady hum of notifications, updates, and likes bringing our "friends" onto our screens with regularity, the structure of the World Wide Web—with its foregrounding of the link as a conceptual structure—encourages writers to understand themselves not as islands but as nodes in networks. This understanding is deeply embedded in the Web. The inventor of the World Wide Web, Tim Berners-Lee, was explicit about this goal: "When I proposed the Web in 1989, the driving force I had in mind was communication through shared knowledge and the driving 'market' for it was collaboration among people at work and at home" (Berners-Lee and Fischetti 174). Thus, the machines that house the software tools that most people use for written composition are never far from the tools people use to connect with one another.

Often, the preferences and practices of print composition will remain stubbornly in place as composers adopt new technologies (still writing on their QWERTY keyboards). But every now and again, we will experience moments of possibility, of perceived weightlessness as the potential of inter-networked digital composing tools makes truly new practices and patterns of composition possible. This book is directed at helping us understand when and how me might realize the promise of writing that lives both in the *heres* of our various writing tools, and the *theres* of the internetworked servers that house our words as we write, known colloquially, and aspirationally, as "the cloud." It is worth noting, in passing, that "the cloud" is typically presented as a singular, even though as a practical matter it includes all the *many* cloud-based services offered by internet giants like Amazon, Apple, Google, and Microsoft, along with hundreds of smaller cloud-based services.

While cloud computing means that we are often composing texts that ultimately reside in servers half a continent or more away, the substitution of these servers for our own hard drives means that these texts are now more available to both our far-flung collaborators and our co-workers down the hallway than they were a decade ago. Opportunities for collaborative composition—solicited and unsolicited—are multiplying exponentially. We might look longingly at Virginia Woolf's hoped for "room of one's own"—a writing space removed from the chatter and challenges of one's personal and familial relationships—and realize that even if such a room could be located, the tool we use to compose texts no longer offers this same sense of apparent distance from others. It is tempting to conclude that writing, as a practice and an art will suffer because of this shift. But this is underestimating the tremendous power of human creativity and the will to write and be understood. We will write differently because we have moved from anti-social writing machines to avowedly social machines, but there is no reason to believe we won't write at least as well as we have through history. In fact, the broad availability of sophisticated writing tools argues that we may be on the verge of one of the most writing-intensive moments in human history. Nimble composers will undoubtedly avail themselves of novel and powerful opportunities within our writing platforms as they respond and recalibrate to technological changes.

2 What We Wrote about When We Wrote about Writing in the 1990s

When living through a moment where there are many observable shifts in both writing technologies and the ways people are using writing technologies, it can be difficult to resist the temptation to embrace novel technologies at the expense of the extant and arguably thoroughly optimized technologies already at hand. This book is an exploration of the internet-worked writing space known colloquially as "the cloud" as a relatively new space for writers and writing, but it is also about the ways in which we adapt our practices to these new spaces, and also about how much of the settled aspects of writing practice persist even within distinctively novel composing spaces. While the remainder of this book will explore the cloud at some length, one core challenge will be finding ways to celebrate the possibilities of these new composing spaces without falling prey to the temptation to position the advent of writing in the cloud as heralding the end of prior writing practices. For guidance in how to respond to this moment, this project is particularly informed by the work of three prominent scholars who worked to understand what writing was becoming at a similar moment of seismic change: Jay David Bolter, Christina Haas, and James E. Porter.

Bolter's 1991 book, *Writing Space: The Computer, Hypertext, and the History of Writing*, features an introductory chapter titled, "The Late Age of Print." In this chapter, the first words are not Bolter's, but Victor Hugo's, from the novel *Notre-Dame de Paris, 1482*. Bolter's carefully chosen Hugo excerpt concludes:

> The archdeacon pondered the giant edifice for a few moments in silence, then with a sigh he stretched his right hand toward the printed book that lay open upon his table and his left hand toward Notre Dame and turned a sad eye from the book to the church.
> "Alas!" he said, "This will destroy that." (qtd in. Bolter 1)

The first words written by Bolter within Bolter's introduction are a gloss of this passage from Hugo's novel:

> The priest remarked "Ceci tuera cela": this book will destroy that building. (Notre Dame Cathedral) He meant not only that printing and literacy would undermine the authority of the church but also that [again quoting Hugo] "human thought . . . would change its mode of expression, that the principal idea of each generation would no longer write itself with the same material and in the same way,

that the book of stone, so solid and durable, would give place to the book made of paper, yet more solid and durable." . . . Of course, the printed book did not eradicate the encyclopedia in stone; it did not even eradicate the medieval art of writing by hand. . . . But printing did displace handwriting; the printed book became the most highly valued form of writing. And printing certainly helped to displace the medieval organization and expression of knowledge. (1–2)

Bolter, writing at the beginning of the 1990s, is inviting readers to consider parallels between print and pre-print civic and cultural life (embodied by Notre-Dame de Paris) and digital and pre-digital civic and cultural life (embodied by the printed paper books that Hugo presents as the prospective destroyers of "books of stone"). And Bolter is cueing the reader to the reality that media forms generally do *not* destroy their predecessors so much as they supplement the existing aggregation of media forms. Indeed, like Notre Dame, print has experienced cycles of revision, renewal, and re-invention.

So why did this (print) fail to destroy that (Notre Dame)? Some might protest that I am being too literal-minded and that print's negative impact on Catholicism or Christianity more broadly is the ultimate point of the archdeacon's prediction. But this is hard to reconcile with the statistical realities of this moment, at which there are over *two billion* Christians on the planet, roughly *half* of whom are Catholic. And, certainly, print was deeply involved in spreading the good words and good news of the Christian faiths across the globe. Far from destroying Notre Dame, print reified it, and subsequent media have reinforced this reification. This leads us to consider the possibility that media do not consume and destroy so such as they accrue and supplement one another. This cannot have been lost on Victor Hugo. His novel's title: *Notre-Dame de Paris, 1482* announces and reinforces the almost 350-year gap between the fictional archdeacon's projection and the lived present in which Hugo was writing, in which Notre Dame still stood, and still mattered.

Indeed, Hugo's novel, better known to English-speaking readers as *The Hunchback of Notre Dame* published in 1831, was—in addition to the familiar story of Quasimodo and Esmeralda—also a call for a form of historic preservation. At the time he wrote this novel, Hugo is known to have objected to the replacement of the cathedral's medieval stained-glass windows with clear glass. While this replacement arguably did violence to the cathedral's aesthetic, it also hardly added up to the wholesale destruction of Notre Dame. Indeed, Hugo's novel reinforced a call for the restoration of Notre Dame which culminated in King Phillippe's 1844 order that Notre Dame (and its windows) be restored. Implicit in Victor Hugo's objections to alterations to Notre Dame cathedral is an important, obvious point: "this" (print) had *not* destroyed "that" (the cathedral). If anything, print had reinforced Notre Dame's status as—at least—a must-see tourist attraction if not as a house of worship. So, in a very real sense, this (print) *restored* that (Notre Dame).

And much as Hugo knew that Notre Dame had somehow withstood the first three centuries of print, so too did Bolter know that Notre Dame endured well into what he, in 1991, termed "the late age of print." Bolter's surfacing of the Hugo quote invites us to consider how and whether media forms (with architecture being understood as one among many) coexist, interrupt, and disrupt one another, and the obvious lesson at hand is that accumulation and supplementation are more common than destruction.

Media forms are not necessarily the proverbial buggy whips that evaporate in the face of new technology. While it is tempting to cross media forms off the master list, or at least file them away as archaic, once they reach critical mass, they have a way of enduring. The plot of the 2020 Academy of Motion Picture Arts and Sciences Best Picture, Bong Joon Ho's *Parasite*, turns, in part, on (spoiler alert) a child's use of *Morse code*. Morse code, adapted for telegraphy, happens to date back to 1844, coincidentally the year the restoration of Notre Dame commenced.

Bolter's *Writing Space* is situated at a remarkable moment in the history of writing technologies. Published in 1991, *Writing Space* was composed after the widespread adoption of so-called personal computers, but before widespread public adoption of the Internet as a communicative channel. Bolter was writing in a context where roughly 2.5 million people worldwide were using the Internet, two years before the Mosaic browser introduced the World Wide Web to a public audience. Indeed, what made "personal" computers *seem* personal was their lack of connection to anything other than the plugs supplying the computers with household current.

Indeed, the subtitle of Bolter's book: *The Computer, Hypertext, and the History of Writing* now dates it with some precision. Throughout the 1980s, much of the theoretical work on the likely impact of digital media on writing processes and practices emphasized hypertext, placing great significance on digital media's capacity for linking *words* to one another. Indeed, the possibility that digital media might link *people* together as well as words seems to glimmer only faintly in Bolter's book. Notably, Bolter positions the precursors to the contemporary Internet as ancestral to hypertext:

> Important anticipations of hypertext can be found in the computerized communication networks such as ARPANET or BITNET, put in place in the 1960s and 1970s. Such a network constitutes the phys-

ical embodiment of hypertext. Each element or *node* in the network is a computer installation, while the connections among these elements are cables and microwave and satellite links. Each computer node serves dozens or hundreds of individual subscribers and these subscribers both produce and read messages created by others within their computing facility, around the nation, or around the world. (29)

In fact, the sequence is the other way around. Ted Nelson coined the term *hypertext* in 1965, and then, in collaboration with Andries Van Dam and a number of students, developed the Hypertext Editing System (HES) in 1967. The planning phases of ARPANET, the first wide-area, packet-switching network, date back to 1966, with the first two nodes, hosted at Stanford and UCLA, getting up and running in 1969. BITNET was a university network that started in 1981 with nodes at Yale and City University of New York. These networks are foundational steps along the path to the contemporary Internet, but from where Bolter was sitting at the time he wrote, the degree to which these networks were physical manifestations of the then-larger phenomenon of hypertext was the significant point.

Observing that Bolter, at that moment, weighted hypertext more heavily than the then-nascent networks populated by dedicated academics, hobbyists, and early adopters is not meant as a criticism. In most respects, Bolter understood both the landscape surrounding him and the prospects for writing technologies better than just about anyone writing about writing in 1991. There are passages in *Writing Space* that feel absolutely prescient. Within the first ten pages of his book, Bolter offers forecasts of technology that have, in the intervening decades, been developed (more or less):

> It is not hard to imagine portable computer with the bulk and weight of a large notebook and whose screen is as legible as a printed page. We can also envision an electronic writing system built into the top of a desk or lectern (like those used in the Middle Ages and the Renaissance) where the writer can work directly by applying a light pen instead of typing on a keyboard. (4).

Notebook computers predated *Writing Space*, so the most distant element in Bolter's forecast is the "screen as legible as a printed page." Arguably the first laptop computer to approach that standard is the third-generation MacBook Pro, released by Apple in 2012. Bolter's forecast of stylus-driven computing is also apt, though all of us at the time Bolter wrote would have had difficulty envisioning a portable tablet being the space for this interface. Even so, the exact product Bolter envisioned now exists: "smart" or "intelligent" lecterns with stylus and/or touchscreen interfaces are expensive, but available, but the far more common configuration is people plugging in their own portable machines to achieve the same effect.

While Bolter could not realistically forecast the specifics of decades of technological development and refinement, *Writing Space* was precise and prescient in its characterizations of what electronic text might feel like as it moved from circulating in the small networks of Bolter's time, to inhabiting the network of networks that is the Internet. Here, Bolter spotlights the degree to which electronic texts foreground the possibility of variable reading experiences for different members of a text's audiences:

> Because an electronic text is not a physical artifact, there is no reason to give it the same conceptual unity as the printed book, no reason not to include disparate materials in one electronic network. The writer or editor need not envision and address only one homogeneous readership; an electronic book may speak with different voices to different readers (and each reader is a different reader each time he or she approaches a text). (7)

While some might argue that this potential has always been inherent in writing, whether print or electronic, the degree to which this latent capacity is pulled to the surface by writings that now inhabit cloud-based spaces is notable. Web-based texts, of course, are also notable for their capacity for mutability and change. The Internet Archive exists largely to address our collective nagging sense that we were *sure* that we saw something on a given site that is no longer there.

It is impossible to revisit a book like Bolter's while writing a book that aspires to do a similar job—of both offering an assessment of where writing stands and offering informed speculation as to where we might be headed—without being aware of the risks involved. On a related note, even with millennias of writing as a relatively stable means of cultural communication and connection, it begins to feel obvious that books that address writing *technologies* will probably never age well. Bolter, to his great credit, was willing to climb out on the occasional limb, and on those occasions where he is not prescient, he offers contemporary readers a clear sense of the limits of what seemed possible before writing and the Internet became folded together. One moment, near the conclusion of *Writing Space*, is notable for the degree to which it teeters between pre- and post-internet understandings of the computer as a writing space:

> The ideal of stability and cultural cohesion will largely disappear. Few will feel the need to assert such cohesion since even the smallest group of writers and readers can function happily in its niche on the elec-

tronic network. The computer can in fact provide a quiet place for readers and writers to pursue such interests, relatively secure from the noise of what remains of shared cultural elements. The computer as a writing space can also be a place to hide from the sensory overload of the daily world of work and leisure and the other electronic media. In this space, all the various definitions of cultural literacy can survive, but no single definition can triumph at the expense of all others. (Bolter 238)

With the benefit of hindsight, and the lived experiences of the intervening thirty years, Bolter's imagining of the computer as "a place to hide from the sensory overload of the daily world of work and leisure and the other electronic media" now seems wildly out of alignment with the lived reality of 2021. Indeed, the computer *is* one of the primary drivers of sensory overload, both in terms of work *and* leisure (especially if we understand smartphones as computers, which, of course, they are). The selective removal of apps from smartphones by users has become a common coping mechanism, with some of my fellow academics arguing in favor of removing work e-mail from their smartphones to stave off the nagging sense of urgency that can be prompted by an 11:00 p.m. e-mail message. The computer as a writing space, especially if it extends to tablets and smartphones, can become a space where it is *always* possible to read and write and thus, promotes a "round the clock" workplace with attendant expectations of almost immediate replies. While Bolter was no doubt right about the degree to which the cloud now facilitates niche audiences, we *are* experiencing sensory overload and most of us no longer view the computer as anything like a "quiet place." It is with this in mind that I now turn to a book from the mid-1990s notable for its laser-like focus on how writers in that moment were describing their experiences of the computer as a material site for the activities of writing.

Christina Haas's 1996 book *Writing Technology: Studies on the Materiality of Literacy* underscores the degree to which Western writing has consistently depended upon (and been limited by) writers' uses of specific, material, writing tools. In, her first chapter, titled "The Technology Question," Haas pulls an array of submerged material aspects of writing into the spotlight:

Writing is situated in the material world in a number of ways. It always occurs in a material setting, employs material tools, and results in material artifacts. Writers sit in well-appointed desks in offices, or they slouch in less well-appointed ones in classrooms. Sometimes writers forego a desk altogether, preferring the kitchen table, or a lap, or the dashboard of a car. Writers use stubby pencils, or felt-tip pens. cheap ball-points or lap-top computers; often writers use a number of these material implements in tandem. Writers compose speeches on the backs of envelopes, make lists on scraps of paper, write essays in spiral notebooks, and compose lab reports or love letters on word processors. Indeed, an observer from another culture might be surprised by how much time people in Western society spend typing on keyboards, or—more surprisingly, perhaps—how much personal, intellectual, economic, and even physical work gets done with pen and pencil in hand. In short, such a visitor would be astonished to see how engaged individuals within Western culture are with the material tools of literacy. (4)

Almost a quarter century later, this key paragraph in Haas's argument remains accurate in spirit, but not in letter. While writing always occurs in material settings and always (for now, at least, employs material tools, it does not *always* result in material artifacts, at least not in the conventional senses of "material." Indeed, virtual artifacts are commonly the by-products of writing. While the mid-1990s required Haas's call for greater attention to the materiality of literacy, the current moment invites our attention to the increasing *immateriality* of literacy. Further, the writers that were on the backs of envelopes, scraps of paper, in spiral notebooks, and with word processors are gravitating to the scaled-down aesthetics of smartphone and tablet interfaces. All but the last of these might have once been considered written ephemera. But when composed in digital spaces, these same bits of writing become bits of information, with digital lives that reverberate well beyond their moment of composition.

As a practical matter, digital storage is so inexpensive that those who can afford a smartphone or tablet can also afford immense amounts of digital storage. Google initially invited users of its Gmail e-mail service to keep their messages "forever." This is, in part, because their business model depends on reinforcing dependence on the Google Suite of applications. But the initial allotments of space offered to me by Google served me well enough. After over fifteen years of insanely heavy use, with messages to and from over a thousand different students (among others), I faced a decision point, whether to selectively delete messages or pony up a little bit of money to avoid the slog through my messages from Friendster and the John Kerry campaign. I chose to more than quintuple my storage for $1.99 a month (to 100 GB of storage). Each gigabyte can easily house roughly 100,000 pages of e-mail. Even as a high-volume user, the price of the 100,000,000 pages worth of storage I might someday need is well within my reach.

It is worth considering the degree to which ephemerality itself is challenged by our increasing reliance on digital composing tools. The default settings, in almost all cases, tilt toward preservation. Even the lowly shopping list might not need to be reinvented from scratch if a copy is kept.

While Christina Haas's emphasis on materiality oriented a generation of scholars toward consideration of the implications of specific tools, stretching roughly from pencil to laptop, for their composing processes, the descendants of the cumbersome laptops available when Haas wrote now produce incredible amounts of functionally immaterial text. This, in turn, has significant implications for another of Haas's key contributions, the notion of "text sense" or, initially, "sense of the text" as one of the writers in one of Haas's studies put it. In a series of empirical studies, Haas guided writers through parallel tasks in pen-and-paper and computer writing environments. These mid-1990s writers spoke to their own challenges in adapting to computer-based writing spaces:

> One of the reading problems that writers frequently mentioned was getting a sense of the text on-line; virtually every writer who mentioned text sense problems reported generating a hard copy printout of their texts in order to compensate for this problem. They often said things like, "I need to generate a hard copy to skim over—just to see where I am going," "It's hard to get the center of gravity of the piece," or "I just don't have a sense of the text when I write on-line." (Haas 118)

Haas clearly drew upon this writer's turn of phrase (echoed by other writers) to develop a key term for her project. She further develops the idea in the following terms:

> What is a sense of the text? Text sense is a mental representation of the structure and meaning of a writer's own text. It is primarily propositional in content, but includes spatial and temporal aspects as well. Although text sense—as an internal construction—is distinct from the written textual artifact, it is tied intimately to that artifact. Text sense in constructed in tandem with the written text and seems to include both a memory of the written text and an episodic memory of its construction. (Haas 118)

Haas's cannily constructed studies underscored the degree to which computer-using writers of the early-to-mid 1990s remained attached to the specifics of print. Many of the people involved in Haas's studies were highly experienced with writing in digital environments. One study's subjects, classed as "experienced writers" included people who worked in "systems design, teaching, and professional writing" (Haas 82). In short, many of

Haas's subjects were, for their time, exceptionally familiar with the practices and challenges of writing in digital environments. But these same people, demographically, all were trained as writers before the widespread adoption of digital writing tools. They might be expected to miss aspects of the writing technologies that corresponded to the ones they experienced as they learned how to write. Were we to conduct parallel studies today, one wonders whether writers would express such concern over not being able to achieve the text sense that they associated with print texts. Indeed, a generation of writers has become habituated to internetworked digital texts as both composing spaces and as deliverables. Today's readers might be able to locate an adequate "text sense" in networked digital spaces because these are the spaces where they were trained to write sustained prose in the first place.

Whether writers can develop an adequate text sense in internetworked digital spaces matters mightily, because smartphones, tablets, and devices with interfaces drawing heavily from their more limited operating systems, are, increasingly the *default* writing spaces. While it was possible for the academy to be initially dismissive of smartphones—as a space where ephemeral and meaningless texting occurred—and further, to be dismissive of texting as a possibly-not-so-important kind of writing that is more a speech than writing *qua* writing, this stance begins to buckle as an entire generation of students is being handed iPads and Chromebooks in K–12 educational settings throughout the United States. It is common for students to be developing their writing projects with operating systems that stem from the iPhone or Android, rather than from Windows or the MacOS.

It is increasingly common for the core writing tool found in K–12 contexts to be a tablet outfitted with a keyboard, or a netbook scale laptop (with Google's Chromebooks being especially popular for this purpose) with a touchscreen as well as a traditional keyboard interface. As a practical matter, this means composition is being taught in spaces that allow students to compose not merely by typing and but also by "touching" their words. Ironically, at a point where composers' texts are residing in cloud spaces that take writing farther from the site of composition than *ever* before, the composers "sense of text" is that the texts are literally "at hand" and sometimes composed by the motion of a single fingertip. While a fingertip pressed against a screen is not *actually* touching text, the screen *does* respond to specific contacts in specific places. The screen is as much an interface as the keyboard, but the writer's sense of distance from the text while typing evaporates as the writer manipulates text via touchscreens. It feels overwhelmingly like physical actions are having physical consequences, even if the writer *knows* that what lies within (or behind) the screen is virtual. In a sense, this gets us closer to text than ever (with the exception of letters directly painted with fingers).

In the second decade of the twenty-first century, it has become commonplace for writers to directly manipulate text via seemingly direct and seemingly physical contact with the letters they are "highlighting" or deleting. Yet, even as this very close finger-to-screen-to-virtual-text connection unfolds, most manipulations are being tracked and recorded in real time within server farms hundreds if not thousands of miles away. The here-and-thereness of digital text is never more pronounced than it is in these moments. The text at the writer's fingertip *feels* so very present when, in fact, it is more absent than any text prior to this time could possibly have been.

The spatial challenges contemporary writers face are, nevertheless, significant. As composers, they are routinely constrained to the limited dimensions of their screens. However large the imagined texts "behind" these screens might be, the texts at hand will be shaped and understood according to the screenspaces available, first to the composer, and then to the reader. On the other hand, this has *always* been the case. To the extent that ink filled the white rectangles of codex books and magazines, the task of writing has always involved shoehorning human thought into constrained spaces. Written composition has, for centuries, involved presenting a portion of a much larger whole within a fairly small rectangular window. In many cases, print windows have proven resistant to the kinds of creativity that writers might have wished to embed into their arguments, but the default writing space for most internetworked writing is a never-ending scroll, extending infinitely *downward* from the space where the composer is writing. Screen-based writing is now easy to conceptualize as the task of filling an almost bottomless vessel with alphanumeric characters.

The challenge then becomes how to teach writing in a culture where the here-and-thereness of digital writing is the default. And a first step involves acknowledging that this experience is unusual within the history of writing. Complicating this is that, relative to past examples of here-and-there writing (text composed in real time for broadcast on television, for example) the here-and-thereness is still largely bound to patterns and expectations that were developed for nineteenth century textual production. What, after all, does a "margin" mean when the same text is—by design—meant to flexibly rearrange itself in response to the reader's preferred reading device? The *New York Times* prepares textual and image content in at least four different ways each day. First, the *Times* prepares its print edition, in which the editors craft an arrangement of articles and decide page breaks. The editors give relative weights to different kinds of text, and thereby guide readers' eyes. For the moment, this remains the starting point and is perceived as the definitive version of the *Times*. The textual content of this print paper is then poured into multiple digital containers, with desktops and laptops receiving a version of the paper, tablets receiving another, and smartphones yet another. In each of these cases, the device effectively informs the text what is workable within the space available, and the text is coded to function within those limitations. Within the smartphone space, *sequence* largely takes the place of typographic weighting. Smartphone-using *Times* readers learn to decode the order of articles within the scrolling *Times* app space, much as they learned to decode the various weightings and typographic variations of print headlines. Each of these coding systems is wholly workable, and both are arguably intuitive. But *they are not the same*. Further, to state the obvious, the presence of even the few rare links within the *Times*'s electronic editions changes the relationship of the reader to the text. The reader is, within the space of the *Times*, routinely invited to move outside the paper's virtual space. This is something that the print edition simply cannot do with a fraction of the efficiency of internetworked writings. And, in some rare cases, the digital content of the online editions of the *Times* is pared down for presentation within the print editions of the *Times*. So, on any given day, *The New York Times* generates an enormous aggregation of content, most of which is then tweaked and manicured to fit the specific digital and print containers by which readers consume the *Times*.

Understanding text (and the visual elements of contemporary composition) as functioning almost as liquid poured into various and variable containers is by no means a new concept. A version of this metaphor of fluidity is front and center in John Perry Barlow's renowned 1994 *Wired* essay titled, "The Economy of Ideas":

> [A]ll the goods of the Information Age—all of the expressions once contained in books or film strips or newsletters—will exist either as pure thought or something very much like thought: voltage conditions darting around the Net at the speed of light, in conditions that one might behold in effect, as glowing pixels or transmitted sounds, but never touch or claim to "own" in the old sense of the word.
>
> Some might argue that information will still require some physical manifestation, such as its magnetic existence on the titanic hard disks of distant servers, but these are bottles which have no macroscopically discrete or personally meaningful form.

Within a year of one another, Barlow and Haas are, effectively, arguing over the significance of the *materiality* of literacy as against the impending *immateriality* of expression. For those of us born into a print-dominated landscape, it has been and sometimes still is difficult to envision futures without the specific interactions with text that were driven by the technology that housed it: the codex book. Noting the variations across, say, various print editions of James Joyce's "Ulysses" is possible in part because there are relatively few editions to review. In a culture of digital abundance, multiplicity of editions is commonplace. From this point forward, readers will have a relative degree of uncertainty with respect to the editions and printings of the texts they read. Indeed, the very concept of an edition is a by-product of the relative stability of ink and paper. The text-based compositions housed within our screens never offer readers this same level of certainty. Controversial tweets are deleted. Factual errors in newspaper articles are corrected, sometimes with notice, sometimes without. Immateriality necessarily implies instability, and until something has been archived or screenshot for posterity, it is subject to revision. This instability was not always the case, even with digital writing. A CD-ROM copy of Microsoft's *Encarta* encyclopedia says nothing today that it did not say in 1993. Wikipedia, by contrast, is changing literally every second. Instability is not a bug, it's a feature.

As a practical matter, we are now often unable to work our way *back* to the Internet of the early 1990s. Even landmarks in internet history are subject to the recursive and revision-intensive structures of HTML. On April 30, 2013, perhaps the most significant web page in internet history made a welcome return to the 'net after a long hiatus. In recognition of the twentieth anniversary of its release of the source code for the World Wide Web on a royalty-free basis, the European Organization for Nuclear Research—more commonly known as CERN—reposted what is now understood as the earliest known web page. Careless reporting often presented the page as if it was the "first" web page dating to the "birth" of the Web. Consider, for example, the CBS News piece "CERN Reactivates First Web Page for 20th Anniversary" that misstates April 30, 1993 as the date of the "birth" of the Web even though it is acknowledged that the site dates to *1992* (Ngak). The story misses that it was CERN's *elimination of royalties* that was a crucial step in the growth of the then-tiny and largely unknown Web. Prior to this point the need for licenses and compensation had curtailed use of the World Wide Web, with most Web users being confined to University campuses and other large-scale institutions that saw enough value in the Web to pay licensing fees to CERN. In February of 1993, the University of Minnesota announced that it would start charging licensing fees for the then-dominant Internet protocol, Gopher. CERN's elimination of fees, when paired with the development and rise of the Mosaic browser (developed by the National Center for Supercomputing Applications at the University of Illinois in January of that year) prompted a profound shift in how people engaged with information on the internet. Indeed, today the Web has become large-

ly synonymous with the Internet—to the point that mainstream news stories about the re-posting of the historic web page carefully disentangled the
'net and the Web for an audience expected not to recognize the distinction.

In April of 2013, those popular press stories that were clearly structured around the notion that the "first" webpage had been "re-animated"
and lived again online—if carefully reported—ended up uncovering a fairly startling fact about the World Wide Web. *We really don't know whether we have
an exact copy of the very first page on the Web!* While it is fair to describe the site
address as the first ever, the *content* of the page—though very limited—likely
evolved repeatedly between the Web's initial launch date of August 6, 1991,
and CERN's opening of the Web for royalty-free participation in 1993. So,
while the world acknowledged Tim Berners-Lee's tremendous contributions to global communication at the London Olympics in 2012, we do not
have an accurate record of the first message via this new medium. We know
by contrast, that "what hath God wrought" was the first telegraph message
with some precision. So, too, do we know Alexander Graham Bell's "Mr.
Watson, come here, I need you" as the first telephone message. In the case
of the Web, we only know *approximately* what that first page looked like in 1991:

World Wide Web

The WorldWideWeb (W3) is a wide-area hypermedia information retrieval initiative aiming to give universal access to a large universe of documents.

Everything there is online about W3 is linked directly or indirectly to this document, including an executive summary of the project, Mailing lists , Policy ,
November's W3 news , Frequently Asked Questions .

What's out there?
    Pointers to the world's online information, subjects , W3 servers, etc.
Help
    on the browser you are using
Software Products
    A list of W3 project components and their current state. (e.g. Line Mode ,X11 Viola , NeXTStep , Servers , Tools , Mail robot , Library)
Technical
    Details of protocols, formats, program internals etc
Bibliography
    Paper documentation on W3 and references.
People
    A list of some people involved in the project.
History
    A summary of the history of the project.
How can I help ?
    If you would like to support the web..
Getting code
    Getting the code by anonymous FTP , etc.

Figure 2.1 The reclaimed version of the "first page" of the World Wide
Web, via CERN.

But this is pretty clearly *not* what the site looked like on "day one" given that
elements of this page clearly depend on the Web having been up and running for some time. Indeed the "day one" iteration of this page would not
have had a prominently featured "What's out there?" link for the simple
reason that *nothing was*.

The World Wide Web is not the only internet phenomenon to suffer
from incomplete archiving. We know even less about the first e-mail mes-

sage than we do about the first website. Taken together, these failures to archive point up a significant series of truths about composition in networked digital spaces:

1. Texts in networked digital spaces are necessarily designed *for circulation*; and

2. The rapid and friction-free circulation of digital texts makes it likely that most texts will be archived for a period of time; and

3. The rapid and friction-free circulation of *more* and *more* digital texts makes it likely that most digital archives will fail to meet even their own stated missions.

Networked digital media, despite being readily amenable to archiving, end up being functionally unstable over time. This instability materializes from any number of directions. The following are some of the major contributing factors to the instability of internetworked digital texts.

James. E. Porter was among the first to recognize that it was important to distinguish between *networked* writing and *internetworked* writing. In his 1998(!) book *Rhetorical Ethics and Internetworked Writing*, Porter draws an appropriately sharp distinction between the work that had been occurring on the various and scattered networks that predated widespread adoption of the Internet, and an array of internet-based activities (extending ultimately to reading, browsing, collecting, and researching) all of which Porter repositions—in an idea that felt new at the time—as kinds of writing:

> This project raises questions of the ethics of *internetworked writing*—by which I mean computer-based electronic writing that makes synchronous or asynchronous links to remote participants or databases. Internetworked writing refers to the creation, design, organization, storage, and distribution of electronic information via wide-area networks. (Electronic information includes not only verbal text, but also audio, visual, and cinematic "text" distributed via the Internet and World Wide Web.) Internetworked writing includes activities such as posting email messages to groups or individuals, browsing and collecting documents from electronic archives, developing electronic text for and maintaining electronic archives and web sites, and synchronous conferencing. *Internetworked writing differs from networked writing in that it involves writing for and on the Internet.* It refers to more than simply closed, local-area classroom or corporate systems, but refers more broadly to what we might consider a wider *public* space (although the exact notion of "public" may vary from technology to technology). It refers to wide-area and public uses of electronic text (as opposed to, for instance, using word processing to create a print document) *In the*

> *sense I am using the term, internetworked writing also refers to more than simply posting text: It includes reading, browsing, and collecting electronic text, as research activities that are also types of writing activities.* (2, emphases added)

At the time Porter wrote, less than five percent of the world's population was using the Internet. The Internet was, overwhelmingly, a space for academics, nerds, and hobbyists of varying stripes. Yet, Porter was prescient enough to understand that the profound shift in digital writing tools brought about by the widespread availability of computers was about to be complemented by an explosion of writing and writing-adjacent practices on the newly public Internet. While writing within networks was arguably almost three decades old in 1998 (if we count from the first e-mail transmission in 1969), *internetworked* writing was very new and had only scratched the surface of its full potential.

Porter describes a then-not-yet-in-existence Internet as "what we might consider a wider *public* space." It is important to note that one of the implications of the wider public space we now inhabit is an associated and inevitable shift in what *public*ation means and does. For half a millennium, the degree to which print publication was both labor and material-intensive necessarily implied that not just anyone's writing could or would find its way to a broader public. The costs involved in pouring alphanumeric characters into codex books prompted a layered system of gatekeepers, charged with decisions large and small as to whether a work was worthy of public consideration and consumption.

Porter also points at the degree to which *internet*worked writing promotes a then-newly expansive understanding of what might count as writing activities. Porter lists reading, browsing, and collecting electronic texts as research activities that, from his standpoint, must also count as *writing* activities. In this paragraph, Porter comes very close to hitting upon the term that would come to describe writerly practices of reading, browsing, and collecting in the twenty-first century: *curation*. In this framing, Porter wisely sidesteps the positioning of print, digital, networked, and internetworked writing as competitors and promotes a more fluid definition of writing that seems better aligned to the fluidity of the texts that would come to inhabit the Internet in the intervening years. By so doing, he finds his way to a writing that clearly builds upon, rather than competes with, the centuries of literate practice leading to the advent of internetworked writing. Indeed, this lesson is one we find not only in our engagement with texts, but also in the ways our engagement with texts intersects with our experience of the material world. Porter's prescient identification of internetworked writing is complemented by a sustained focus on writing spaces and writing technologies. At this moment, we find writers gravitating to spaces in cloud-based software and services. To the extent that these writers carry forward, optimize, and reinvent their preferred practices from print ecologies, writing in clouds does not destroy, but complements, the writing we have known under previous technological circumstances.

On April 15, 2019, like many others around the world, I watched Notre Dame cathedral burn in real time via streaming news coverage on the World Wide Web. As an agnostic with no deep ties to any faith tradition (who had nevertheless visited Notre Dame on a trip to Paris decades ago), I felt a vague sickness as the damage to this cherished structure became increasingly pronounced. I watched Parisians sing hymns as this profoundly significant church building was burnt, bent, and broken by fire.

It now seems clear—despite the archdeacon's projection *and* the fire—that Notre Dame will endure. Neither print nor its supposed successors (cinema, radio, television, and the Internet to name four of the more prominent candidates) have displaced Notre Dame as a space for gathering, reflection, and contemplation. Indeed, the Internet became a gathering space for the words and thoughts of those grieving the building's damage as it burned. Two days after the start of the fire, with what remained of the cathedral still smoldering, French Prime Minister Emmanuel Macron pledged to restore and renew Notre Dame: "We will rebuild Notre Dame, more beautiful than before—and I want it done in the next five years. We can do it. After the time of testing comes a time of reflection and then of action" (Lyons and agencies).

Notre Dame will endure in no small part *because* of its enduring place within the textual and visual media that have been developed since it was erected. Initial construction on Notre Dame commenced in 1160, in a time of script literacy. The Gutenberg Bible, printed in the 1450s, is an edition of the Vulgate, which would go on to become the Catholic Church's endorsed version of The Bible. This text, was then carried on missions throughout the rest of the world, reinforcing the significance of cathedrals like Notre Dame throughout Europe. To this we add Hugo's nineteenth-century novel *Notre Dame de Paris* that drove the restoration of the cathedral's stained glass, and prompted *dozens* of adaptations into all of the various media invented since print: cinema, radio, television, comics (and many more adaptations in a range of forms including music, musical theater, ballet, opera). *All* these many adaptations—all of which were, to varying degrees, facilitated by print—have served to inscribe Notre Dame into the cultural consciousness to a degree that even if largely destroyed by fire, a shared sense of Notre Dame's cultural significance *requires* that it be rebuilt.

This (print) does not destroy that (Notre Dame). Indeed, once the ongoing restoration is completed, it will be fair to say that print has *saved* Notre Dame. Twice.

Nor will internetworked writing destroy print. As our composing spaces have migrated to cloud spaces, internetworked writing is, increasingly, the means by which people connect themselves to collaborators, and ultimately, to larger communities of composers. Indeed, as the following pages will demonstrate, internetworked writing is the very thing that will help preserve most of the aspects of print that are worth saving.

3 Clouds, Composers, and Collaboration

The concept of *cloud computing* as something more than a vague metaphor has a relatively short history. The concept began to gain traction after Netscape co-founder Marc Andreessen's September, 1999, founding of a business known as Loudcloud. Loudcloud's business was not precisely *cloud computing* in current terms, but rather a turnkey all-in-one website service (Venkat). That said, the terminology at the heart of this business corresponded closely to the current rhetoric surrounding server-driven computing. In a 2000 article for *Wired*, David Sheff describes Loudcloud's initial engagement with its customers in terms that would not be out of place in our current and more overtly cloudy context: "Customers start by choosing from a menu of Clouds: a Database Cloud, an Application Server Cloud, a Mail Cloud, a full Web Cloud, et cetera" (Sheff). Thus, Andreessen and his team members played a key role in the conceptualization of networked arrays of distributed servers as *clouds*.

One of the earliest *mainstream* media references to the cloud as a space for composing, creating, or housing information appears in a 2000 *New York Times* article titled "The Future, Through Microsoft's Glasses." Drawing heavily on Microsoft's product demonstrations, reporter Sam Howe Verhovek provides a snapshot of a technology giant amid a major course correction:

> [W]hat is Microsoft's vision for its next generation of services, which the company calls ".NET" (pronounced dot-net)?
>
> In essence, according to the demonstrations at the company's conference center here on Thursday, Microsoft.NET is about offering what is often called a "cloud" of services on the Internet, to be accessed by a range of personal devices, including hand-held "tablets" and organizers, cell phones, cameras and whatever else inventors dream up.
>
> It promises a world of incredibly instant gratification.

It is important to underscore that at the time this was written, the list of "personal devices" at the end of this article was almost wholly speculative. The overwhelming majority of cell phones at that time had no functional connectivity to the Internet. In the United States, only extreme early adopters were text messaging in 2000, as less than thirty percent of the United States population even owned a *cell* phone. (Tuckel and O'Neill 4002). The *New York Times* reported that only three percent of all mobile phone users "intentionally use the message service" (Hafner). Affordable and functional tablet computers were a solid decade away. It's fair to say that at this point, clouds were more vision than practical reality.

To both Andreessen and Microsoft's credit, they understood the resonance of the idea of the cloud as a conceptual space for human-computer interaction. The nuts-and-bolts reality of the spaces in which online computing takes place borders on depressing. Server farms filled with racks upon racks of high-powered computers, almost innumerable skeins of wiring, and immense investments in cooling technologies offer a dark—if not dystopian—portrait of the spaces in which online composers write, create, and express themselves. A generation of computer users had initially been sold on the notion that the personal computer's primary advantage over the old mainframe-and-client model was the degree to which PCs were, indeed, *personal*. Before always-on broadband connections to the Internet became standard, it was possible to draw sharp distinctions between the stuff on one's own hard drive and the *other* stuff *out* on the Internet.

And the stuff out on the Internet was often viewed with a mixture of wonder and fear. *Time* magazine's now infamous 1994 cover depicting the "strange new world of the Internet" is emblematic of the cultural uncertainty that hovered over the Internet throughout the 1990s. While browsers like Andreessen's Netscape Navigator and Microsoft's Internet Explorer did an amazing job of *normalizing* the look and feel of the Internet—allowing Internet information to adopt forms not far removed from newspaper and magazine layouts—many lay users of the Internet were reasonably wary of the privacy implications of linking their personal computers to the purportedly strange worlds of the Internet. The enterprise-level server-client infrastructures that offered protected paths to a mainframe computer were walled gardens that felt secure. Among the dominant metaphors used to describe the Internet were *the frontier* (with more than a whiff of *Star Trek* geek aspiration in tow), and *the Wild West* (with a pungent aroma redolent of lawlessness and might making right).

It is all but impossible to isolate the precise moment when the cloud began displacing these metaphoric frames as the preferred descriptor of the spaces outside users' personal machines housing their ideas, compositions, and data. Even so, the above snapshots of leading Internet innovators coalescing around the idea of the cloud underscores the metaphor's importance as a rhetorical framing device. Among other things, positioning the external spaces of Internet-based computing as *up* (rather than the more accurate *out* or *down*) carries with it a host of positive associations.

Andrew Blum's 2012 book titled, *Tubes: A Journey to the Center of the Internet*, documents Blum's global journey to understand the physical technologies that facilitate the Internet. It is surprising how much of this journey takes Blum *down* into spaces like abandoned subway tunnels under Manhattan, and ever lower, to the ocean-bottom-scraping trans-Atlantic cables stretching from the east coast of the United States to the coast of Cornwall in the United Kingdom (also known as Land's End). At one point, Blum interviews a Facebook representative while sitting in a data center in a small town in Oregon, and suddenly Blum realizes that he is, effectively, sitting mere steps away from the cloud that likely houses a good bit of the data that he has produced as a Facebook user:

> I couldn't avoid the breathtaking obviousness of what was physically in front of me: A room. Cold and empty. It all seemed so mechanical. What had I handed over to machines—these machines in particular?

> "If you blew the 'cloud' away, you know what would be there?" Patchett asked. "This. This is the cloud. All of those buildings like this around the planet create the cloud. The cloud is a building. It works like a factory. Bits come in, they get massaged and put together in the right way, then packaged up and sent out. But everybody you see on this site has one job, that's to keep these servers right here alive at all times." (Blum 256)

With due respect to the satellites that participate in our ability to access the Internet via mobile devices, most of the technologies that make up what we now understand as cloud spaces are transmitted via wires that we could see . . . *if* we knew where to look. Among the tangible markers of the cloud are: wires underground, wires undersea, and wires within ecologically suspect server farms where thousands of computers whir away while processing terabytes of data. The *upness* of clouds as the metaphoric spaces in which we now work so much of the time directs our attention above and away from the practical realities that facilitate these spaces.

Further, in a Western context, there is a substantial bias toward traveling skyward, whether literally or figuratively (ideas of ascension, especially those associated with Christian depictions of Heaven, are perhaps the most important here). The virtual cloud metaphor is clearly directed at only a thin strip of what clouds are and mean in terrestrial contexts. When the Internet clouds are depicted in advertisements and popular media, the illustrations are typically of fluffy cumulus clouds, neatly sidestepping the practical reality that some types of clouds (yes, we're looking at you, cumulonimbus!) are overtly threatening in nature.

In an expansive and much needed historicization of the steps that led us to accepting the cloud metaphor, Tung-Hui Hu rightly casts a wary eye toward the relationships between cloud users and cloud providers:

Seen correctly, the cloud is a topography or architecture of our own
desire. Much of the cloud's data consists of our own data, the photographs and content uploaded from our hard drives and mobile
phones; in an era of user-generated content, the cloud is, most obviously, our cloud (this is the promise of the "I" in Apple's "iCloud,"
or to use an older reference, the "my" in "mySpace"). Yet these fan-
tasies—that the cloud gives us a new form of ownership over our data,
or a new form of individualized participation—are nevertheless structured by older, preexisting discourses. (xvii)

Indeed, one of the baseline challenges we now face when composing in
cloud-based writing spaces is the degree to which our work now often depends on the maintenance of our relationships with providers of cloud services. The big four in this area are Amazon, Apple, Google, and Microsoft.
The former is in the cloud business to sell stuff to us, and the other three
are all in business to sell information about us to the people who wish to sell
stuff to us. Contemplating this fact at any length is enough to prompt most
composers to at least consider the possible merits of composing tools that
are incapable of connection to the Internet. But that path ultimately leads
to recalling all the risks involved with composing tools that produce just a
single physical copy of a given text.

When 350 pages of Ralph Ellison's long-hoped-for follow-up to *Invisible Man* burned in a fire at his cabin, *that work product was destroyed*. These pages, and the countless hours of work they represented, went up in smoke.
Unpublished paper pages were always fragile and sometimes precious. But
Ellison would have a hard time actually losing manuscript pages in a contemporary context. The dogs that famously ate homework are largely re-
tired now that homework exists in the both here and there spaces of various clouds. But as our texts live both in front of us and apart from us, our
sense of ownership in those texts inevitably erodes. United States copyright
laws felt intuitive when writers produced a single manuscript that *because of its
singularity* had pronounced value. The right to *copy* that manuscript has special significance because the manuscript itself was precious. Of course, one
reason why writers can no longer feel the level of near exclusive ownership over their manuscripts is because they are aware, however dimly, that
they are now writing in spaces that others own. At the moment I am typing
these words, this manuscript resides more fully in Dropbox than it does on
my laptop.

To the extent that texts are composed in spaces facilitated and
maintained by Amazon, Apple, Google, and Microsoft—even if these corporations make no significant claims on this work—writers write with at least

a faint awareness that their work is not as unequivocally owned by them to the same degree that texts were when housed in previous technologies. Possession, as the saying goes, is nine tenths of the law, but a text that lives within the composer's machine *and* on multiple servers is, to say the least, a complicated possession. In many cases, the composer accepts the implicit quid-pro-quo with reasonably open eyes because paper was so very fragile. The catastrophic losses of work that extended up to and through the fire that consumed Ellison's 350 draft pages, and the numerous data-destroying computer crashes from the mid 1980s to the mid 2010s likely persuaded most digital composers that having back-ups sprinkled in servers scattered across the planet is in their interest. The price points for the relative peace of mind that internetworked backups offer feel reasonable, and composers are, arguably, free to select services in alignment with their own comfort levels.

Each of the major providers of online storage has a tentacle or two wrapped around each of the composers using its services. These spaces, are, by design, widely distributed. They exist only because some companies can scale their services to the level needed to ensure that if a hypothetical Godzilla stomps the server farm in Orem, Utah, my manuscript will still exist in numerous other sites, some presumably far from Godzilla's likely footfalls. So, while I would be adamant about my own legal ownership of my written work products, my sense of ownership is ever-so-slightly eroded by my lingering awareness that my work is now housed in spaces that are both facilitated and owned by corporations.

Further, the degree to which cloud-based writing spaces facilitate collaborative writing—both synchronously and asynchronously, makes them especially attractive to people working in many disciplines within academia, and in a broad range of institutional and professional settings. We do well to note, though, that while collaborative writing seems both common and "natural" in our contemporary contexts, this has not always been widely understood, even after the widespread adoption of digital writing technologies. In their 1992 book, *Singular Texts/Plural Authors*, Andrea Lunsford and Lisa Ede conducted a series of surveys that arrived at the then-noteworthy conclusion that: "collaboration is not specific to a limited number of documents, but rather . . . it is a frequently used strategy in producing documents of all kinds" (63). That collaborative writing was also a relatively new phenomenon in non-medical disciplines in the early 1990s is also underscored by Ede and Lunsford's reports that their tenure and promotion committees struggled with how and whether to count their collaborative writings as part of their academic work products. While some might shrug in response, believing single-authored texts are *the* model that has served readers well for centuries, that shrug would now be occurring at the precise moment that cloud technologies are delivering remarkable opportunities to collaborative writers. One indicator of this is the degree to which people could now choose from broad array of cloud-based tools that facilitate collaborative writing and composition.

For those working in academia (or indeed, in most educational settings) such choices are routinely made on their behalf at the institutional level. My campus (the University of Minnesota) is a Google campus and as a practical matter, that means it is impractical for me to attempt to opt out of Google's cloud-based services. While there are many programs that I prefer to Google's office suite and Google Drive, the university's license exerts enough of a push on me and my colleagues that abstention from certain Google cloud apps would effectively exclude me from much of the day-to-day communication of my department, my college, and university life more broadly. Indeed, Google's relationship with my university recalls the soft-drink contracts that transformed campuses into "Pepsi campuses" and "Coke campuses" in the 1990s. Navigating away from Google at my campus is about as easy as locating a vending machine with Pepsi products on my "Coke campus," which is to say, borderline impossible. There is no direct cost to me for Google's suite of services, though it is likely my university is paying two to four dollars per user for Gmail, Google Drive, and all of the associated apps (Abamu). The so-called "G Suite" is not a big revenue driver for Google, but it does achieve another goal, making *all* of Google's online services "stickier" in the sense that I am more likely to use Google's search tools because they are contiguous with the suite of applications my university has purchased for me to use and as the *lingua franca* for our campus.

Thus, one of the leading candidates for my "default" writing space, Google Docs is one tentacle in a Google squid that is intent on pulling me back toward Google's search tools, and, given Google's dominance in the search category, the quid pro quo is a bit more imbalanced in Google's favor, with my search history being datamined to sell me stuff I may or may not really want or need. This remains the case despite the availability of dozens of open source and open access options for those who would prefer to opt out of the sometimes-invasive ways in which the leading corporate clouds monetize the services they offer. For better and for worse, many of us now feel dependent on the quid pro quos established with our employers by some of the largest multinational communication companies in human history.

For the arguments that follow, I will usually be bracketing the question of whether one *should* enter into these bargains. While in this book I will often celebrate the possibilities cloud computing offers to composers of texts, especially collaborative writers and multimedia composers, this must not be understood as an endorsement of the skewed bargains those same composers often face. For the moment, the tools that are working most efficiently, or that have the largest user bases, are those backed by multinationals, but it is quite possible to envision a future in which the cloud features users prefer migrate into spaces with greater respect for their privacy, and less interest in turning them into commercial targets.

The benefits of real-time collaboration at a distance and cloud storage are genies that seem squarely removed from their respective bottles. For years, writers were at risk of forgetting to save their work. Now saving of progress is routinely automatic and constant. When writers forget, algorithms remember. The amount of effort required to actually lose digital work has spiked dramatically. The egregious cut-and-paste disasters still occur, but most of them can be unwound with a quick trip up to the "undo" command. While writers might find better-balanced bargains with respect to their own rights and privacy—or we all might choose to *build* such spaces—it is difficult to imagine writers willingly returning to the paper-thin fragility and enforced solitude of typewriter-based textual production across the board.

Within the fields of rhetoric and composition studies, Johndan Johnson-Eilola's 2006 monograph *Datacloud: Toward a New Theory of Online Work* was among the first to embrace the concept of the cloud and to begin to investigate its implications for processes of composition and rhetorical invention. Johnson-Eilola writes:

> We are in a networked culture, both in the sense of communication networks and concepts, objects, and subjects being considered by interconnected social and technical forces. . . . The possibility of agency within these apparently chaotic contexts requires us to adjust some of our assumptions. Our existing models of both communication and work tend to support relatively linear, orderly, modernistic activities and objects. Work in the information age, however, increasingly requires a different approach. . . . From a datacloud way of thinking, we need simultaneous access to multiple channels, information overload be damned. (9–10)

Johnson-Eilola here rightly argues that the shift toward the cloud as a conceptual space is not without cost. While machines (like the typewriter) that both enabled and enforced the isolation of textual composers arguably facilitated processes in which the composer spiraled ever deeper into an at least *semi*-personal space, the insistent call of the cloud within our composing tools places a new array of demands before twenty-first century composers.

To cite one obvious example, for research-based composers, the very real physical limits of library collections and textual accessibility allowed composers to say—with at least a degree of confidence—that the research phase of a writing project was complete. Composing in the cloud, by contrast, leaves researchers in a state of nagging uncertainty as to whether and how to locate parallel stopping points when—after all—just one more (or new) source is always no more than a few clicks away.

Research in the age of cloud computing is—in many respects—easier than ever before. Substantial research efforts can be pursued without ever setting foot in a library. A staggering portion of the extant published corpus of scholarly writing can be found online. The major search engines do a remarkable job of leading researchers to key phrases and ideas. Targeted tools like Google Scholar facilitate the kinds of focused searches that allow researchers a degree of confidence about the scope of prior work in their chosen areas of study. The opportunity to pursue keyword and key phrase searches in texts further serves to bring texts into conversation with one another. Some scholars, though, mourn the potential loss of the "serendipity factor" that many scholars acknowledge as occurring when they arrive at bookshelves arranged according to a cataloging system like the Dewey Decimal System. These scholars will testify that these trips to physical libraries routinely result in them leaving with significantly more texts than those initially sought. Of course, this is not really serendipity. The purpose of cataloging systems is to group like texts together, with Melville Dewey's system pioneering an approach that allowed for repeated subdivisions of a given catalog number to *ensure* that closely related texts would end up in close proximity to one another. But whether serendipitous or by design, to the extent that some current library editions are electronic, rather than physical, this opportunity for researchers to identify connections among texts may be compromised.

This concern has been taken seriously enough that academics have repeatedly dedicated themselves to recreating this "serendipity factor" in virtual spaces, and—potentially—expanding opportunities for these kinds of "lightbulb" moments. One notable example of these attempts to port the physical serendipity factor into cloud-based spaces was a 2012 SIG-CHI project titled "The Bohemian Bookshelf" by Alice Thudt, Uta Hinrichs, and Sheelagh Carpendale. This project offers a malleable visual interface that would allow its users to pursue links among texts in many ways over and beyond what is typically possible in library spaces. The "Bohemian Bookshelf" prototype invited participants to pursue links among texts through not just keywords, but also author names, timeframe, cover color, and number of pages. While this interface was calibrated for use with–

in physical libraries on a large interactive display, the general concept has obvious potential for a wide range of virtual spaces. As the authors write: "There are many digital data collections that could benefit from a serendipitous approach to information exploration such as news feeds, photos, videos, or music collections" (Thudt et al. 9) More recently, a 2019 project by Harvard-based researchers with the intuitive name BookVIS attempts to provide a parallel serendipity factor by allowing its users to screenshot the cover of a book and then receive links to arguably similar books based on the Goodreads database. Notably, the starting point for this enquiry into similar books is the selection of a physical book from a shelf in a library or bookstore. Maintenance of serendipity in virtual spaces is an ongoing site of study and innovation, but the supposed strengths of the physical library space hang heavily over this body of scholarship. It is likely that we remain too tethered to print conceptions of writing spaces to envision a fuller array of serendipity possibilities offered by virtual tools.

Contemporary researchers have usually had many experiences where a simple search of a key term has led to a journey through a chain of links providing depth, context, or shading to the term that prompted the initial search. Research tools like Zotero and Mendeley that not only intuitively manage much of the citation, reference, and bibliography work formerly done by hand also offer opportunities for researchers to share references with like-minded scholars, thereby opening up the possibility of "crowdsourced serendipity." Research, like writing, has too often been a lonely enterprise. The ever-increasing aggregations of data *and people* in cloud-facilitated spaces offers significant potential to transform the experience of research, though the increasing presence of colleagues within one's research process is not an unalloyed positive.

Universities remain structurally biased toward rewarding *individual* achievement. Co-authorship in some disciplines is still understood more as a "problem" to be managed rather than as a reflection of contemporary composers responding to current opportunities for collaboration, many of which are facilitated by cloud-based tools as fundamental as the writing module within Google Docs. Given the structural biases toward sole authorship, some academics may reasonably resist even the low-level cooperation involved in sharing curated lists of citations. Further, when the research involves projects with significant financial potential, it may well be wise for researchers to keep their "cards" face down.

Further, most publishing models are structured around protecting information until the point at which no significant revenue can be extracted from it. While researchers at major universities can depend on access to *most* of the proprietary databases housing *most* of the research from their peers, the prices for scholarly journals have skyrocketed over the past few decades. As a practical matter, research processes are often slowed by the distribution of pertinent articles across a series of proprietary silos that are not designed to effectively interconnect with one another. This model reinforces understanding of an article as a freestanding argument rather than as a participant in a *network* of interconnected arguments. The question at hand is whether and how the publishing industry can develop a model that effectively leverages the added value of *participation* in these networks in a way that maintains revenue streams. If not, peer review—the hallmark of academic publishing—may well migrate to spaces outside of the traditional journal structure. The Public Library of Science has—for almost two decades—published an expanding array of peer-reviewed scholarly journals all of which are open access and funded by fees charged to the contributing authors. Of course, this model is not sustainable across all scholarly disciplines, and the presence of payment from authors raises ethical concerns that become pronounced when other journals without PLOS's strong reputation pursue contributions (both textual *and* financial) from scholarly authors.

To the extent that the twenty-first century university system is structured around acknowledging and rewarding *authorship* it runs the risk of being unable to see significant scholarly *writing* in all the many ways it now happens. Specifically, it lacks a toolkit that is equipped to process huge swaths of significant scholarly work that now radiates throughout the Internet in the form of websites, blogs, podcasts, YouTube videos, *Medium* articles, and even the occasional precisely calibrated tweet. Kathleen Fitzpatrick sounded an alarm with respect to the challenges of academics properly weighting online compositions in her 2011 book, *Planned Obsolescence: Publishing, Technology, and the Future of the Academy.*

> [W]e'll . . . need to let go of some of our fixation on the notion of originality in scholarly production, recognizing that, in an environment in which more and more discourse is available, some of the most important work that we can do as scholars may more closely resemble contemporary editorial or curatorial practices, bringing together, highlighting, and remixing significant ideas in existing texts rather than remaining solely focused on the production of more ostensibly original texts. We must find ways for the new modes of authorship that digital networks will no doubt facilitate—process-focused, collaborative, remix-oriented—to "count" within our systems of valuation and priority. (12 –13)

A decade after Fitzpatrick's call for an expanded playing field, the university is still—by and large—seeking and valorizing *authors* while many of its most talented composers are routing at least some of their ideas through alternative and even social media. For the most part, this work doesn't count. And, because of the way it takes shape, it may *never* count precisely because it is *hard* to count.

In cases of organic online collaborations, it can also be difficult to unravel who contributed what. It is often the case that people contribute freely before they recognize they are producing something that has value to a larger audience. Many years ago, I went to a Minneapolis bar to meet with Markos Moulitsas, the founder of the *Daily Kos* political blog. As the name implies, *Daily Kos* had initially been a personal project for Moulitsas ("Kos" being a nickname based on the final syllable of his first name). When I met Moulitsas, I had a single question for him, and that was: "At what point did you realize that the site had moved from a space in which you and a small group of hand-selected bloggers were the dominant voices, to a vast community-authored project which sometimes appears to function almost without a center?" Moulitsas's answer seems obvious now, but it wasn't at the time. He explained that there was *never* an identifiable breaking point in which his initially sole-authored- and then small-team-authored blog turned a corner and the people involved recognized that they were in a wholly new—and massively collaborative—space. Rather, the growth had been—at least as the *Daily Kos* team processed it—incremental to the point that it was hard for him to locate major decisions that led to this outcome, characterizing it instead as the cumulative effect of aggregations of minor decisions.

This is, to some degree, the way of the Web. We see this same dynamic in place in the circulations of memes, with only an occasional sense of the moment at which a brief spark of creativity sets the terms of the latest argument, character, dynamic, or meme. Academic conferences have, historically, been the spaces where scholars gather to feel the crackle of collective ideas being built out in real time, but cloud composing spaces offer opportunities for synchronous and all-but-synchronous composition. While it is easy to dismiss memes as ephemeral snippets of pop culture, the dynamic authorship models visible in memetic production exemplify a fluid, collective creativity that has a demonstrated ability to scale within small windows of time. And no one who lived through the 2016 election ought to be broadly dismissive of memes as a means by which significant political content *can* be distributed.

Yet, though most memes are probably meant as ephemeral contributions to an imaginary shared refrigerator door, they have rightly become objects of sustained scholarly inquiry. This is, in no small part, because memes productively complicate questions of authorship, ownership, and invention. Limor Shifman's 2014 book *Memes in Digital Culture* outlines collaborative and responsive production patterns as of the ways memetic content defies the critical tools applied to traditional texts:

> [A]n Internet meme is always a collection of texts. You can identify a single video and say "This is a viral video" without referring to any other text, but this would not make much sense when describing an Internet meme. A single video is not an Internet meme but part of a meme—one manifestation of a group of texts that together can be described as the meme. . . . [M]emetic content is closer to the original idea of the meme as a living and changing entity that is incorporated in the body and mind of its hosts. [Emphasis in original.] (56)

Thus, if a meme falls on the Internet and there is no one there to riff upon, remix, or recirculate it, *then we really don't have a meme at all.* We might have a composition with a shape or structure that recalls other memes. This composition might attempt to mimic recognized memetic genres like the "stock character" memes that have, in the past, featured "Bad Luck Brian" or "Overly Attached Girlfriend," usually accompanied by a legend in the outlined variant of the **IMPACT FONT**, but in the absence of uptake and participation by composers who find something to build off of in the initial composition, we have not arrived at memetic composition.

Indeed, memetic composition is a demonstrably internet-specific phenomenon (notwithstanding some overreaching efforts to shoehorn pre-internet examples of viral ideas into the contemporary memetic model). Whitney Phillips and Ryan M. Milner's description of memetic composition in their 2017 book, *The Ambivalent Internet: Mischief, Oddity, and Antagonism Online*, is shot through with illustrative examples that underscore how memetic composers depend on the affordances of internetworked writing tools:

> [A]s more and more people create and explore and tinker with themselves across a variety of digital platforms. And reduced social risk, often spurred on by anonymity, allows these tinkerings to veer into territory that participants might be inclined to avoid in embodied spaces, for better and for worse.
>
> What emerges from this cacophony isn't a singular, self-contained, easily traceable litany of texts, authors, and meanings. Rather, online spaces are tangled with tissues upon tissues of quotations, multiplicities upon multiplicities of authors, and densely knotted meanings hinging not on who made what thing, or even on the thing itself, but on what memetic motifs resonate with an unknown number

of unseen audiences, who can further their own resonant meanings simply by posting a link. (202)

Elsewhere within this project I have identified spaces where there is striking continuity between writing's past and writing's present. Much of the current moment reflects a lingering attachment to the habits of print production. But in the case of memetic compositions, we see composing strategies that feel significantly and distinctively internet specific and even cloud specific. The rapid collaborative layering and escalation of memetic composition probably has ancestral ties to the writer's table for sketch comedy shows. But the levels of effectively simultaneous improvisation and play facilitated by digital spaces *combined* with the richness of graphical tools allows us to point to the internet meme as a new genre of writing, and one with inventional patterns that are distinctive to this internetworked moment in communicative technologies.

Memetic compositions are distinctively cloud-based compositions. They depend upon the affordances of clouds for their raw materials. They further depend upon specific dynamics of textual consumption and production facilitated by cloud spaces. Memes are tiny compositions meant to live and multiply in a writing space that did not exist in the twentieth century. In the summer of 2019, "Woman Yelling at a Cat" had a brief run as the arguable meme of the moment. The meme, juxtaposing a shouting woman and a purportedly confused cat, has become a flexible structure for tweaking the overwrought responses people sometime have to trivial matters, and the degrees of confusion that these overwrought responses can cause.

The remarkable meme research site KnowYourMeme.com has identified all the steps and sources for this meme, and taken together they are as follows:

1. December 6, 2011: The newspaper *The Daily Mail*, publishes a dramatic screen capture/photo of *Real Housewives of Beverly Hills* cast member Taylor Armstrong shouting and pointing.

2. June 19, 2018: Tumblr user deadbefordeath posts an image of a confused white cat sitting at a dining room table surveying a plate of green vegetables, with the caption "he no like vegetals." The subsequent uptake of this photo had the unexpected consequence of making the cat in the picture, Smudge, an icon for some blend of confusion and/or justifiable disappointment.

3. May 1, 2019: Twitter user @MISSINGEGIRL, who composed a tweet pairing both of the images in the now familiar side-by-side format and then wrote: "These photos together is making me lose it."

Figure 3.1: An example of the "Woman Yelling at a Cat" meme, from memeRIOT.com

4. May 2, 2019: Twitter user @lc28_ who refined the side-by-side images for a meme-structured post labeled: "Me accusing my cat of cuddling with other people when I come home drunk after bottomless brunch."

5. June 2, 2019: Reddit user PerpetualWinter is the first to exploit the contrast between the two images with the image of the shouting Taylor Armstrong and her friend being labeled: "KNICKS FANS AND NY MEDIA NEXT YEAR" and the cat being labeled: "KRISTAPS PORZINGIS JUST PLAYING BASKETBALL."

6. June 9, 2019: Reddit user -69— posts a template with the two images to the /r/memes subreddit.

7. June 9, 2019: Redditor Apple-Trump uses the template to post: "Girls when they see a spider/The spider." This version of the

> "Women Yelling at a Cat" meme is the first to be significantly viral, receiving 38,600 upvotes in 12 days. (adapted from Phillipp and chevyrolet)

Each contribution to the meme is incremental and, clearly, no single contributor deserves significant credit for having developed the meme. Notably, in this case, PerpetualWinter is the first to establish the left/right contrast that has since become the hallmark of the meme, but because this example hinges on knowledge of New York Knickerbockers basketball, there was little uptake or commentary in response to this composition. Apple-Trump's composition is a more accessible version of PerpetualWinter's joke, albeit with a dash of gender stereotyping. With Apple-Trump's iteration of the meme, the terms of the game are clarified, the relationship between the images is stabilized, and the meme then becomes a flexible template for certain kinds of observations about conflict and confusion.

Memes are typically defiantly and delightfully authorless. While the first example of what goes on to become a meme might have a single composer, what makes it a meme is the uptake by a larger pool of composers, each of whom has a potential to shift the understanding and the meaning of the original composition. Nor would I argue that the world would be better if we pushed the "authorship" button in cases like this and required attribution for either the incremental steps or the meme as a whole. Indeed, part of the charm of the meme as a genre is the degree to which it flies below the radar. It is often a space where—for better and for worse—people say the things they would not say if attribution were part of the equation. And there is only so much control that any individual can exercise over that uptake. More than one creator of a composition or concept that became memetic has issued a Prufrockian cry of *"That is not what I meant, at all"* only to learn that the composition's new life and new meaning are so entrenched as to obscure the possibility of ever returning to the original intention or meaning.

This, of course is true of *all* compositions with any popular uptake. At this point there is not THE *Adventures of Huckleberry Finn* so much as there are *Adventures of Huckleberry Finn*—a point that rhetorical critic Steven Mailloux makes in his 1998 book *Reception Histories: Rhetoric, Pragmatism, and American Cultural Politics*. But while Mailloux traced the shifting understandings of an inarguably significant American novel and its measurably painful racial characterizations over decades, the meme ecology invites us to consider micro-compositions with brief lifespans. Twain's work is a whale to a meme's mosquito, and while we do well to pay attention to how these works are received and how their meanings change over time, the toolkits we use must acknowledge the difference between a lifespan measured in centuries as opposed to a lifespan measured in weeks.

And while we might be inclined to dismiss even the very best variations on the "Woman Yelling at a Cat" meme as trivial, the compositional structures and patterns that underpin memetic composition are potentially profound. Generations of composers are now sensitized to the specifics of typography and juxtapositions of texts and images that intertwine to produce a successful contribution to a larger body of memes. They are—on many social media platforms—able to track audience uptake and approval in something approaching real time. Memetic compositions are one of the ways people will learn to compose image-rich texts in coming years. Taking memes seriously as a form of cloud-based composition—whether the memes themselves are meant to be taken seriously or not—offers ways to discuss invention, collaboration, uptake, and audience. To the extent memes emphasize these aspects of writing in clouds, they provide entry-level lessons in embracing more collaborative and connective modes of internetworked writing.

4 Arranging Invention: The Rise of the Second Rhetorical Canon in Internetworked Writing

One of the most profound implications of our escalating reliance on cloud-based spaces for written composition is the degree to which these spaces have the potential to prompt shifts in invention practices and strategies. To the extent that cloud composing spaces are designed to facilitate collaboration, they offer a significant intervention into the theories that have been derived from the communication technologies associated with rhetorical invention. As has so often been the case, the relationship between communications technologies and communication theories and pedagogies is highly intertwined, with many moments where which drove the other is as debatable as the initial sequencing of chicken and egg.

In a Western context, the rise of rhetorical theories recognized as such coincides with the advent of alphabetic literacy. Greek rhetoric is very closely intertwined with the hot new communication technology of the fifth century BCE: the Greek alphabet. That said, tracing the history of how the predominantly speech-focused theories of Greece were adopted and adapted to writing over five centuries, is instructive. These adaptations, culminating in a distinctively Roman approach to rhetoric are instructive, and reflect the degree to which conceptions of invention are in large part the by-products of the available composing technologies at any given cultural moment.

For most of the history of rhetorical theory, the rhetorical canon of invention has held a status that borders on "first among equals" at best and "some canons are more equal than others" at worst. Invention is literally the first, sequentially, of the five rhetorical canons—invention, arrangement, style, memory, and delivery—stabilized in *Rhetorica ad Herrennium*—a Latin text from the first century BCE without a reliably identifiable writer (attributions to Cicero are not accurate). The rhetorical canons are properly understood as a series of steps leading from initiation to delivery of rhetorical discourse, with an orally delivered speech serving as the paradigmatic case of the kind of composition a rhetorician might invent. The orientation of the rhetorical canons toward spoken delivery is made clear by the fourth canon: memory, which in its initial formulation referred primarily to the rote memorization of an already-composed speech for the purposes of oral delivery.

But the lie embedded within the initial framing of the canons of rhetoric is that any of the canons can be wholly pried apart from any of the others. To the extent that invention, arrangement, style, memory, and delivery can be ported to a contemporary circumstance, we immediately understand these canons to be participants in overlapping recursive processes rather than discrete steps. The compositional activities associated with each canon circulate *throughout* composing processes, never in isolation, and certainly not in a stable sequence.

In the intervening millennia between the initial discussions of invention by Western theorists and today, invention has overwhelmingly been understood as the first, and thereby the most important of the canons. Further, invention has often been presented as the step a writer takes *in isolation*. Beginning composers are routinely advised to go somewhere quiet and get in tune with their presumed inner voices. Others' words and ideas are, in these frameworks, corruptions of something authentic and internal. But to the extent that we accept visual aspects of composition as a significant aspect of many contemporary compositions, there is little to pry apart the canons of invention and arrangement, *especially in internetworked digital composing spaces.*

Indeed, the rhetorical canon of arrangement now stands as the canon that seems most adapted to the practical realities of digital composition. In certain contemporary cases, arrangement is indistinguishable from invention. For example, in the production of a meme, a composer repurposes an image from popular culture with specific typographic effects. Whether an identifiable idea is conceived prior to the execution of the meme is debatable, but to the extent this invention exists, it is thin, and yet some memes—especially those with political content—have demonstrable cultural impacts.

The collapse of the canons into one another is a reflection of the complexities of our current cultural moment. The rise of digital and internetworked media prompted Collin Gifford Brooke to undertake a wholesale revision of the canons in his 2009 book, *Lingua Fracta: Towards a Rhetoric of New Media.* Brooke's rebooted and updated canons are proraesis / pattern / perspective / persistence / performance, with proraesis and pattern aligning roughly with invention and arrangement. Brooke's positioning of proraieses, which is an ancient Greek term describing the act of choosing one thing before another is especially significant, as it posits that the start of the composing process might be less like manifesting the heretofore-non-existent from scratch and more like selecting from among existing options or, perhaps, extant compositions. In constructing his "canonical" proraesis, Brooke turns to, as an illustrative example, the "social bookmarking" services that were then especially popular among academics, including del.icio.us. Brooke writes:

> The practice of bookmarking and using one of these services is a perfect example of proraietic invention and how that invention can be intrinsic to a particular interface. The addition of each bookmark changes the site, reinforcing certain connections, adding new ones, and expanding the network in small but important ways. It enables a process of associational research and exploration that resists closure. (85)

Brooke's canons seem responsive to his moment, and helpfully counter some of the limitations embededded in the ancient formulations, but as an advocate of using the term *composer* in places where "author" and "writer" typically occur, I remain attached to invention and arrangement as key terms in the composing process encapsulated by the canons. The ancient terms offer ready gateways to understanding written composition by way of analogy to *musical* composition, and this often has the effect of demystifying composition for those who are not yet able to see themselves as composers. Brooke's proraietic invention blurs the lines between traditional arrangement and invention and reminds readers to understand canons as permeable and not separated by firewalls.

Krista Kennedy offers pathways to arrangement-rich modes of invention in her 2016 book *Textual Curation: Authorship, Agency, and Technology in Wikipedia Chambers's Cyclopaedia*. Kennedy's argument draws upon her studies of the encyclopedia genre as a space, and foregrounds the importance of arrangement in contemporary writing spaces:

> Arranging, interconnecting, and recomposing are essential skills; these skills may manifest themselves in the everyday life of a writer through something as simple as a carefully ordered stack of books relevant to a chapter that is under construction or as complex as a cross-referenced, tagged, categorized reading blog that also links to external sources. Such structuring is deeply familiar work to any writer who works extensively with digital information. This understanding of the labor processes associated with composing in current digital environments leads us to a different conceptualization of collaboratively produced digital information structures, whatever their genre: open, interconnected, and not necessarily finished in the ways that we previously deemed projects to be complete once they were published and distributed as print artifacts.

While Kennedy's work is anchored in the curatorial practices that are foundational to the encyclopedia genre, this paragraph sees her speaking more broadly to compositional practices across genres (and Kennedy should be taken at her word when she invokes "composing in current digital environments"). Also worthy of note is the degree to which "collaboratively produced digital information structures" seem in Kennedy's framework to be not peripheral genres, but significant participants in what writing is and means in the current moment. Because Kennedy emphasizes collaborative production, we do well to remind ourselves that composition has, throughout Western history, swung from privileging individual composers to emphasizing collective contributions. And further, that literacy technologies play a profound role in shaping our perceptions of who composers are and should be.

In the 2005 edition of *The Printing Revolution in Early Modern Europe*, Elizabeth L. Eisenstein presents the advent of print as having profound cultural consequences that include—in her formulation—the recognition of a "drive for fame" that, in Eisenstein's framing, had not been as present or pronounced prior to Gutenberg:

> The "drive for fame" itself may have been affected by print-made immortality. The urge to scribble was manifested in Juvenal's day as it was in Petrarch's. The wish to see one's work in print (fixed forever with one's name in card files and anthologies) is different from the desire to pen lines that could never be fixed in a permanent form, might be lost forever, altered by copying, or—if truly memorable—be carried by oral transmission and assigned ultimately to "anon." Until it became possible to distinguish between composing a poem and reciting one, or writing a book and copying one; until books could be classified by something other than incipits; the modern game of books and authors could not be played. (94 –95)

Eisenstein goes on to build her argument by offering an oft-cited passage from a thirteenth century Franciscan, St. Bonaventura, in which he stair-steps from scribe to compiler to commentator to, finally, "author," which is defined as "one who writes both his own work and others' but with his own work in principal place adding others' for purposes of confirmation" (95). As Eisenstein notes this passage is "remarkable . . . for its omission of completely original composition" (95). Indeed, at the time St. Bonaventura wrote, it was unimaginable that an author (admittedly, of *non*-fictional works like essays and treatises) would ever be able to construct a text that was not significantly entangled with the works of others. Indeed, circa the thirteenth century, the possibility of a wholly original text appears to have been unimaginable.

The omission of putatively "completely original composition" is all the more remarkable when Eisenstein's "modern game of books and authors" is set against the longer history of rhetorical invention in Greco-Roman contexts. The very first text included in *The Rhetorical Tradition*, an overtly field-defining anthology of Western rhetoric, is Gorgias' *Encomium of Helen*. The *Encomium* is notable for the degree to which it is an exercise in fluid play between the composing patterns endemic to speech and to writing and an exercise in complexifying the relationships among composers and audiences. Nowhere is this more evident than in the following passage, where Gorgias superficially ascribes great power to speech while simultaneously asserting *his own power* as a composer:

> Speech is a powerful lord, which by means of the finest and most invisible body effects the divinest works: it can stop fear and banish grief and create joy and nurture pity. I shall show how this is the case, since it is necessary to offer proof to the opinion of my hearers: I both deem and define all poetry as speech with meter. Fearful shuddering and tearful pity and grievous longing come upon its hearers, and at the actions and physical sufferings of others in good fortunes and in evil fortunes, through the agency of words, the soul is wont to experience a suffering of its own. But come, I shall turn from one argument to another. (41)

By the close of the *Encomium*, Gorgias repeatedly celebrates the power of logos as being concentrated in him as an intending agent:

> I have by means of speech removed disgrace from a woman; I have observed the procedure which I set up at the beginning of the speech; I have tried to end the injustice of blame and the ignorance of opinion; I wished to write a speech which would be a praise of Helen and a diversion to myself. (54)

This assertion of both willful invention and of ownership over the resultant text places Gorgias remarkably close to invoking a roughly modern construction of authorship. But this relatively clear articulation of what seems almost like authorial intention was not consistent among leading theorists of invention and composition who succeeded Gorgias.

A Western construction of rhetorical invention begins to take shape in remarkably challenging examples of writing from this period that remain sites of ongoing study and speculation. For example, Plato's *Phaedrus* is a dialogue featuring *only* Socrates and Phaedrus as discussants (with a sort of guest appearance in the form of a speech, presented in full, composed by the sophist Lysias). The *Phaedrus* is, in all likelihood, a literary construction composed by Plato, based on—at most—a recollected historical interaction described to Plato after the fact. Yet, this literary construct famously contains Socrates leveraging what is presented as a mythic tale of an Egyptian god of the underworld(!) inventing writing, which is decried in this myth as the destroyer of memory. As many have pointed out, perhaps none more powerfully than Jacques Derrida in his essay "Plato's Pharmacy," the *Phaedrus* is a dialogue that appears to argue for its own non-existence. There are a lot of layers to this particular onion. We leave Plato's dialogue understanding that rhetors invent in both spoken and written genres, but without substantial guidance as to how we ought to do so.

Similarly, despite his pedagogic bent and his facility with taxonomies, Aristotle's *On Rhetoric* defies readers seeking a clear articulation of how rhetorical invention functions and what might constitute optimal inventional practices. In a 1986 *Rhetoric Review* article titled "Aristotle's *Rhetoric*: Reinterpreting Invention," Ellen Quandahl points up the difficulties facing those who wish to mine the text for a clear account of rhetorical invention:

> [T]he *Rhetoric* is difficult to read, full of discrepancies, gaps, and repetitions. It was composed, as far as we know, in three segments and over a long period of time. It combines theoretical statements, commonsense descriptions, and references to the rhetorical practices and teaching of Aristotle's contemporaries. If the text itself is exigent, scholarship makes it more so. We have to read the Rhetoric against a tradition that has interpreted it as a philosophical rhetoric, but often reduced that philosophy to a logic of argument or to taxonomies of discourse, and separated it from questions of language and style. And over the past two decades the controversies have gone on among teachers of speech communication more than among teachers of literature and composition. For all of these reasons, the Rhetoric doesn't seem an available pedagogical resource, in spite of the general recognition of its historical importance. (128)

The import of Quandahl's critique is that to the extent Aristotle addresses invention, he does so in a way that is not likely to be accessible to most contemporary students. While, for example, Aristotle's *ethos, logos, and pathos* appeals are now commonly taught as critical lenses, the ways in which one ought to use the appeals to construct discourse are more implicit than explicit in *On Rhetoric*.

The best current translation of Aristotle's *On Rhetoric*, George Kennedy's 2007 second edition, subtitled, "A Theory of Civic Discourse," offers only two index entries for "invention." The first is to Kennedy's headnote for Book 1, in which Kennedy arguably undercuts the very idea of Aristotelian invention *qua* invention. Kennedy writes:

> Books 1 and 2 discuss the means of persuasion available to a pub-
> lic speaker by presentation of the speaker's character as trustworthy,
> by use of persuasive arguments, and by moving the emotions of the
> audience. Although this part of rhetoric has come to be known as
> "invention" (from Latin, *inventio*) Aristotle himself offers no general
> term for it until the transition section at the end of Book 2, where it
> is referred to as *dianoia*, "thought." (27)

Kennedy's presentation here underscores the degree to which Roman rhetoricians were responsible for stabilizing a conception of invention (centuries after the composition of *On Rhetoric*) that was then projected *backward*
onto Aristotle's text. This retro-projection is further underscored by Kennedy's other indexed reference to invention, which appears as "39n" but is
clearly directed at note 37 on page 38. In this section, Kennedy is translat-
ing Aristotle's discussion of *pisteis*, often translated as "proofs." Kennedy's
translation reads:

> Of the *pisteis*, some are atechnic ("non-artistic"). Some entechnic
> ("embodied in art, artistic"). I call *atechnic* those that are not provided
> by "us" [i.e., the potential speaker] but are pre-existing: for example,
> witnesses, testimony from torture, contracts, and such like; and *en-
> technic* whatever can be prepared by method and by "us"; thus one must
> use the former and invent the latter. (38)

Kennedy promptly drops note 37 after this use of "invent" where he explains: "*Heurein.* 'to find'; *heuresis* becomes the regular Greek word for rhetorical invention" (38). But before we accept this transformation as a *fait
accompli* it is probably wise to take Aristotle at his words as he wrote them.
With respect to the challenges facing a rhetor (in this example, the surrounding frame is clearly a judicial proceeding) the rhetor has externally
supplied pre-existent information and then additional discourse that must
be "found" effectively *within* the rhetor, by means of art. Kennedy has already, by this point, translated the famous beginning of Book 1, Chapter 2
of *On Rhetoric* as: "Let rhetoric be [defined as] an ability in each [particular]
case to see the available means of persuasion" (37). Thus, a rhetor grounded
in Aristotelian rhetoric would be skilled in, for example, diagnosing whether a particular circumstance called for an epideictic speech, and might then
gravitate toward Aristotle's exemplary epideictic argument forms—praising
and blaming—because the rhetor rightly sees them as available, but how and
where the praise or blame comes into existence is, for the most part, un-
clear. In Book 2, Chapters 20 –26 Aristotle offers lists of common modes
of persuasion and common topics, all of which function as kinds of a struc-

tural or conceptual "sourdough starter" for arguments. Even so, for a book that is sometimes inaccurately cited as the source for the rhetorical canons of invention, arrangement, style, memory, and delivery, Aristotle delivers faint guidance on how invention *happens*. *On Rhetoric* is strong on diagnostics, routinely offering structures and strategies keyed to particular discursive situations. It is less helpful with respect to where arguments come from in the first place, providing models and examples where one might expect to find training in inventional processes. In effect, Aristotle's emphasis falls on inviting rhetors to *find* arguments by means of an internal art rather than clearly articulating *how to construct* them.

The namesake for this Parlor Press series, Janice Lauer, accurately describes the post-Gorgias rise of rhetorical theory and practice in Greece as a space where invention is a fascinatingly complex and confusing topic. This complexity is compounded by significant disagreements among contemporary scholars. Lauer closes her review of the rise of rhetoric in the fifth century BCE with the following summation:

> As the above discussions of Greek views of invention illustrate, issues abound among the Sophists, Plato, and Aristotle as well as among their interpreters. Differences exist over which inventional acts and arts are included in the texts: *kairos* and *status* [ed. note: more commonly known as *stasis*] as initiators of discourse; special and common topics as exploratory arts; *dissoi logoi*, enthymeme, example or dialogue as forms of rhetorical reasoning; and probability, truth, or certainty as rhetorical epistemologies. They also disagree over the purposes of invention: initiating discourse with questions, issues, or contradictions, creating knowledge, reaching probable judgment, finding arguments to support existing theses, communicating truths or supporting persuasive propositions. (22)

Lauer is here pointing up the degree to which the texts themselves are at times confusing, and so, by extension, is the scholarship attempting to wrangle these works into something like a coherent theory. Given the emphasis on Greek contributions to rhetorical theory, it is notable that Roman rhetoricians bear substantial responsibility for bringing a measure of order to the topic. But that order occurs in defiance of the breaks and disruptions among the extant texts.

Rhetorica ad Herrennium, while offering the first extant stabilized account of the rhetorical canons, remains a strikingly mysterious text. We do not know the composer, though misattributions to Cicero are common. We do not know much about the addressee, Gaius Herennius, beyond his name. We can timestamp the text to roughly 80 BCE, but beyond that, we are unable to fully reconstruct the circumstances of the text's composition. That said, *Rhetorica ad Herennium* is arguably a repository of significant extensions of Aristotelian rhetorical theory, including framing invention being used for "six parts of a discourse," namely: introduction, statement of facts, division, proof, refutation, and conclusion. A compressed version of this same framework is, of course, taught as the "five step essay" or "five paragraph essay" to this day. The *Rhetorica ad Herennium* composer argues that a speaker should possess the "faculty" of invention (along with each of the other canons, which are all described as faculties that a speaker should possess). The composer glosses invention as "the devising of matter, true or plausible, that would make the case convincing" and goes on to explain:

> All these faculties we can acquire by three means: Theory, Imitation, and Practice. By theory is meant a set of rules that provide a definite method and system of speaking. Imitation stimulates us to attain, in accordance with a studied method, the effectiveness of certain models in speaking. Practice is assiduous exercise and experience in speaking. (Book I)

When, later in the text, the *Rhetorica ad Herennium* composer refers, in passing, to "the theory of Invention," the reader is able to scan back through the text and see a theoretical understanding of what it means to invent discourse taking shape.

Given the title, Cicero's *De Inventione* would seem likely to be an especially important intervention into the Western history of invention theories, but it does not rise to that level. Or, to be fair, the *surviving* volumes (two books of four) do not represent an especially strong contribution to the overall arc of Western understandings of inventional strategies in rhetoric and writing. Cicero's *De Oratore* is more commonly cited by scholars seeking an account of Cicero's views of Invention, but because *De Oratore* is a dialogue, scholars should exercise care with respect to whether the ideas voiced by the characters reflect Cicero's own views. Lauer's summarizing paragraph addressing Cicero's contributions to the history of Western understandings of invention is notably muted:

> The dialogic format of *De Oratore* enabled Cicero to review several positions on the nature, purpose, and epistemology of invention. As seasoned rhetorical performers, Crassus and Antonius privileged their talent and interaction with the rhetorical situation as causes of their rhetorical success although their rhetorical education in invention was evident in the conversation. Such a position is understand-

able since as prominent rhetors they had by then internalized their education and had used it to enhance their own powers. (26)

So, while invention is first and implicitly most important of the rhetorical canons stabilized in *Rhetorica Ad Herennium*, Cicero's contribution to a broader theory of invention is often internalized, implicit, and inferential. It is, perhaps unsurprisingly, a project directed at the *teaching* of rhetoric that harnesses these discussions of invention into a more recognizable and—for Westerners—familiar form.

In a project directed at the pedagogical strategies needed to build an "ideal orator," the Roman rhetorical scholar and teacher Quintilian eventually arrives at very contemporary constructions of invention and authorship. This, Quintilian's best-known project, *Institutes of Oratory*, is often criticized for Quintilian's unusually high degree of dependence upon the works of others throughout the text. Quintilian rarely advances in argument in the first nine books of *Institutes* without grounding it in copious citations of his predecessors' works. Indeed, *Institutes* is one of the best available summations of many texts since lost to the fires, floods, and other various destroyers of written words. Yet, both the beginning and the ending of *Institutes of Oratory* find Quintilian in a space where his claims squarely anticipate Eisenstein's purportedly "modern game of books and authors."

First, Quintilian suggests that the *Institutes* came into existence only because literary pirates were circulating works under his name. Quintilian wrote the Institutes late in life, after decades of building his reputation as an instructor. His lack of written output eventually prompted others to attempt to trade on his reputation in a very early indication of a functional book trade in the West. Quintilian's prologue refers to "two books on the art of rhetoric which are at present circulating under my name, although never published by me or composed for such a purpose" (I.PR.7). Quintilian, by his own account a reluctant writer, is here positioning his own composition as an effort to use publication to regain ownership over what he perceives to be a distinctive array of ideas. That said, the nature of this distinction is worthy of examination.

Quintilian's pedagogical model is grounded in a painstaking sequence of imitations of extant models. Once a student has demonstrated a capacity for imitation, that student is afforded opportunities for invention, which increase as the student demonstrates competence at each step. Quintilian ends up arriving at a standard that has become a key element in how—in addition to publication—we separate writers from authors:

> It does not follow that because we should select one author for special imitation, he should be our only model. What then? Is it not

sufficient to model our every utterance on Cicero? For my own part, I should consider it sufficient, if I could always imitate him successfully. But what harm is there in occasionally borrowing the vigour of Caesar, the precision of Pollio or the sound judgment of Calvus? For quite apart from the fact that *a wise man should always, if possible, make whatever is best in each individual author his own*, we shall find that, in view of the extreme difficulty of our subject, those who fix their eyes on one model only will always find some one quality which it is almost impossible to acquire therefrom. Consequently, since it is practically impossible for mortal powers to produce a perfect and complete copy of any one chosen author, we shall do well to keep a number of different excellences before our eyes, so that different qualities from different authors may impress themselves on our minds, to be adopted for use in the place that becomes them best. (X.ii.24 –6, emphasis added)

This baseline standard of taking the work of others and making it one's own is celebrated variously as the dividing line between writers and authors, plagiarism and originality, and kitsch and art. Note, that there is good stuff to be found at both ends of these putative poles, but there can be no question which of each of these terms is the more culturally favored.

The final chapter of Quintilian's *Institutes* is notable for Quintilian's poetic treatment of his feeling of having moved beyond the body of extant work. Here Quintilian announces himself as having met his own standard, and having taken in and understood the works of others to the point where he now feels free to offer a distinctive contribution that should rightly travel under his own name:

Now there is "Nothing before and nothing behind but the sky and the Ocean." One only can I discern in all of the boundless waste of waters, Marcus Tullius Cicero, and even he, though the ship in which he entered the seas is of such size and so well found, begins to lessen sail and to row a slower stroke, and is content to speak merely of the kind of speech to be employed by the perfect orator. But my temerity is such that I shall essay to form my orator's character and to teach him his duties. Thus I have no predecessor to guide my steps and must press far, far on, as my theme may demand. (XII.Intr.4)

For Quintilian, *imitation* is the mother of invention. The rhetor is the space wherein the internalization of good models meshes with wisdom (or, perhaps, judgment) to lead to distinctive and novel discourses that are rightly understood to be the property of their composers.

All of this underscores a somewhat obvious truth: what Eisenstein refers to as "the modern game of books and authors" has deep roots in Western discursive practice, and especially, within a long conversation within rhetorical theory with respect to the nature and meaning of invention. Significantly, the notion of textual ownership did *not* arise as a by-product of print, though the stabilization of laws codifying authors as owners of certain textual discourses *did* follow in print's wake. To state the obvious, the need for a copyright law is predicated on there being mass-produced (i.e., print) copies with significant monetary value, and to which more than one individual might plausibly assert an ownership right.

Simply put, while there is value to be had in framing shifts and developments in the ways people communicate with one another as "revolutionary" when looked at within the space of even a century or two, most communication patterns and practices remain roughly constant. David Levy's 2001 book *Scrolling Forward: Making Sense of Documents in the Digital Age* features a passage in which Levy, taking a wide-lens view, marvels at how consistent human discursive practices have been to that point:

> For most of five thousand years of writing history, all our techniques and technologies have been directed at making visible marks stick to surfaces. It is only in the last hundred years that radically different mechanisms have been invented. . . . And now, thanks to computers, we are developing still other mechanisms and forms. These include "everything," as David Weinberger puts it, "from a text-only word-processing file to a Java-soaked interactive Web page."
>
> Are these new forms really a breed apart, as David Weinberger argues? Not really—certainly not to the extent he suggests. Are text files and spreadsheets and Web pages talking things? Of course they are. They speak through still and moving images—the same basic communicative repertoire we had before computers appeared on the scene. (34–35)

As Levy's invocations of Weinberger suggest here, the onslaught of digital communication is, in part, the function of significantly more ephemeral communication being recorded. But the degree to which ephemeral communication is now rendered into written forms rather than speech forms necessarily implies that we must again consider how, whether, and when our definitions of authors and audiences ought to be bounded.

Historically, the implied honorific of author has been maintained not simply for people who write, but for those whose writing bespeaks some level of artistic or literary aspiration. In this framework, Sir Arthur Conan Doyle and Charles Dickens, both of whom initially published their works serially in periodicals are now understood to be authors, but Bob Woodward and Carl Bernstein, whose book, *All the President's Men*, grew out of their work as reporters for *The Washington Post* would not initially be understood as *authors*, so much as they remained reporters, or writers *of a sort*. There is a line people draw between writers and authors, and in most cases they do so intuitively.

It is common for those who wish to pry the two terms apart to attempt to do so on the basis of whether the composer's output has been published or not. Thus, one would be a writer of that which has not been published, but once a work goes through the steps required for publication, that pushed one toward authorship territory, depending on the nature of the writing involved. The question we now face is whether—in the absence of print publication serving as a clear demarcation line—we now ought to acknowledge a similarly blurry line between writers and authors. What we find is the degree to which the figure of the author is enmeshed in a foundationally imbalanced, exclusionary, and ultimately unfair framework for cultural production makes the figure of the author a hard case for rehabilitation.

But if publication is the dividing line between writers and authors, we must reckon with the practical realities of publication throughout at least the last few centuries. And opportunities to reach the rarified standing of "author" have generally been disproportionately distributed, with an immense bias toward, well, people demographically like me (and in my case, that's cis white male). In "A Room of One's Own" (now thought of as an essay, but first delivered as a reading/speech), Virginia Woolf makes this point clearly and powerfully:

> In the first place, to have a room of her own, let alone a quiet room or a soundproof room, was out of the question, unless her parents were exceptionally rich or very noble, even up to the beginning of the nineteenth century. Since her pin money, which depended on the goodwill of her father, was only enough to keep her clothed, she was debarred from such alleviations as came even to Keats or Tennyson or Carlyle, all poor men, from a walking tour, a little journey to France, from the separate lodging which, even if it were miserable enough, sheltered them from the claims and tyrannies of their families. (51)

Woolf is, of course, speaking to the writing opportunities available to *women* as of 1929, but, of course, in an Anglo-American context aspects of these same challenges were faced by most of the population owing to some combination of gender, ethnicity, or family/economic status.

Woolf's woman-writer-wishing-to-be-an-author likely needs that room of her own for two reasons. First, the writer's room must be *sound-*

proof to give the writer space to think and reflect. Woolf writes wistfully of the contemplative spaces she found on England's most elite college campuses:

> [I]f the spirit of peace dwells anywhere, it is in the courts and quad-rangles of Oxbridge on a fine October morning. Strolling through those colleges past those ancient halls the roughness of the present seemed smoothed away; the body seemed contained in a miraculous glass cabinet through which no sound could penetrate, and the mind, freed from any contact with facts (unless one trespassed on the turf again), was at liberty to settle down upon whatever meditation was in harmony with the moment. (5)

But the second reason for Woolf's emphasis on soundproofing is likely that she is conscious of the likelihood that even aspirational writers of her time *might be using a typewriter and thus making a lot of noise*. In addition to the needed room, to the extent that machine composition was favored (and in some cases necessary) for twentieth century authors, this required a substantial investment in the writing machine itself, costing between $50 and $250 for 1929's top-of the line Electromatic Typewriter, which, when adjusted for inflation, would range from roughly $500 –$3700 in current dollars. Re-markably, the cost of writing machines from the 1910s is roughly equivalent to the cost of contemporary writing tools when adjusted for inflation. And the cost of writing machines has, until recently, pretty much *always* been a lot of money.

In a very real sense, for most of the history of the concept, author-ship has been a country club membership. And opportunities for writers to become authors have been distributed roughly as fairly and equitably as country club memberships. The entire raison d'etre for country clubs was exclusion. In 1907, John Gordon Steele labeled country clubs "the very es-sence of American upper-class," and that maintenance of that upper class was facilitated by membership restrictions that routinely excluded Jews, Catholics, people of color, and women. Though country clubs have, over the past half century, slowly, often grudgingly, and often under threat of lit-igation, retooled their admissions policies so that anyone can be a member, this does not necessarily mean that all the people historically excluded now wish to be members. This also creates a dynamic where country club mem-bers from historically excluded groups are often those most comfortable with the existing culture of the country clubs. In her 2009 essay "The View from the Country Club: Wealthy Whites and the Matrix of Privilege," Jessi-ca Holden Sherwood underscores the degree to which the price of admis-sion is often assimilation:

Today, nonwhites are granted admission; but the contexts remain culturally white. Those nonwhites—indeed, any non-WASPs—who belong to the clubs in this study are assimilated enough that they do not disturb the "comfort zone" that dominates members' conception of who does and does not belong. (139)

Sherwood's research, drawing on interviews with country club members, documents the degrees to which race, class, and gender become functional obstacles to club membership:

Given the American ideals of open access and equal opportunity, club members must account for the fact that their clubs only admit new members by selective invitation. They account for their exclusion in either of two ways: by arguing that there is really no meaningful exclusion taking place, or, if exclusion is acknowledged, by excusing and justifying it. Variants of the first theme range from simply denying that there is any screening to saying that the only filter is social ties, or residence, or affordability, to saying that virtually anyone could afford to belong. (138)

Further, gender roles within country clubs are traditional and male dominated, with marriage often being the pathway for women receiving second-tier limited memberships. Sherwood's assessment of the gender roles within country clubs is pointed:

Gender segregation is more culturally accepted than explicit racial segregation. Some club members speak approvingly of separating the sexes, in a way that they would not, today, of separating "the races." This may be, ironically, because gender subordinates are in many ways closer to their dominators than class and race subordinates. (149)

Notwithstanding this relative "closeness," the elite Muirfield Golf Club—a host to many British Open tournaments—held a vote where members failed to reach the 2/3 majority needed to include women as full members *in 2016*. While the vote was overturned in 2017, the recency of this insult testifies to the degree to which the prejudices and bigotries of the past shape our present.

With these painful realities in mind, we are prepared to grapple with the implications of Groucho Marx's pointed one-liner: "I wouldn't belong to any club that would have me for a member." On the surface, this appears to be Marx making a joke at his own expense. Groucho's obstreperousness was a well-established part of his comedic persona at the time this quote circulated. When the Marx Brothers visited the races, the opera, a university, or a big store, generally those sites came out somewhat damaged in the encounter. But there's another meaning embedded in this joke—one that had to resonate with at least *some* members of the audience who heard Marx's quip. At the time Marx made his joke, many clubs—country clubs and others —refused admission to Jews. A second tier of country clubs serving Jews who had been excluded from elite country clubs rose up in the first half of the twentieth century. Marx, an avid golfer, was a longtime member of Hillcrest Country Club, a historically Jewish country club in Los Angeles. Thus, when Marx jokes about not wanting to belong to a club that *would* have him as a member—that is, a club that accepts Jews—an aspect of this joke is about the obvious differences between the well-established elite clubs serving white populations and the newer clubs that served Jewish populations whose families had emigrated to the United States relatively recently. Marx, is, of course, operating on a number of levels here. It is not that he doesn't mean that any club that would accept the Groucho character would not be worth joining. But the joke *has* to also address the dynamics of clubs and clubbiness in the United States that surrounded Marx as he ascended into mid-century celebrity in the twentieth century.

Golf courses are not merely recreational spaces. They are spaces where social connections and status are reinforced. They are spaces where deals get made. The exclusionary power of spaces like country clubs cannot be fully addressed by building parallel spaces for those excluded. That strategy can be neatly summarized as "separate but equal," and it has an embarrassing track record in the United States. The degree to which literate life in an Anglo-American context has followed a parallel trajectory to the exclusionary patterns of country clubs is visibly apparent. To use one available benchmark as to which authors count most in United States culture, we can observe a 2 –1 bias in favor of men's writing over women's writing in the Pulitzer Prize for Fiction (previously known as the Pulitzer Prize for the Novel). While the twenty-first century has served as a corrective to a degree, the twentieth century's Pulitzers for fiction writers also has an observably immense bias against non-white writers. Membership in this elite "club" has been slow in coming. This speaks to the degree to which nearly every aspect of cultural life in the twentieth century was marked and marred by reluctantly proffered pathways toward recognition of non-white and/or non-male peoples as full members of the clubs that dominate national cultural conversations.

When instructors approach the tasks of training students in rhetorical invention as a *pathway to authorship*, they must do so with an awareness that most of the students in *any* given classroom carry with them at least one demographic characteristic that in the very recent past would have complicated their aspirations toward claiming "author" as a title for themselves. Gender identity, race, faith, and family circumstance have all been mobilized to suggest that while there is an author's club that is open to *others*, it is not necessarily open to the likes of *you*.

Adam Banks's scholarship suggests that the degree to which authorship's doors have been closed is a multidirectional loss, both for the students who feel left out, and for United States cultures at large. In his 2011 book *Digital Griots: African–American Rhetoric in A multimedia Age*, Banks speaks to available opportunities in the recalibrations of invention and arrangement (signaled here by his invocation of remix) made possible by digital media:

> Because technology use, production, and design (and the role each plays in the public imagination) are all so thoroughly embedded in rhetorical acts, one could argue that technologies themselves are rhetorical in nature. This rhetorical nature extends from the first imaginings that lead to *invention* and design to decisions about which designs to pursue; writing practices of students or the practices we want them to develop or the rhetorical practices that take place in a remix culture, I'm interested in the rhetorical possibilities that emerge from the culture that gave us the remix. The preacher, storyteller, standup comic, everyday black people in conversation, and the DJ can help black students see themselves reflected more genuinely in writing classrooms and theory and can benefit all students looking for a greater appreciation of the multiple connected and diverging cultural influences on writing in a society that is (very slowly) becoming coming more genuinely inclusive and multicultural. (14, emphasis added)

When Banks points toward "the culture that gave us the remix," he is referencing African American culture, and indeed the rap and hip-hop cultures of the early 1980s provided numerous innovative composing models that have since been ported into internetworked writing spaces. But the journey to contemporary remix cultures, and, implicitly, to new understandings of the role of the canon of arrangement, is both remarkable and complicated.

One obvious ancestor to contemporary remix is the *dub* techniques of Lee "Scratch" Perry who was a leader in developing an offshoot of reggae in which studio production took centerstage in the late 1960s. Perry's *dub* versions of often-familiar reggae tracks involved dense reverb, removal or transformation of vocals, and heavy emphasis of the rhythm section (drums and bass). Perry's work sometimes consisted of cascading "versions" in which a single song was sometimes so radically transformed by Perry's studio wizardry that two versions of the same song might not—on first listen—seem to share a common ancestor. It is thus likely not coincidental that two of the most prominent members of the 1980s wave of pioneering hip-hop turntablists hail from regions where Perry's sonic experimentalism was in wider circulation than in the United States. DJ Kool Herc moved from Kingston, Jamaica, to the Bronx in 1967 where he developed the *break*—an extended dance break created by mixing between the dance breaks of two copies of the same record. Grandmaster Flash moved from Barbados to the Bronx as a child and went on to develop scratching and an early version of sampling. These techniques, achieved with turntables, vinyl records, and mixing boards, are conceptual ancestors to the cut-and-paste possibilities made more generally accessible by digital media.

Remix also arrived at its current form owing to the less-discussed creativity of Tom Moulton, who was arguably the first United States-based composer to be celebrated for remixes as an artistic achievement. Moulton's work is only rarely cited in scholarship addressing the movement of remix from its roots in musical production to a broader cultural strategy facilitated by digital tools, with Lev Manovich, who has repeatedly emphasized the importance Moulton's contributions, being a notable exception. Moulton initially popularized remixing to tape, and his tapes became a notable draw in the gay club scenes on Fire Island in the early 1970s. Within this club culture, Moulton is recognized as a true innovator. Andrew Mason's richly multimedia 2011 article for *Wax Poetics* speaks to Moulton's substantial contributions to remix as we now understand it:

> Tom Moulton did not invent music, discos, dancing, or vinyl records. But he has a fair claim to the patents on several of the most important innovations rising from the combination of those ingredients. "He pretty much singlehandedly created the art of extended remix," states Dimitri From Paris, one of today's leading practitioners of the art. Along with this creation came its natural partner, the 12-inch single. And what about those long, soloed sections of percussion beloved by dancers and disc jockeys, known as the "disco break"? Another Moulton invention. (par. 1–2)

What separates the "extended dance remix" of the late 1970s from the artefacts prized in contemporary remix cultures is their lack of interpolation. Interpolation, simply defined, is the introduction of part of an existing composition into another distinct composition. Moulton's dance remixes, by contrast, were extended by means of reproducing existing elements of songs—usually especially danceable grooves—and repeating them, effectively creating a longer version of the same composition, and effectively creating a longer version of the same composition, and effectively creating a longer version of the same composition, and effectively creating a longer version of the same composition. This composition strategy anticipates the ease with which text can be cut and pasted in digital spaces. It also opens questions about when and whether a given composition should be understood to have arrived at its final form.

For a significant swath of the twentieth century, popular song lengths were constrained by the available space on a 45 rpm single, which could accommodate—at most—about five minutes of music. If a composer had a song that lasted longer than that—Don McLean's "American Pie" and James Brown's "Get Up (I Feel Like Being a) Sex Machine" are two examples—the accepted approach was to release the song broken into two parts, each of which would take up one side of the record. This *clearly* did violence to the experience of engaging with the compositions as the composers had envisioned them. Stopping, pausing, flipping the record over, and dropping the needle on the vinyl interrupts the flow of getting the Chevy to the levy *or* shaking your moneymaker. But the limits of the technology defined what did and did not fit, and it was left to the most committed composers to push back against these medium-based limitations.

The advent of tape and the twelve-inch vinyl single changed the landscape of possibility for recorded music. These formats allowed composers like Tom Moulton to extend compositions for the audiences inhabiting dance floors, in some cases making hits out of songs that had not caught on in their more abbreviated versions. In practical terms that means there are, for example, multiple distinct versions of a song like Gloria Gaynor's version of "Never Can Say Goodbye" tailored to different media and the different audiences associated with those media. The song was released as part of a nineteen-minute "disco suite" produced by Moulton, on a vinyl LP of the same name. The song was also extracted from that suite and issued on a twelve-inch vinyl single lasting six minutes and twenty seconds, and also issued on a 45rpm seven-inch single at three minutes flat. Each of these might stake a claim to being the definitive version of Gaynor's song, but it might be fairer to say that there *is* no definitive version (although the three-minute version feels a bit spare to anyone who has heard the longer versions). This transformation of a core work as it moves through a range of media spaces (in 1974!) offers a preview of the ways content would move through digital media a few decades later. The technical skills modeled by the innovators of early dance and hip-hop would be echoed in the tools built into operating systems and software. Copying, pasting, and rearranging are among the most important *and* accessible features of digital media.

By the late 1970s these two streams began to intersect. The vinyl twelve-inch single became the site for the initial wave of remix, in which the extension of the most danceable parts of a song gave way to the interpolation of James Brown's screams, grunts, and exhortations, and then certain favored break beats (the most notable of these being the "Apache" Break which is now instantly familiar to most consumers of pop music under fifty). The academic narrative that argues that we, as a culture, have ported remix strategies to digital writing spaces writing often emphasizes the Jamaica to New York connection but only rarely addresses the degree to which Moulton's contributions (along with Perry's) set the stage for that work. Taking all of these narratives together, an important point emerges: so-called minority populations in the United States found their way to remix strategies well before mainstream US cultures were able to process or understand these distinctive approaches to composition. Even so, after the advent of digital technologies, these same composing strategies seemed obviously ancestral to the composition strategies facilitated by digital tools.

In *Digital Griots*, Adam Banks offers a focused definition of remix, paired with an explanation of its particular appeal to teachers of writing:

> The remix is a common, if somewhat floating, signifier among compositionists. It is usually meant as any reuse of an original text, as a repurposing of that text, or sometimes as any recombination of elements from many sources in the creation of a new text of any kind. These conceptions are much closer to how DJs mean and use the mix than how I am using remix here. The remix as employed by these scholars is prized as a concept because of how it values a sense of play with texts and various nontextual elements and because it allows teachers and students generic possibilities beyond those immediately rooted in the standard academic essay. It is also valued because of its semantic proximity to postmodern notions of pastiche and because it gives teachers a concept of revision that their students can easily grasp, thanks to its ubiquity in popular culture. (87–88)

The import of Banks's argument is clear. Twenty-first century *writing* students will benefit from the incorporation of remix strategies into the writing classroom. And they will benefit *because* the remix DJ offers an illustrative example of a composer who moves toward invention *by way of arrangement*:

> DJs are not mere ventriloquists, playing or telling other people's stories for us; rather, their arranging, layering, sampling, and remixing are inventions too, keeping the culture, telling their stories and ours, binding time as they move the crowd and create and maintain community. (Banks 24)

To the extent that students take up these strategies, their relationship to the contents of pages changes. The internetworked digital page is revealed as a space where one might be an author, owner, or inventor, but might also be an arranger, remixer, or collaborator.

The words "Produser" (Bruns, 2005) and "Prosumer" (Toffler, 1980) are relatively recent coinages directed at better understanding the shifting relationships between traditional composers of information, their use of existing media in their compositions, and their audiences. Implicit in each of these terms is a recognition that the boundaries between producers of information and the consumers or users of that information have become more permeable than in the print-dominated past. Neither term, to my eye, offers more than the word "composer," which has always been understood to range from a solitary maker working in isolation to a maker in dynamic conversation with others and their works. But Bruns and Toffler's coinages are anticipatory of the ways internetworked digital media offer audiences opportunities to shift into the role of producers while using or consuming other's compositions.

Online annotation tools like Diigo have the potential to transform virtually any page that exists within a browser into a space that can be highlighted, annotated, marked-up, and shared with others. While each of these activities are also possible with printed pages, marking print pages is a transformative process that eliminates the option of anyone reading the *unhigh*lighted or *un*annotated version of the text. Further sharing of these "marginal thoughts" requires sharing the physical copy of the text. Cloud-based texts eliminate that hurdle. At present, Amazon's Kindle offers fairly robust options for ebook readers to share their highlighting and annotations. Ultimately all these arguments underscore a profound shift in *proximity* between not only composers and their audiences, but among audience members in relation to one another.

Even the most baseline literate activities in internetworked digital spaces prompt reassessments of the relationships between consumption and production. The permeability of digital formats prompts a baseline hum that functions as a rolling invitation to comment on, complement, and challenge the text at hand. These opportunities were never as richly available in a print context. The advent of internetworked digital texts throws into sharp relief questions that perhaps should have been asked more pointedly in the past, the most important of which is probably: *to whom does the page belong?* When presented with this question, the answer that would most likely surface is "the author," as the centuries since the development of copyright laws testify to an increasing emphasis on the figure of the author *as owner* of words. The contrarian answer that has arisen in the more recent past is that the page belongs, ultimately, to the reader. This aligns neatly with Aristotle's assessment that it is the *hearer* who determines a speech's end and object, an injunction that had to have resonated in Stanley Fish's mind to some degree as he worked toward to the development of what came to be known as reader-response criticism. Past alternative candidates for the ultimate ownership of the page might have included "The Muse," or God, or some form of inspiration welling up out of nature. But by collective social agreement, we designated the subset of composers called *authors* an exclusive ownership right in their writings, even if we always had reason to suspect that the stories of how given books came to be was more complicated than the story of a lone composer filled with inspiration sitting before a writing machine and making words appear on a page.

This emphasis on the author and the author's putative wellsprings of inspiration have had the effect of obscuring the elaborate publishing infrastructure that—for the last few centuries—participated mightily in shaping (or, more to this chapter's point, *rearranging*) writings with significant commercial potential. For example, the 2015 publication of *Go Set A Watchman*, a novel attributed to Harper Lee, is an illustration of the degree to which such publishing structures can and sometimes *should have* intervened in the creative processes that are widely understood as the author's to own and decide. While the initial publicity surrounding *Go Set A Watchman* suggested that it might be a long-hoped-for sequel to Lee's first and, to that point, only book, *To Kill a Mockingbird*, it eventually became clear to readers and critics that *Go Set A Watchman* was an early and *failed* draft of the book that would eventually become *To Kill A Mockingbird*.

While the differences between this earlier draft and the final novel are primarily attributable to Lee's own labor, in this specific case, the efforts of a strong-willed literary editor, Tay Hohoff (a.k.a. Therese von Hohoff Torrey), are marked and substantial. The title of Jonathan Mahler's 2015 *New York Times* article speaks to the richness of Hohoff and Lee's collaboration, referring to Hohoff as "The Invisible Hand Behind Harper Lee's 'To Kill a Mockingbird.'" Mahler reports on the deeply collaborative process between Lee and Hohoff. "When [Lee] disagreed with a suggestion, we talked it out, sometimes for hours," Hohoff wrote, "and sometimes she came around to my way of thinking, sometimes I to hers, sometimes the discussion would open up an entirely new line of country." It is notable, though, that while Hohoff clearly had a profound impact on the movement from what we now know as *Go Set a Watchman* to *To Kill a Mockingbird*, Hohoff was careful to foreground Lee's ownership of these choices and changes, writing: "After a couple of false starts, the story-line, interplay of characters, and fall of emphasis grew clearer, and with each revision—there were many minor changes as the story grew in strength and in her own vision of it—the true stature of the novel became evident."

It seems unlikely that literary partnerships of this depth will persist in an increasingly digitized publishing landscape. Cloud spaces invite rapid publication, and in some cases, abhor "middlemen." Amazon, for one example, now offers Kindle Direct Publishing, a self-publishing service it describes in the following terms:

> Self-publish ebooks and paperbacks for free with Kindle Direct Publishing, and reach millions of readers on Amazon.
> Get to market fast. Publishing takes less than 5 minutes and your book appears on Kindle stores worldwide within 24 –48 hours. (par. 1)

Amazon here gleefully sidesteps the gatekeepers and offers a five-minute pathway to publication. Having built the Kindle platform, and the immense cloud-based infrastructure that supports it, Amazon's costs for extending access to self-publishing composers is minimal. Simply put, *digital pages have a relatively minimal opportunity cost relative to their print predecessors.* Some reader somewhere's likely willingness to spend ninety-nine cents on an unedited, unvetted text, rather than the layered ecology of print production, are now determining whether words see the light of day or not. Further, the economic pressures that drove a well-positioned editor like Hohoff to famously carve away three hundred of the five hundred initial pages of Nicholas Delbanco's second novel, *Grasse 3/23/66*, are less burdensome in a context where multiple edits of the same text (or, especially film) are likely to be released when a work achieves significant popular uptake. It is too early to say whether this points toward better or worse writing in the coming decades. It is to say, though, that the labor once undertaken by editors at publishing houses will not occur as frequently or consistently as it did in the past. We will have access to the deluge, and, likely, we will be both better and worse for it. We will face a landscape filled with "director's cuts" of prose, and we may or may not find ourselves longing for the interventions of the gatekeepers of a pre-digital era.

Those of us who are teachers of writing now often teach arrangement as not a successor to invention, but as a co-equal pathway to invention. One favored and admittedly old-fashioned exercise, handed down to me as lore from my disciplinary forebears, involves scissors and space. I have often recommended to writers struggling with an extended writing assignment that they find the largest table available in their homes and cut the current draft of their projects apart at each paragraph break. I then invite them to "shuffle" the paragraphs and, without being tied to their original order, pursue placing them in what seems like the most effective order on the table. Students routinely report considerable rearrangement of their paragraphs. Often, they find that this exercise illuminates "missing" spaces in their arguments, which they then go on to fill in with additional writing. This is not a perfect exercise, but it does do a lot to encourage writers to step out from the continued linear development of their projects. The exercise allows writers an opportunity to reconsider the *shape* of their arguments. The "scissoring" of paper texts and rearranging them by paragraphs is also doable, to a degree, within screen spaces, but in most interfaces the composer only gets to see the text a window at a time. That said, while I am confident this exercise is really helpful to at least some students now, I can also anticipate that a generation of students habituated to working with smartphone-sized writing spaces will—of necessity—develop skills in envisioning and organizing the writing that exists outside their available screen spaces. The rearrangement I now ask students to perform with scissors may well be something that future students can manage virtually, owing to their increased sense of the text that dwells outside the illuminated rectangles that house their writings in the clouds.

The argument here is simply that no one approach to writing ought to be understood as paradigmatic. Neither the maximally isolated work of those who self-select for deep dives into their own internal spaces, nor the teched-up hyperconnected, constantly updated collaboratory will serve all composers and all audiences at all times. Having established these poles, I need to also make clear that I am not suggesting that some sort of sweet spot exists between them. These specific poles are each great *for certain types of writing*. Various points between these poles are also great *for certain types of writing*. This requires approaches to teaching writing where flexibility, fluidity, and adaptability are emphasized. In addition to foregrounding opportunities for collaborative composition, cloud-based writing spaces facilitate remixing and rearranging texts in ways that blur distinctions between the canon of arrangement in with the "first" canon of invention. Early returns suggest we will have much to learn from the new modes of composition that are made possible by this rearrangement of the rhetorical canons.

5 Looking Back at PureText: The "Black & White" Writing of Our Past

The experience of twenty-first century writing spaces is often one in which bright icons and badges constantly pop and chirp, elbowing onto the screen and pleading for the composer's attention. This is not always a negative. For example, a composer concerned about the outcome of an election *might* appreciate the security of knowing that an alert will pop up if there is a change in the vote count. Then again, perhaps not.

Pushing beyond the obvious first step of bemoaning the levels of interruptive chatter that people face in internetworked digital composing spaces, we might consider what is being gained and lost when we resituate the physical site of composition as an interaction within an overtly social tool.

When Karen Burke LeFevre wrote *Invention as a Social Act* in 1987, there was, effectively, no public Internet. LeFevre's work re-situates rhetorical and literary modes of invention as embedded within the texture and interactions of broader communities. LeFevre offers the following assessment:

> Informal associations between people play a significant role in enabling creative thinking. Perhaps it is misleading to refer to these as part of the "social context," if the term implies that such relationships are merely a background in which creative acts of individuals occur. The varied type of collaborations — loose or structured, in pairs or groups, lasting for minutes or years — deserve recognition as an integral part of invention. (78)

LeFevre here is working to challenge the romantic construction of authorship, which routinely foregrounded isolation from society as a necessary step in achieving the contemplative/reflective intellectual space needed to compose long-form writings. But the isolated author was *always* a construct. As a practical matter, composers of all texts have participated in networks of exchange. We give the name author to central nodes in these networks, but they have histories, contexts, and they are all shaped, not only by their connections, but also by their preferred writing tools, and by the spaces they hope to see their texts occupy.

Positioning invention as *social* likely feels obvious and intuitive to scholars and readers anchored in the twenty-first century. In 1987, it was not. Then-dominant writing technologies had the practical effect of distancing writers from one another. The austere, minimalist aesthestic of most scholarly publications had the effect of isolating the composer as an author and thereby enforcing distance between one composer and another. Further, this aesthetic reinforced an ethos grounded in abjuring anything that might be understood as "decorative." *Even the presence of* color within scholarly spaces tended to raise suspicions with respect to the seriousness of the arguments presented. By contrast, scholars are now leveraging available technologies to emerge from a time in which writing spaces have been maximally constrained, both in terms of the relationships among the (usually multiple) composers of any given text, and with respect to what the economics of dominant technologies make viable within page spaces.

The concept of *The Gutenberg Parenthesis*, generally attributed to Lars Ole Saurberg, points up the degree to which the last half millennium might come to be understood as an anomalous and *especially regimented and linear* moment within the broader history of human communication:

> With the invention of moveable type and the printing press, the conditions for communication of and access to information and knowledge changed radically. The change affected not merely the material appearance of information and knowledge dissemination but also, in the process, the nature of cognition.
>
> In a cognitive context the mass-produced and mass-distributed book has been of the greatest significance for the way we approach the world. In the transition from the printed book to digitalized textuality the mode of cognition is being moved from a metaphorics of linearity and reflection to a-linearity and co-production of "reality." This means moving from the rationality accompanied by the printed book to an altogether different way of processing, characterized by interactivity and much faster pace.
>
> The book as privileged mode of cognition is, it seems, being marginalized and transformed. Our experience of being in the world is now determined by cognitive parameters originating as often as not in multi-medial manifestations as an endlessly varied and variable process, competing with a pursuit of uniformity and standardization. (Saurberg 79)

The promise of the Gutenberg Parenthesis is one of eventual and recognizable closure. But the opening parenthesis is far easier to identify and stabilize than the closing parenthesis. We are able, with some confidence, to point to 1439 (plus or minus a year or two) as the point at which Gutenberg's moveable type printing press was added to the array of already available printing techniques (with moveable type itself, significantly, dating to about four hundred years earlier in China). The printing press is a dramatic leap in terms of *efficiency*, and this, in turn, prompted shifts in the distribution and consumption of texts. The impact of Gutenberg's innovation can be traced in the exponential increase of printed texts, first in Europe, and then throughout the world. Those who developed the concept of the Gutenberg Parenthesis have a clear opening parenthesis, but has it closed? Will it?

One possible answer as to how we might locate the Gutenberg close parenthesis comes from acknowledging that for most of the history of the printed codex, both images and color have been prohibitively expensive. This is hardwired into the very foundations of the Western print codex. Gutenberg's Bibles are notable for their mix of black printing and red hand-lettering (rubrication) and the vine-like decorations that were woven in and around the beautiful typography. But when one visits the British Library's online copy of the paper Gutenberg Bible, the Library offers an explanatory note:

The rubric from Fol 5 recto, the beginning of Genesis

The British Library's paper copy has no printed rubrication. The handwritten rubrication does not follow the guidance sheet. The rubrics seem to be the work of more than one rubricator. Smaller initials, chapter-numbers, and headlines are supplied in red, but the headlines do not appear to be by the same hand. Small capitals have been marked in red or yellow.

Decoration

The style and the extent depended on how much money the owner wanted to spend. The British Library's paper copy has very lavish decoration, but on three pages only.

Figure 5.1: The British Library's acknowledgment that their Gutenberg Bible has only three pages of decoration, screenshot from The British Library's "Treasures in Full" site.

Thus, in the case of the British Library's precious copy of this incredibly significant book, the apparent answer to how much *this* owner wanted to spend is "not much." Since Gutenberg, the print codex has always managed black text on white rectangular pages reasonably well, but anything over and above that has at least prompted extra expense, and at worst, served as an unwelcome interruption to the unspooling of alphabetic and numeric characters, preferably all the same type size.

The challenge involved with invoking notions of hard closure with respect to writing technologies is that, for the most part, they never really go away. Rather, they usually continue to be produced, often for collectors and connoisseurs. Gutenberg's letterpress printing method has largely been supplanted by offset printing, but letterpress is now a distinctive "craft" printing technique that is prized for the handmade elements of its production process, and the tactile richness of letterpress pages. While contemporary writing technologies automate and obviate many of the elements of what made the moveable type printing press so striking, we are nowhere near a place where we can point to the "Gutenberg Era" as a thing that ended or that will definitely have ended anytime soon.

One space where the Gutenberg Parenthesis *does* look particularly parenthetical is with respect to the look and feel of pages. If we understand the Gutenberg Parenthesis as a time in which richly colored and lavishly decorated illuminated manuscripts gave way to the black-and-white, sterile linearity of mass-produced machine printing, then we can begin to see open and close parentheses take shape.

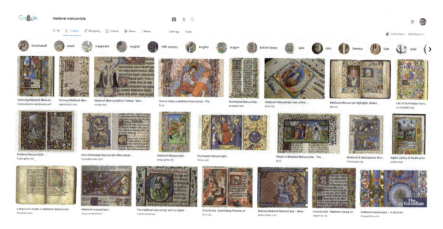

Figure 5.2: A Google Image search for "Medieval Manuscripts" (i.e., pre-Gutenberg) results in an explosion of colors.

Pre-Gutenberg texts, crafted by hand, are notable for their dramatic investment in color, especially when compared to the pages that would be ushered in by the print ecologies that arose in the centuries following Gutenberg. Gutenberg's invention opens the door to mass audiences that in turn, exert pressure to streamline and optimize printing as a machine-based process that can be made more efficient and thereby, less expensive. The least expensive approach to printing is one in which pages are filled with nothing but alphanumeric characters. Four hundred years after Gutenberg, pages reflect an increasing bias toward speed, and an increasing recognition that color and images, and even significant variations in typography cost time, energy, and money.

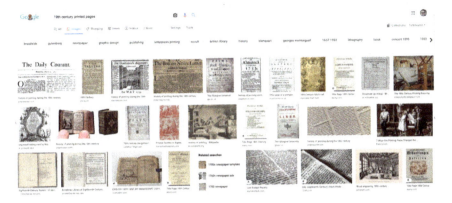

Figure 5.3: A Google Image search for "19th Century Printed Pages" reflects an increasing emphasis on alphanumeric characters at the expense of color and images.

Viewing roughly representative samples of medieval manuscripts, nineteenth-century printed pages, and contemporary web pages underscores the degree to which the available technologies for the delivery of writing and the expanding audience for that writing transformed the specifics of and the experience of reading.

Figure 5.4: A Google Image search for "web pages" reflects a pendulum swing back toward color as a notable element in the look and feel of most pages.

Internetworked writing tools throw into relief just how much choice is involved in foregoing the other possibilities latent in any page, whether real or virtual. Pages are remarkably flexible, and they can house just about any imaginable text, visual, or color. Pages cannot typically offer dimensionality (although the data visualization specialist Edward Tufte once challenged this limitation by including a fold-it-yourself three-dimensional pyramid in one of his books). This is not to suggest that there is anything wrong with filling two-dimensional white rectangles with black ink. Indeed, this is a time-tested approach to communication that will likely remain effective indefinitely.

98

In 1987, Vilém Flusser composed a book (notably also released on a pair of floppy disks) titled *Does Writing Have a Future?* In a critical chapter titled "The Digital," Flusser positions digital media as a new entrant into a millennia-old contest between text and image. The essay's final paragraph begins, "As the alphabet originally advanced against pictograms, digital codes today advance against letters to overtake them" (147). Later, Flusser expands on this argument, writing:

> [A]s images defended themselves from history, from being strangled by texts, the alphabet is setting up its defenses at present so as not to be strangled by the new codes — only a small consolation to those who continue their engagement with writing texts, for the whole thing has been accelerating. Only in the eighteenth century, after a three-thousand year struggle, did texts succeed in pushing images, with their magic and myth, into such corners as the museums and the unconscious. The current struggle won't take so long. Digital thinking will triumph much more quickly. It is true the twentieth century is marked by a reactionary revolt of images. Should we anticipate a reactionary revolt of repressed texts against computer programs in an unpredictable future? (147)

Indeed this "reactionary revolt" is a regular feature of contemporary conversations about a perceived contest between digital and print texts.

I once stepped outside of my core disciplinary communities and ended up at a conference titled "The Crisis of the Book: Worlds of Opportunity, Worlds of Change." While the sessions I visited may not have been representative of the conference as a whole, most of the presentations I saw featured speakers tilting heavily toward "crisis" rather than opportunity. This dovetails with a broader phenomenon of dismissal of digital and internetworked writing that is observable within some scholarly communities. When academics self-identify as "book lovers," what, specifically, drives this love? Is it paper itself? Or "cloth" bindings (typically made of textured paper)? The cardboard within the "cloth?" The smell of the glue binding the pages to the spine? Or the musty combination of mold and rot that perfumes most used bookstores? Perhaps for some book lovers it is some or all of these. But for most, it is the *content* delivered by the codex that drive these feelings of love. For me, for example, my love for codex books arises from the interaction between the text of F. Scott Fitzgerald's novel and the haunting dust jacket cover by Francis Cugat (completed before the novel and subsequently incorporated into the novel's text). The love I hold for codex books is also inspired by Ernst Reichl's typographic play in the 1934 Random House edition of James Joyce's *Ulysses*, in which the capital "S" inaugurating the book in a sentence describing "Stately plump Buck Mulligan" is itself stately and, well, plump. Or, to take the argument away from canonical works of fiction to a more contemporary space, I and others feel emotionally awakened by the ravishing pages Edward Tufte's self-published books on data graphics, prepared with a meticulous attention to the look and feel of each page, and thereby underscoring Tufte's larger arguments about the care with which data must be presented in print spaces.

All these—especially Tufte's works—are examples of texts prepared with particular attention to latent opportunities within the codex as a medium. They all feature effects that would suffer if and when they were ported to current ebook spaces. They are understandable objects of bibliophiles' love. And they are *in no way representative* of most codex books.

Most of the time codices serve as what are meant to be neutral delivery vehicles for the alphabet, numerals, and punctuation marks. The majority of books are—except for their covers—what I refer to as *PureText*. In PureText books, little if any attention is paid to the look and feel of pages. Typography is lightly considered, with typefaces drawn from the default settings of a publishing house, usually something along the lines of Palatino or Bodoni. PureText eschews the decorative in favor of the direct. PureText aspires to neutrality as a delivery medium. PureText defers wholly to a construction of the textual composer as a maker of *ideas* that travel via words and attaches no special significance to the fact that those words find *expression* in a medium that is significantly removed from the actions of that composer's mind or hands. PureText aspires to be a clear channel back toward the interior of that distant mind. PureText aspires to transparency.

The ideas at the heart of PureText have long been a site of critical consideration by scholars of digital and internetworked writing. In his 2007 book *The Economics of Attention: Style and Substance in the Age of Information* Richard Lanham walks his readers through a meaningful distinction between looking *at* alphanumeric characters with engaging surfaces and looking *through* those characters to understand their meaning. He then speaks to the stress some readers feel when electronic texts begin participating in the delivery of prose alongside print texts:

Beyond the "touch and smell" nostalgia for the printed book, electronic text elicits deeper and more serious fears. For nonfictional prose, the central fear is the blurring of conceptual thought that comes with a thinking alphabet. Just as Havelock argues, only by transcending the alphabet that thinks can conceptual thought find a condign notation. Only the aesthetics of subtraction that alphabetic notation creates can allow us to ignore the expressive surface, filter out extraneous signals, and concentrate on the conceptual meaning. Look through rather than at. It is a legitimate fear. We don't want coffee-shop chatter in the library of our mind. We feel we must preserve the unselfconscious transparency of the medium if we are truly to "lose ourselves in a book." A bi-stable form of notation, like a bi-stable economics, that switches from at to through and back, from stuff to nonstuff and back, makes us queasy. (Lanham 136)

But suppose some readers *do* want coffee shop chatter in the libraries of their minds? Suppose they don't necessarily prize the sense of one-on-one communion with the composer that comes from being able to "look through" PureText? What if the presence of others within a text actually *helps* them concentrate on the conceptual meaning?

Academic conferences I attended over the past decade often featured print-codex-loving scholars voicing canards about supposed limitations of ebooks. Chief among these were the purported impossibilities of highlighting or commenting upon texts. In fact, for the past decade ebook applications have offered robust tools for both commenting and highlighting. In 2010, Amazon's update to Kindle (version 2.5) introduced a feature called "Popular Highlights" that offered readers the opportunity to see the aggregated highlights of other readers. Now there are obvious circumstances in which this feature would function as an unwelcome intrusion in the interchange between the reader and the composer. A Kindle edition of Emily Dickinson's poetry might well be sharply compromised by the distracting presence of Popular Highlights. But like most ebook features, these highlights can be toggled on or off at the reader's discretion. In 2011, Amazon added a parallel feature for its annotation system, titled Public Note, allowing readers to opt in to sharing their own annotations with other Kindle readers.

And while poetry might not benefit from the virtual presence of others chiming in on the merits of the poet's choices, many other texts might. Shortly after the introduction of Popular Highlights the most highlighted Kindle passage was a snippet from Malcolm Gladwell's *Outliers: The Story of Success* in which Gladwell outlined three qualities that he argued were necessary for satisfying work. In this instance, the aggregated Kindle readership had collectively zeroed in on a passage that encapsulated Gladwell's much larger argument. Given the nature of Gladwell's text, the Kindle edition offers clear value added over a print edition. Hands-off critics of *what they believe ebooks to be and do* need to step up to the challenge of explaining how and why—for example—having the option to engage with an aggregated pool of annotations is somehow less helpful than having only one's own notes in a codex.

In cases where print codex books have offered nothing more than PureText, the "pouring" of text into ebook "containers" often represents an arguable improvement upon what those codices offered. One of the obvious risks of the shift toward ebooks is the reinforcement of the constrained aesthetics of PureText as the default. The leading commercial ebook software applications offer a very limited pool of fonts as options for readers. Amazon's Kindle platform showed some deference to the initial design of the text by offering "Publisher Font" as an option, though the software is unable to reproduce that font for purposes of comparison in the menu offering the pool of ten available font choices. That said, even the choice of Publisher Font in no way guarantees that the page design the reader sees will even roughly approximate the layout of the original print pages. This is compounded by the options for readers to resize the size of the characters, margins, line spacing, and alignment. Indeed, the positioning of words on pages is apparently seen as a minor consideration, readily traded off in exchange for the flexibility offered to readers by allowing them to tailor the look and feel of the textual content to align with their personal preferences. So yes, contemporary ebooks are the destroyers and defacers of aesthetically striking works like those of Cugat/Fitzgerald, Reichl/Joyce, and Tufte. But these works were, by design, exceptional within a broader body of codices that were, by design, unremarkable. The overwhelming majority of print codex books deliver PureText and nothing more.

Over time, the machined perfection of PureText became an intimidatingly authoritative marker of especially worthy texts. For the first year of my honors English program I was enrolled in a then-in-vogue "Great Books" class sequence. We marched week by week through canonical texts like *The Iliad* and *Paradise Lost*, with skilled professors elucidating common themes that had, presumably, animated the composers of these texts. I *never* made a note on any of the print pages of these texts. I was too intimidated. Who was I to mark up an edited, typographically set page that carried words from Homer, Plato, Milton, or Shakespeare? I persuaded myself that I could offload the notes to my spiral-bound notebooks, but over time it became clear to me that I was not keeping up with my peers who annotated the margins of their texts with their real-time responses. They were able to use their notes to track how they had felt as they read, and to jot down questions whenever they encountered obstacles to their understanding.

The advent of digital texts offered me a welcome respite from the stress I felt when despoiling neatly arrayed rectangles of typeset alphanumeric characters with my already-crabbed handwriting. Digital annotations allow my words to appear as clean and as clear as the text at hand. More importantly, my notes can be made to appear and disappear at my discretion. I have the opportunity to see Sophocles *with or without* my passing commentary. This is a difference that makes a big difference to me as a consumer of texts.

Scholars can quite reasonably mourn the loss of what might possibly be recovered from reading the notes of others. I understand this. I once painstakingly copied Thornton Wilder's annotations from his copy of *Finnegans Wake* to a fresh copy of my own, developing an elaborate color-coding scheme in hopes of divining a clear sense of what Wilder was chasing as he read Joyce's *magnum opus*. But Wilder's copy of Joyce's *Wake* lived (only) in the rare books room of the Beinecke Library at Yale. The price of trying to surmise how Wilder was responding to the *Wake* as he read was my own travel to that physical space, and my painstaking mimicry of Wilder's notes on his pages. This was not an opportunity readily available to all of those who might have shared my interests. Indeed, without a generous grant from my graduate program, it would not have been available to me. Today, I might might be able to gain parallel access to a significant scholar or theorist's annotations for the price of a "follow" on a note-sharing platform, or perhaps a friendly e-mail. And an especially knotty text like *Finnegans Wake* becomes a hive of shared activity online, with scholars reaching across continents to share their insights.

So many possibilities open because contemporary ebooks are, by definition, *networked*. They are constructed to live not so much within devices but *in the cloud* because of their implicit promise to be available *across* readers' various e-devices. If a Kindle or Kobo book is expected to open to the page where you left off reading, with either your own annotations or those of others (based on your preference) highlighted in yellow as you move from your ereader to desktop to smartphone, then clearly, the book itself cannot be said to reside in any one of these devices. Further, it does not reside only in any one reader's devices.

In his 2011 essay, "Post-Artifact Books and Publishing," Writer and designer Craig Mod argues that digital texts on the Kindle platform participate in a wholly different ecosystem from print texts precisely because of the degree to which readers themselves leave traces of their readership in cloud-based texts:

For only the briefest of instances—*seconds, perhaps, for popular authors*—does the digital edition of a book exist in this static, classic, 'complete' form. The moment a Kindle edition of a book is downloaded and highlighted it has been altered. The next person to download a copy of that book will be downloading the 'complete' form plus all associated marginalia. And the greater the integration of systems of marginalia, the greater the impact that subsequent conversations around the book will have on future readers.

Consider the moment an exhausted reader closes the cover of a print codex book and sets it on a nightstand. To state the obvious, that book is truly "off" until the following morning, offering no meaning or value to anyone until the cover is re-opened. Now consider the same exhausted reader flicking the switch on a Kindle and setting it on a nightstand. Unlike the print text, the Kindle text never "sleeps." As the reader rests, the text is potentially being transformed by other, less somnambulant readers (or those in different time zones). Whether or not a given reader opts in to viewing these highlights, the text itself is, highlight by highlight, *changing* ever so slightly. So too did the reader's own highlights transform the text, leaving algorithms to continually adjust and reset the terms of what counts as a "popular" highlight among the number of readers of a given text. Thus, Kindle books are transformed throughout the day by their readers, accumulating and generating data.

The Google Doc as a writing space is also, potentially, a document that transforms as composers sleep. In my work as a professor, it is not uncommon for me to abandon my own contributions to a shared Google Doc in the wee small hours of the morning only to discover, the following morning, that a colleague has trumped my own insomnia and contributed mightily to that same document between 4:00 and 5:00 a.m. In this small way, the timestamps of our shared writings offer us a window into others' lives that dances on the edge of invasiveness.

Internetworked digital compositions are so malleable that they undercut the sense of fixity readers attach to print texts. Where print offered readers a sense of closure, writing in the clouds repositions texts as nodes in a networked conversation.

The practical experience of digital text is, again and again, one in which documents that felt "owned" in a print context are readily and regularly transformed by others, even as we sleep. While writers and readers are offered a *measure* of discretion over the circulation and availability of their texts to others, there are also cases where choice is circumscribed. While I can choose whether to see others' highlights, I am not given the option of refusing to have my own highlights be counted by Kindle. While my highlight is effectively anonymous—one among many and invisible unless the highlight hits the "popular" threshold—I *still* might wish that no one (and no machine) ever know what I found so intriguing about that one page in Jonathan Lethem's *The Ecstasy of Influence*.

The prospect of communities built around the sharing of online annotations makes clear that reading need not always be a solitary activity that involves only reader and text. That said, we will soon be facing new kinds of questions about how we engage with texts in online spaces. If the comments and highlights of an ebook edition of *Mein Kampf* becomes a gathering place for twenty-first century nazis, what are the obligations of an ebook seller like Amazon? Ought they allow ethically bankrupt and morally repugnant exchanges to unfold within the semi-publicly shared space of the book's pages? Further, suppose two competing communities, one scholarly and reasoned, and the other aggressively and confrontationally racist, begin battling within the margins of the text, with the volume of ad-hoc commentary ultimately exceeding the text itself? Clearly, we will need to think through how these spaces can be made equitable, fair, and functional. The guiding principle will need to be placing significant choice and control in the hands of readers, much as readers are now free to view the comments on webpages—or not—as they see fit.

Internetworked digital media have the potential to make the broader conversations that circulate around and within texts visible—to make them functional and, in many cases, to extend these conversations beyond the academic machineries developed to sustain and perpetuate them. There is much to be gained by developing and sustaining structures that accommodate conversations about the texts that inspire, confuse, and challenge audiences. The Web is only a partial realization of this potential.

While living through times of rapid change, it is tempting to seek endpoints, or to try to identify moments in one's own lifetime as the breaking points between then and now. I write very differently today—speaking strictly in terms of my engagement with the technologies of writing—than I did as a senior in high school, when I was a creative writing major working on my mother's handed-down Olympia portable typewriter. Some might argue that the tools likely made little difference in my composing strategies . . . that I always possessed an aggregation of internal inspirations and expressions that would be realized in roughly the same ways whether typed, processed, or tapped. This is, from *my* perspective, clearly not the case. I had no choices to make with respect to the size, color, and typeface of my manuscripts. I footnote fairly freely now, but like many college students of of my generation, I dreaded any assignment that required footnotes because of the guesswork involved in gauging how much of the page would be needed to accommodate the footnotes. I strongly suspect that instructors who called for footnotes simply wished to receive second or third drafts of the projects they received because typing a clean first draft of a footnoted project on a typewriter bordered on impossible. The luxuries of computer-managed cut and paste remain profound to me, and they have encouraged me to write more freely than I ever did when the limitations of the typewriter exacted their toll on my time and energy. Further, the flexibility of my writing tools with respect to the look and feel of characters and words feels like an immense luxury. At every point in my history as a writer, but *especially* since the advent of digital media, my writing has been shaped by the tools I had at hand.

The experience of writing in internetworked spaces is one in which I as a writer am always conscious of my proximity to others' ideas, texts, and sometimes their realtime textual co-production. Even though the virtual writing spaces I inhabit are often overtly directed at reconstructing key elements of the experience of using a mechanical typewriter, the comparative ephemerality and fluidity of my texts continually shapes my sense of the possibilities for each project. A misplaced paragraph is quickly relocated. A co-composer and I can start revising at opposite ends of that paragraph and "race" each other toward the middle. Writing in virtual spaces addresses my three greatest frustrations with typescript as a medium: (1) *fixity* and the technical challenges associated with corrections or adjustments; and (2) *isolation* (in no small part because of the anti-social character of the typewriter as a tool); and (3) *dependence*, because typescript was routinely understood as a medium in which to deliver interim documents with a look and feel that would then be refined by editors and designers. Now, for better and for worse, composers have opportunities to shape the look and feel of their own documents to a great degree.

The challenge we face, as we seek to understand written composition in this moment, is finding ways to wrap our heads around two things that are happening simultaneously. On one hand, the shifts in technology *feel* decisive. There are times when we are able to mark clear shifts in our composing practices in response to writing-associated technologies. For example, there are compositional practices pre- and post- photocopy that can now—with the benefit of hindsight—be pried apart from one another. On the other hand, when the lens is widened, there is immense continuity in how writing is taught and which modes of writing are most valorized with in the United States.

As Marshall McLuhan wrote: "When faced with a totally new situation, we tend always to attach ourselves to the objects, the flavor of the most recent past. We look at the present through a rear-view mirror. We march backwards into the future" (74 –5). It often takes a surprising amount of time before we stop understanding today's technology in terms of yesterday's. We too often look backwards for our preferred practices at the expense of exploring possibilities that are now readily at hand. The gap between past practices and current potentialities is perhaps most pronounced with respect to the incorporation of visual information into contemporary compositions.

Perhaps the most obvious example of the degree to which we project writing's past into writing's present is our relationship to color as an element in written compositions. The use of color as a marker of meaning in written compositions remains rare. This is true despite the intuitive associations and resonances that most audiences have with specific colors. This is, in no small part, because writers to this point have largely contented themselves with managing the one hundred or so alphanumeric and punctuation characters that have sufficed for most written communication. Questions of color, like questions of typography, were theoretically the bailiwicks of others in an imagined publication process. The substantial costs of color print production reinforced this separation. Color print production was (and is) strikingly expensive relative to black-and-white printing. Even home printing of color remains expensive, with inkjet ink costing at least double the price of Dom Perignon champagne on a per-ounce basis (Bufete). In internetworked digital contexts, though, the costs for color are nominal because, in most cases, written compositions *are not meant to be printed at all*. Within screen spaces, no color costs more than any other. The continuing cultural bias toward black alphanumeric text within white rectangles is attributable, in part, to the maximal visual contrast between black and white. But it is also, simply put, the by-product of habit.

Given that when writing in the cloud, color is effectively free, it is reasonable to wonder how long it will take for color to migrate from our screens into "serious" long-form compositions. Even basic websites from the 1990s explored the possibilities of using color as visual cues. The early Web featured a common visual cue for links often consisting of a small red ball accompanying underlined blue text to indicate the presence of links.

Figure 5.5: The "red ball/blue underline" design ethic of the early Internet, excite image courtesy of The Internet Archive Wayback Machine

Within the space of a decade, a rough color-coding system for different types of information became part of understanding writing on the

World Wide Web. While the red balls have thankfully receded from view, color remains one of the primary ways we are invited to navigate the Web. Like excite, contemporary pages use color to alert readers to the presence of sections within the site, and further, to help readers understand the weightings and relationships among information on a given page.

In print contexts, by contrast, the use of color remains a challenging and expensive endeavor. One example of how challenging it can be to make use of color as an aspect of written expression in print is the 2012 novel *Sacré Bleu: A Comedy D'Art*, by Christopher Moore. The first edition—and pointedly *only* the first edition—of Moore's novel is printed in a lush indigo ink. Moore's book also features reproductions of paintings by Toulouse-Lautrec, Manet, and Van Gogh. That these visual delights appeared only in a single edition made intuitive sense. Readers understood that the steps involved in shifting from black to indigo ink must be labor-intensive and costly. Moore himself marketed the first edition on the grounds that it would be the only edition presented in its intended format: "Remember, only the first printing of *Sacré Bleu* will have color art and print. After they [sic] it will be in black and white, so jump on these if you're not near a tour city. If you order before the 8th, these will be the color, first printings." Thus, the first print edition of Moore's book is both a curiosity and a rarity. Eyes habituated to the optimized black-type-on-a-white page default are first confused, then delighted by Moore's subtle play with convention. But because this indigo edition is arguably the closest to Moore's vision for the project, we do well to ask why color was seen as expendable not merely for the subsequent paper editions but also (by and large) for electronic editions.

This is in part attributable to the limitations of platforms like Amazon's Kindle platform. Indeed, the limited degree of control these platforms offer to readers is a selling point.

Despite generations of refinement, we are still working within the limitations of web- and browser-safe color palettes. To send ideas through clouds, we need to lop off some bandwidth, much as audio CDs and MP3s stripped away the presumably inaudible data lying above and below the standard spectrum that can be heard by a typical human ear. So, while my laptop cheerfully offers "millions of colors" as an option, the Internet routinely pares this down to a few hundred. This is a loss that only occasionally registers with us as readers. More often than not, we don't know what we are missing. The functional cost of color has plummeted to the point that it is a readily available element of writing, but it simply is not an element of writing that composers are habituated to using. Further, the institutional structures that manage the movement of literary works toward publication are generally not equipped to consider color as a potentially significant element of what writing is and means.

As J. R. Carpenter points out in her 2019 essay, "Writing on the Cusp of Becoming Something Else," the trajectory we are now on is wholly precedented. We have experienced similar hangovers with the arrival of relatively recent media forms:

> The browser-based web as we know it has only been around for twenty-three years or so, at the time of this writing—a short amount of time in terms of both practice and discourse. It took much longer yet for photography to be written about 'not' in terms of painting, for cinema to be written about 'not' in terms of theatre. How long will it take for digital writing to be written about 'not' in terms of a publishing industry built on the back of the book as a contained unit of commodity? We don't quite know what we're writing yet; let alone how to write about it. Critical and creative focus within both academic digital literary scholarship and within digital publishing would benefit from studying and supporting the new structures for reading and writing that digital writers and their writing are revealing through as yet experimental processes. Writing performs differently on the page, on the screen, and online. We need to think and write about writing as not residing in any of these media but rather operating across and through multiple media at multiple times. (304 –5)

Too often we use twenty-first-century tools to prepare eighteenth-century texts for twenty-first-century readers, who are encountering these texts within tools that can present, reconfigure, and collage these texts. We need to sharpen our sense of the distinctions that are increasingly apparent among the kinds of texts we are making, some of which are meant to interconnect in internetworked spaces, and others of which live comfortably in PureText, whether in print or online.

Craig Mod has helpfully clarified distinctions in the presentation of text/image content that are thrown into relief by internetworked digital texts. As far back as a March 2010 richly illustrated essay on "Books in the Age of the iPad," Mod was explaining the impact of tablet spaces on how we *would* be thinking about the content on their screens:

> Let's divide content into two broad groups.
>
> · Content without well-defined form (Formless Content . . .)
> · Content with well-defined form (Definite Content . . .)

Formless Content can be reflowed into different formats and not lose any intrinsic meaning. It's content divorced from layout. Most novels and works of non-fiction are Formless. When Danielle Steele sits at her computer, she doesn't think much about how the text will look printed. She thinks about the story as a waterfall of text, as something that can be poured into any container. (Actually, she probably just thinks awkward and sexy things, but awkward and sexy things without regard for final form.) Content with form—Definite Content—is almost totally the opposite of Formless Content. Most texts composed with images, charts, graphs or poetry fall under this umbrella. It may be reflowable, but depending on how it's reflowed, inherent meaning and quality of the text may change. (par. 15 –17)

Mod continues his argument with attention to the question of how and whether composed content *depends* on specific arrangement on the available page spaces to communicate meaning. In rhetorical terms, Formless Content is the by-product of invention and arrangement with respect to the order of words and concepts *within alphanumeric characters*, while Definite Content is directed at the arrangement of words and images in specific ways within specific page spaces. Mod writes:

> In the context of the book as an object, the key difference between Formless and Definite Content is the interaction between the content and the page. Formless Content doesn't see the page or its boundaries. Whereas Definite Content is not only aware of the page, but embraces it. It edits, shifts and resizes itself to fit the page. In a sense, Definite Content approaches the page as a canvas—something with dimensions and limitations—and leverages these attributes to both elevate the object and the content to a more complete whole. Put very simply, Formless Content is unaware of the container. Definite Content embraces the container as a canvas. Formless content is usually only text. Definite content usually has some visual elements along with text. (par. 21)

Mod's distinction between formless and definite content is profound (though I will forego his capitalizations) in that this distinction is the one that *should* explain the current attachment to the print book as a cultural phenomenon. Whether the content of an argument is formless or definite is too rarely addressed in these terms in conventional academic practice, and, worse, it is the basis for a culture of inattention to the possibility that the needed presentation for a particular argument might indeed be definite, rather than formless.

A tour through the stacks of a graduate research library at any major institution will reveal a general academic bias toward formless content. The covers of academic journals are often content-delivery systems with surprising levels of inattention to the possibility that typography, color, or use of white space might powerfully establish the ethos of the journal. Consider, for example, the cover of the November 2020 issue of the *Quarterly Journal of Economics*, an academic journal published since 1886, and the leading journal in the field of economics:

Figure 5.6: The cover of the November 2020 edition of the *Quarterly Journal of Economics*, from Oxford Academic

This presentation is almost entirely formless content. There appear to be no more than four typefaces total, and scale is used in only three ways: to indicate the importance of the title, to call attention to the issue's volume/ number/date, and to highlight the name of the press that maintains the journal. The remainder of the cover is a steady parade of alphanumeric information presented with scant attention to the possibilities of contemporary typography. Indeed, the ethos of this particular journal is that it is data-focused and data-driven, and one could argue that it is not in the *Quar-*

terly Journal of Economics' own interest to offer more than a cursory nod toward the art of page layout. Indeed, the *Quarterly Journal of Economics* has held fast to this design for well over a century. The very first issue's cover is, in terms of visual structure and presentation, a clear model for the look and feel of the journal to this day:

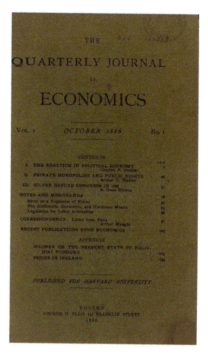

Figure 5.7: The cover of the October 1886 (and first) issue of *Quarterly Journal of Economics*, courtesy Zhaladshar, Wikimedia Commons.

Arguably the only element of the 2020 journal's cover that has received faint attention to questions of design is the logo, and even that has been only slightly revised relative to the journal's first issue in 1886. Thus, it is fair to say that this particular journal is committed to its status as formless content, but for the occasional table or chart, which needs to appear in close proximity to the associated arguments. *This is fine.* What would not be fine is an argument that there is something particularly valuable or powerful about the paper journal format as a container for this particular content. Indeed, given that this is an object of academic consideration and study, the many opportunities afforded by digitization of the journal's articles for scholarly readers (e.g., keyword searches, resizing type, relative portability) suggest that the vast sums devoted to delivering print copies of *QJE* to university libraries might be better directed at maximizing digital access to this and neighboring formless content. But this is clearly not the case for journals in other disciplines. Having positioned *Quarterly Journal of Economics* as an exemplary quantitative journal with an ethos that might well encourage it to abjure anything that smacks of the decorative, I now turn to a roughly polar example, that of *Art Journal*, formerly known as *College Art Journal* and *Parnassus*, but in all cases published by the College Art Association of America (CAA). Where *QJE* arrived at an ethos and a visual identity that easily aligns with Mod's characterizations of formless content, it is reasonable to presume that *Art Journal* would insistently announce itself as definite content. Indeed, the Summer 2019 cover of *Art Journal* is a clear example of definite content:

Figure 5.8: The cover of the Summer, 2019 issue of *Art Journal*, incorporating "Not the Face" by Deborah Roberts, via CollegeArt.Org

Relative to the *QJE* cover, *Art Journal* emphasizes an image *almost* to the exclusion of text. Further, given that this image in question is a *collage*, we can observe that considerable attention has been devoted to the arrangement of the constituent parts of this image. By contrast, we have only three bits of textual content on this cover: the name of the journal, the publication date, and the organization responsible for the journal (CAA). *All* this information is parked hard against the right edge of the cover to give it room to breathe. That said, the colors of both the word "art" in the title and the CAA logo are red for this issue, to harmonize with the colors of the chosen cover image. To state the obvious, the design and stylistic choices on this cover have been made with attention to the image, and it seems clear that a cover *a la QJE* would be entirely inappropriate for a journal with *Art Journal*'s stated mission.

Yet.

This is the cover for the first issue of the publication that would eventually become *Art Journal*. It has almost precisely the same amount of textual content as the Summer 2019 issue, but it looks like a cousin to the early issues of the *Quarterly Journal of Economics* with the cover offering no real indication that this journal is up to anything other than the delivery of formless content:

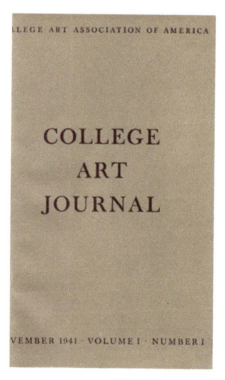

Figure 5.9: The cover of the November, 1941 issue of Art Journal, via CollegeArt.org.

We do well to wonder why a journal dedicated to the sustained examination of visual art settled into such a generic presentation. We can read between the lines of Howard Singerman's celebratory account of *Art Journal*'s first fifty years and recognize that the substantial costs of image reproduction in print technology likely had much to do with the spare look and feel of the journal in its initial years:

> Fitting for its role as CAA's newsletter, *College Art Journal* debuted at eight and a quarter by five and a quarter inches and was printed on inexpensive, uncoated paper. [T]here were no ads in the new *College Art Journal* and, until 1945, no illustrations of any sort. When advertisements reappear in 1946, they are ads not for dealers, but for other art magazines—*The Art Digest*, *Art Quarterly*, *Artibus Asiae*—and book publishers; illustrations return that same year, first as line reproductions of graphic works by artists such as Henri Matisse, Paul Klee, Henry Moore, Oskar Kokoschka, and Max Beckmann. Halftone illustrations accompanying articles begin to appear regularly only after 1952.

It does not take a great leap to surmise that the years 1941 to 1945 were lean years for many publications, and especially those tied to academia and educational budgets. It seems likely that the lack of visual appeal for *College Art Journal* was a reflection of the more general challenges of life during wartime. The likelihood that *College Art Journal* had to forego images as an austerity measure is reinforced by even a brief review of its immediate ancestor, *Parnassus*. Technically and visually, *Parnassus* was a lush and vibrant space. Singerman's account of the journey toward *College Art Journal* celebrates the significant investment in *Parnassus* as a space for art. He writes: "The most obvious differences between *College Art Journal* and Longman's *Parnassus* were physical: *Parnassus* began life in 1929 with a cut size of eleven by eight inches, but from 1934 until its demise it ran a bit larger, and always on coated stock." Thus, while *College Art Journal* was, for a brief time, almost visually indistinguishable from *Quarterly Journal of Economics*, a review of the publication's broader history reveals it to be a clear—if not paradigmatic—example of definite content. And certainly, as we look at *Art Journal* across its media iterations today, page spaces are designed and specific, and calibrated to the space available.

As these cases illustrate, the current moment is one in which publishers are clearly having to pay greater attention to whether their books are formless or not—and how to build structures that honor the graphic richness of their content. Because these questions are new to many in these fields, we are bearing witness to growing pains. Recently, I had the responsibility of choosing a specific text for a course titled Visual Rhetoric and Document Design. As the course title suggests, the class is a sustained examination of the specifics of visual communication within a range of spaces, with a particular emphasis on digital spaces included, for example, infographics. After settling on a preferred text for the class, I contacted the publisher to gain access to the digital "desk copy" that most publishers extend to teaching faculty as a courtesy. What I found (as I have found in the past) was the publisher was unprepared to deliver a functional digital edition of the text. Most striking in this most recent example was the publisher's insistence that literally *every* page of the text carry a crude footer with two separate copyright notices in two different typefaces. These graphically hostile interventions into the elegantly designed spaces of the text made the publisher's edition of the text an obviously unworkable example of effective design.

While not wishing to drive business to Amazon, I found it notable that Amazon sold this same text without the copyright notices and with an admission that the text would *only* be workable within desktop computers and tablets and *not* within most Kindle devices. Thus, Amazon was able to sell a superior product to the one *the publisher itself* was offering because Amazon has been able to afford to make a massive investment in understanding how ebooks work and, further, in how to work with the limitations imposed by ebooks with definite content.

For the moment, both academic publishers and digital spaces themselves are biased toward the relative ease of formless content. In academia, the gravitational pull of "hard science" fields leads to defaults for the look and feel of academic journals, and a culture of wariness toward anything that smacks of the decorative. While the twentieth century featured newsstands filled with glossy magazines, most academic journals contented themselves with black-and-white printing, traditional serifed typefaces, and occasional visuals (with tables being preferred over photography). Purveyors of ebooks, in the name of efficiency, favor platforms that "pour" text into rectangular "buckets." These cultural spaces lean towards formless content, and this invites us to consider when and where definite content might hold sway.

Coffee table and art books and art and fashion magazines will likely continue to have buyers and subscribers specifically because they represent ideal technologies for the kinds of content they house—full color photographs, carefully typeset texts, and richly colorful visuals. They demonstrate that a certain (and perhaps thinning) strip of readers is willing to pay a premium for the scale and richness of well-executed print pages. To the extent that contemporary digital technologies for book-like projects fail to offer rich experiences of definite content, they will, for a time, be rejected by readers and consumers habituated to the possibilities of high-end full-color print.

The question we should be asking at this moment is not *which of these media forms should "win?"* but instead, *which of the available media is suited to the nature and character of this discursive act?* The answer to this question will necessarily vary from text to text.

Indeed, the task of answering the above question will swing on the answers to a series of questions, all of which are pulled to the foreground when composing in a context where internetworked writing is increasingly the default. Effective composers whose works will inhabit cloud-based spaces should now ask themselves:

- What is the role of images in this text?
- What is the significance of color in this text?
- What is the role of typography in this text?
- Does the delivery medium need to offer more than access to a specific configuration of alphanumeric characters?
- To what degree should the audience be allowed to adjust the text to their tastes?
- What reading activities should be supported by the preferred medium
- To what degree is the reader invited to participate in the co-construction of this text?
- Ought this text engage all readers in the same way?
- To what degree does fixity matter for this text?
- To what degree does fluidity matter for this text?

When these questions are considered as a group, we intuitively begin sorting texts according to our understandings of the hoped-for relationships between specific texts and specific audiences. The digital is revealed not as an enemy, not as the destroyer of print, but rather as an extension of a long process of balancing and rebalancing text and image in relation to the writing technologies at hand.

6 The Android and "i": The Politics of Twenty-First Century Writing Interfaces

Contemporary desktop and laptop word-processing programs—in trying to be all things to all composers—have become perhaps *the* paradigmatic examples of the contemporary phenomenon of "bloatware." Over time, software developers have added feature upon feature hoping to anticipate practically *all* the varied choices a hypothetical textual composer might wish to make. Microsoft Word, in particular, stands out as the software equivalent of the now-discontinued "Wenger Giant" Swiss Army Knife, which boasts eighty-seven separate implements that perform 141 distinct functions. The knife is *twelve inches wide*, making it an absurd cartoon of the "pocket" knives from which it descended. While Microsoft Word does a better job of nesting the cascade of functions available within its current offerings, we still can fairly observe that the challenge of meeting most imaginable writerly needs is often at odds with meeting the basic needs of most writers most of the time.

Figure 6.1: An array of over sixty distinct choices greeting the user of the current MacOS version of Microsoft Word

It now seems likely that one significant driver of the increasing adoption of touchscreen tablet computers is the implied promise of simplified interfaces. While desktops and laptops continue to offer "office suites" with incredibly complex applications, tablets employ micro-applications to perform relatively small tasks. Within the smartphone and tablet ecologies, apps have only been adopted on a widespread basis since the advent of Apple's App Store in June of 2007. Google's Android Market (since notably renamed the "Google Play Store") opened for business in October of 2008. The dominant "desktop" word processor—Microsoft Word—was not for sale as such in either Apple's App Store or the Google Play Store until 2019 because the application, at root, was calibrated for desktops and not tablets as a composing space.

The smartphone and tablet ecologies' comparatively low ceilings for application size and scope has not proven a bar to creativity. Rather, they have prompted an explosion of more narrowly calibrated composing tools. Desktop programs like Microsoft Word and Apple's Pages word processor can and do overwhelm users with their arrays of options. But tablet-based textual composers are presented with different challenges, starting with the challenge of locating the small-bore tools they need amidst gateways to candy that needs crushing or to zombie-repelling plants in need of assistance. This task is further complicated by the contrasting aesthetics of the two major tablet operating systems, with Apple often streamlining interactions to the degree that a single button or gesture is all that is required, while Google's Android interfaces tending more toward miniaturized versions of the "big screen" interfaces. With many twenty-first century university students deciding to forego the desktop/laptop levels of computers altogether, and major manufacturers introducing "business class" versions of their signature tablets, we do well to understand the possibilities opened up by these tools and their limitations.

Though the graphical user interfaces of desktop computers have remained remarkably stable throughout the last thirty-five years, the interfaces for smartphones and tablets have been relatively (and productively) elastic since the introduction of the iPhone in June of 2007. The iPhone was notable for the degree to which it relied upon apps and icons to help its users navigate the compressed screen space between the user and the computer at the iPhone's core. Because it popularized an app-driven interface, the iPhone stands out as an especially significant development in the history of internetworked writing. But its status as the leading edge for an app-based ecology is attributable to a canny decision by Apple to pair the interface with another, more familiar set of tools and practices. According to multiple interviews with Steve Jobs, the idea for the iPad tablet preceded the iPhone:

> I had this idea about having a glass display, a display you could type on. I asked our people about it. And six months later they came back with this amazing display. And I gave it to one of our really brilliant UI guys. He then got inertial scrolling working and some other things, and I thought, "my god, we can build a phone with this" and we put the tablet aside, and we went to work on the phone. (qtd. in Zee)

The decision to invest in the phone, as opposed to the tablet, was likely critical to the success of what was then a radically new interface for a digital tool. The iPhone operating system, which prompted the reliance upon icons, asked iPhone users to engage with screens *without* a keyboard, preferring instead touchscreen interactions driven by each user's fingertips. These physical differences in interaction with the technology, in turn, prompted dramatic shifts in the design and aesthetics of computing within what would come to be known as the iOS, Apple's distinct operating system for its "i" devices (the iPhone and, in 2010, the iPad).

Recognizing the significance of Apple's innovations, in 2008, Google introduced the HTC Dream, a flagship smartphone intended to compete with the Apple iPhone. For a year, I used *both* the Apple iPhone and the Google's HTC Dream in parallel—one as my work phone and one as my personal phone—and through this side-by-side comparison I came to understand that the two phones were being designed with entirely different usage patterns in mind (This unusual side-by-side comparison was made possible by an Imagine Fund Grant from the College of Liberal Arts at the University of Minnesota-Twin Cities).

Figure 6.2: The superficially Windows-like interface of Google's HTC Dream smartphone. Photo by Michael Oryl. Image courtesy of Flickr.

The HTC Dream interface was crafted to resemble a miniaturized desktop computer. Once the screen was slid into the open position, the HTC Dream offered a tiny forty-eight-key keyboard with keys the size of Chicklets. The HTC Dream was offering its users about sixty percent of the keys commonly found on a laptop (with, for example, no row of function keys owing to the limited space available). The base of the phone featured five additional physical keys and a rubberized trackball slightly smaller than a pencil eraser. Apps on the HTC Dream typically had icons that resembled conventional icons for desktop computers. Indeed, the look and feel of these apps was often closely parallel to the look and feel of Windows applications. The HTC Dream offered capabilities that the iPhone didn't at the time. Most notably, Dream users could cut and paste text. The process was cumbersome—with users needing to painstakingly highlight words with the tiny trackball—but because the Dream was modeled after laptops of the era, this basic laptop function was included.

The differences between the most popular desktop interfaces and the portable interfaces that have, over time, gravitated toward iOS are important considerations as we consider writing ecologies two decades into the twenty-first century. One difference is subtle but critically important. A word-processing program like Microsoft Word lives in a metaphoric window "atop" the desktop. There is a clear home base within GUI interfaces, and this home base is modeled after common elements of a cube farm workspace. The desktop is positioned near a filing cabinet and what might be termed a wastepaper basket in physical spaces. The metaphoric files and folders of this workspace are teetering on the edge of incomprehensibility for children born in this millennium, for whom a filing cabinet is an increasingly rare and archaic piece of furniture. Physical filing cabinets house pieces of information that are notable for their initial disconnection. Paper files are available only to the extent that the cabinet's organization scheme is intuitively clear. These files are not readily searchable. In physical files, the possibility that a keyword occurs repeatedly throughout different folders in a filing cabinet might *never* be apparent. Searching digital spaces is unquestionably more efficient, and more likely to identify connections across files. Nevertheless, the GUI desktop invokes this increasingly outmoded physical space to serve as a metaphor for one of the spaces where digital texts clearly offer their users far more than their print predecessors.

Unlike desktop interfaces, contemporary app ecologies typically feature apps taking over *all* the available screen space. The taskbars, docks, and core OS functions that hover around the activities transpiring in desktop and laptop spaces are nowhere apparent when an app is active on a smartphone or tablet. This is in part because space is at a premium in smartphones and tablets, but it also reflects the degree to which these interfaces construct their users in very different ways.

Since 2011, the MacOS has offered users a "Launchpad" that pushes the desktop interface ever closer to the iOS interface, but the desktop still lurks in the background, framing the activities that transpire as occurring within a model corporate workspace. Smartphones and tablets, by contrast *give themselves over* to whatever a particular app sets out to do, be it a game, a social media app, or a fitness app. It seems inevitable that app-driven spaces like the MacOS Launchpad will eventually be the core of future laptop and even desktop operating systems. Alternatively, Google is building a model in which the browser is the base of operations for users of its Chromebooks. When the desktop GUI frame, having just passed its fiftieth year as I write, is no longer the metaphoric frame for digital technologies as writing spaces, it seems inevitable that new horizons for writing with digital tools will open up. That will be the moment when digital tools will decisively move beyond being the "better pencil" invoked in the title of Dennis Baron's 2009 *A Better Pencil: Readers, Writers, and the Digital Revolution*. Or, more properly, the eventual abandonment of the desktop metaphor will be the point where digital writing tools escape the gravitational pull of their most immediate predecessors, typewriters.

This shift should be welcomed because, in addition to other limitations, the gender politics of typewriters are notable and, by and large, deplorable. In common office layouts, the perimeters of the office spaces (i.e., the windowed offices) were spaces in which men wrote, typically in longhand, or dictated into successive generations of recording devices. People known as "typewriters" typically occupied an internal, open, shared space in which women worked to render the dictation or longhand writing into typescript. To the extent the desktop frames the internal space of computers as a conventional twentieth century office, these operating systems draw upon a heavily sexist power structure. In a 2019 *Medium* article, Adrienne Grimes rightly calls attention to a sign carried by a woman in the first few minutes of a 2014 documentary about the social steps leading to the United States feminist movement, titled *She's Beautiful When She's Angry*. The sign reads: "WOMEN & TYPEWRITERS ARE NOT INSEPERABLE."[sic.] This compact argument speaks to a practical reality of the world I was born into. Women were, overwhelmingly, the operators of typewriters. Their responsibility when using these writing tools was the rendering of men's words into recognizable written prose.

In addition to the sexist structuring of the spaces invoked by "desktop" interface, the desktop frame also carries with it more than a whiff of the benchmark for successful writing being how many words per minute are being produced. And images slow the processing of words down. Way down. For all the effort invested into word processor interfaces, they still wobble when it comes to addressing images. Word processors are still catching up to the degree to which contemporary composers rarely consider the production of words without also considering the visual appearance of those words and the images that might travel with those words.

The icon-driven interfaces of tablet computers reflect (and inform) broader shifts in international cultures. Businesses are clearly recognizing the value of consistent branding that can scale from the signage for physical structures down to the icon on the screen of a smartwatch. As a practical matter, this means that designs that communicate a lot with relatively few colors and without complex shapes are increasingly favored. Contemporary interfaces are thus shaped by (and, they, in turn, shape) two phenomena that were readily observable in commercial culture prior to the advent of computers. They are *dealphabetization* and *iconification*.

Dealphabetization is the readily observable phenomenon of businesses, organizations, and composers more generally eliminating words from existing logos, signs, or marks in deference to the power of images. There are numerous drivers for dealphabetization in commercial communications. The two most significant are:

1. Increasingly international markets, which prompt movement toward logos that are less heavily dependent on alphabetic characters; and

2. Increasing reliance on icon-driven smartphone interfaces as the means by which consumers navigate the Internet.

The decades-long trend toward dealphabetization feeds into iconification, a more expansive phenomenon in which composers self-consciously attempt to develop recognizable images that help readers navigate interfaces, writing spaces, and compositions more generally.

Even a cursory review of major international brands over the past half century demonstrates the degree to which their public-facing communications have tended toward dealphabetization and iconification. For example, the McDonald's restaurant signs of my youth conveyed *a lot* of textual information, commonly including:

- · the name of the restaurant
- · that the core food sold was hamburgers
- · the remarkably high number of hamburgers McDonald's had sold (a by-the-million countdown eventually gave way to the legend "Over 100 million sold")
- · whether the specific restaurant location had a drive-through option (always spelled "drive-thru")
- · whether the particular restaurant was a licensee of the "Speedee Service System"
- · the *price* of the hamburgers, held aloft on a placard by a charming "strolling hamburger" mascot, known as "Speedee"

At present, it is not uncommon for a McDonald's highway sign to bear no words at all, with the exception of the arcing "M" formed by the "golden arches."

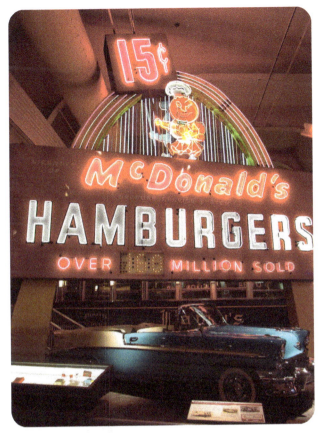

Figure 6.3: Dealphabetization and iconification in action. The Henry Ford Museum's "vintage" McDonald's sign is full of words and data, but contemporary signs routinely feature neither, courtesy of the Henry Ford Museum and McDonalds.com.

McDonald's has whittled its signage down to a spare icon in part because it is one of the most recognizable global brands. But this rejection of alphabetic information in favor of iconification of the brand (with most of the information on the older signs now understood to be either unnecessary or implied by the icon) is emblematic of larger cultural trends. Nike is another obvious example of a brand that—over time—moved to strip the alphabet from its branding and its products, moving instead to foreground first the signature "swoosh" and second, the "jumpman" silhouette of NBA legend Michael Jordan.

The trends toward dealphabetization and iconification take on special significance when the companies and designers involved play a large part in the construction of contemporary writing spaces. One of the most dramatic examples of a shift toward a dealphabetized and iconified presentation is Apple Computer's branding over the years. Apple's original 1976 logo, designed by Robert Wayne, is almost impossible to understand as ancestral to the current iconic logo. Designed to resemble an engraving, the logo features Isaac Newton, on a pastoral hillside, quill pen in hand, perusing a codex book. An apple—presumably the one that legend says prompted Newton to develop a theory of gravity—hovers over Newton's head, waiting to inspire him. Embedded in a thin frame around the depiction of Newton, in a jarring all-capital sans-serif typeface, are the words: "Newton . . . A Mind Forever Voyaging Through Strange Seas of Thought . . . Alone."

Figure 6.4: The conceptual and typographic failure that was the original Apple logo, via Wikimedia Commons.

The image also features a three-part "windswept" banner reading "Apple Computer Co." As this description makes clear, the aesthetics of the time prompted Robert Wayne to pack a lot of visual content into the logo for this fledgling computer company. The logo positions Apple's then-nascent approach to computing as echoing Newton's contributions to the Enlightenment.

This busy and overly complicated logo was quickly supplanted by version of the now-recognizable Apple silhouette with a bite out of the right side, designed by Rob Janoff. From 1977 to 1998, this iteration of the logo featured the colors of the rainbow (albeit in an unconventional order, with green at the top, and blue at the bottom).

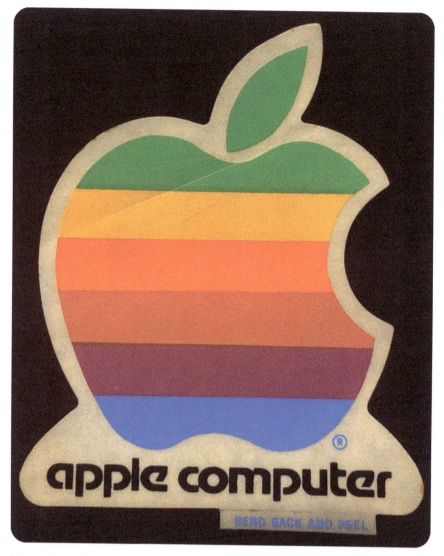

Figure 6.5: The "rainbow" Apple logo designed by Rob Janoff, photo by John Logie.

Apple then opted for monochromatic presentations of Janoff's logo, which have persisted—with minor alterations—to the present moment. Over the years, the textual content dwindled to zero, and the image content was reduced to a single color.

One early non-corporate example of the potential value of iconi-fication—and of the limits of word processors and related software—was the 1993 decision by the performer then known as Prince to replace his name with a typographic glyph, meant to be unspoken. This symbol, ☿ , was delivered to newspapers and media outlets on floppy disks. This decision fell within weeks of the launch of the Mosaic browser, which opened the World Wide Web to a broader public. But it is illustrative that physical media were still needed to deliver this specific glyph to the computers used for newspaper and magazine layout, and that the symbol could not be reliably cut and pasted in the available fonts on most computers. To a degree, this challenge persists to this day. As Emily VanDerWerff notes, in her 2016 retrospective on the Prince glyph: "the symbol itself cannot be replicated in the fonts most publications use. (Indeed, I can't replicate it within the fonts *Vox* uses, which is why I'm just calling it "the symbol" throughout this article.)" My hope and expectation is that this production challenge will be perplexing to many readers of this book. After all, the level of labor involved in combining text and images has become modest and unremarkable. 😏. That said, the amount of effort needed to embed emojis in the Microsoft Word software I'm using to prepare this manuscript is far more complicated than the relatively intuitive technique common to all contemporary smartphones. 🤭.

From 1993 to the present, there has only been an incremental improvement in the image-handling capacity of the machines we tend to rely upon for long-form composition. While composers using internetworked tools can often feel a high degree of creative freedom, it is too often the case that these tools and interfaces place functional limits on the full range of possible expression. Not everyone has the time, resources, or sheer stubbornness of Prince when it comes to hacking around these limitations. Ben McCorkle's 2012 monograph *Rhetorical Delivery as Technological Discourse: A Cross-Historical Study*, speaks to the degree to which both the materiality of texts and established media forms are factors shaping all discursive acts:

> Today, we are beginning to realize a more complete historical picture of how the materiality of texts contributes to the overall rhetorical process. Moreover, the act of rhetorical genesis rests in sites other than the single human being traditionally credited with a text's production (orator, author, designer). An entire communications environment comprising not only machinery but also accumulated media forms and genres, institutions that vet and disseminate the production of texts, and the people circulating in and around such institutions contributes to the eventual shape and ultimate persuasiveness of that text. We are beginning to understand that, to varying degrees, technologies of writing and communication have always had the capacity within them to communicate via their form. (Chapter 6)

In the case of internetworked writing technologies, their form incorporates an obviously counter-intuitive, but conventional interface, perpetuating both the desktop metaphor and the QWERTY keyboard, both of which speak to the needs of the cultural and technological past.

It needs to be said directly that no particular method of inputting text is inherently better than any other. There is nothing particularly elegant about QWERTY other than its clever arrangement of keys so that most of the most-used keys fall in alignment with the most nimble fingers. Here, the needs of the machine and the needs of human operators aligned somewhat serendipitously. But the ultimate driver behind QWERTY is the goal of preventing mechanical keys from piling into one another and interrupting the typing process. And this is no longer a significant concern for internetworked writers.

Richard Rawnsley offers insight into why we have remained stuck with QWERTY in his 2012 essay on the development of writing technologies:

> The fact that the QWERTY keyboard arrangement dominates computer as well as typewriter keyboards is not a testament to any ergonomic thought on Christopher Latham Sholes's part, but to the difficulty people encounter when first learning to type and their refusal to change their operating habits for more efficient methods. This difficulty is caused by several aspects of the keyboard: first, touch typing requires very complex and rapid movement of all ten fingers in conjunction with mental activities that vary with the type of work being performed, from transcription to taking dictation to generative typing. Second, the experience of learning to type is fraught with so much work and frustration that the thought of learning to use another keyboard layout, whether more efficient or not, is repulsive to most typists. So, we are faced with a paradox: for the sake of efficiency, learning even the clumsy QWERTY keyboard is worth the effort, yet few desire to apply the limited effort needed to gain the considerable advantages learning an even more efficient keyboard arrangement offers. (49)

At the end of this passage, Rawnsley points toward the tantalizing prospect of moving beyond the limitations of QWERTY, but the spaces in which we see developers trying to do so speak to the paradox Rawnsley identifies. Even though inventive alternatives to QWERTY exist, facility with QWERTY typing is one of the core markers of functional literacy in United States culture. And in many cases, the first step in exploring a new communicative space is determining how best to wedge the old interface into that space.

Intriguingly, one of the spaces where we see developers beginning to develop viable alternatives to the QWERTY keyboard is the watchOS platform, developed for the Apple Watch. Because the Apple Watch currently caps out at a forty-four millimeter display size (or 448 x 368 pixels) traditional approaches to text generation simply don't fit. The limits of physical keys were likely hit when Blackberry ported QWERTY to Chicklet-sized physical keys. In the even smaller virtual keys found within smartphone screens, the reduction of the QWERTY keyboard appears to have finally hit its limit. Apple's response to this problem—in WatchOS3—was to try having Apple Watch users "draw" letters on their screens. This proved quite cumbersome, recalling the balky text recognition on Apple's Newton line of personal digital assistants in the early 1990s. As it turns out, there is a huge difference between tapping an icon with one's chosen letter and, in the alternative, painstakingly drawing a capital letter "T" only to have it be processed as a "7." Bluntly put, a generation of writers has become habituated to thumbtapping out messages, and the timesink involved in drawing individual letters on the screen, especially with misinterpretations of letters being as common as they are, means that this is not a viable approach to writing within contemporary smartwatch spaces.

In response, at least one developer simply shrank the QWERTY keyboard down to a set of pinhead-sized keys. with depressing results—the amount of time and effort needed to type the word "hello" (*fifteen seconds!*) underscored the degree to which new approaches were needed.

Figure 6.6: A sadly unworkable attempt at miniaturizing the QWERTY keyboard for a smartwatch screenspace, photo by John Logie.

A WatchOS app called FlickType attempts to port the QWERTY interface to the watchOS by eliminating the "keys" in the traditional keyboard and simply placing the QWERTY keyboard onscreen as bare capital letters, in a presentation reminiscent of the lines on an eyechart. Flicktype makes fingertip typing workable by using artificial intelligence to deliver very forgiving analyses of writers' taps, often self-correcting when letters are obviously wrong. In practice, Flicktype also requires writers to swipe right after every single word typed, which is not that different than hitting a space bar, to be fair, but which also takes getting used to. These efforts largely underscore the degree to which QWERTY is not really reducible to watch-sized screen spaces. It packs too many letters in too little space and leads to cumbersome approaches to punctuation.

Figure 6.7: Flicktype improves smartwatch QWERTY functionality by dispensing with the idea of virtual "buttons." Still from "FlickType for Apple Watch: keyboard typing on your wrist!" by iDB via YouTube.

One of the most inventive approaches to "typing" on smarthones and smartwatches is Ian Hanson's "Modality" keyboard that *actually groups letters by their shapes*. Within Modality, letters are grouped by Red/**A)** straight lines with diagonals (e.g. A, K), and M; Yellow/**B)** a mixture of straight and curved lines (e.g. B, D, and J); Blue/**C)** curved lines (e.g. C, O, and Q) and Green/**E)** straight lines at 90 degree angles.

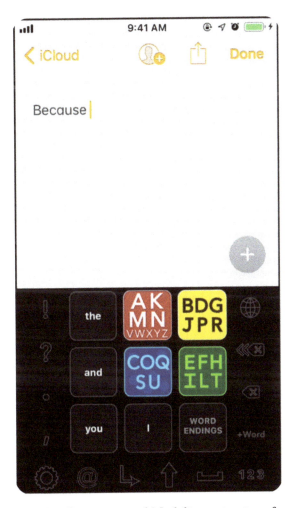

Figure 6.8: The radically re-invented Modality typing interface, courtesy Joyful Machines

Thus, to type the word "wrote," one would move from red/A (because "w" is made up of diagonals) to yellow/B (because "r" is a mix of straight lines and curves) to blue/C ("o" is curved) to green/E (with this last being tapped twice for both the T and the E. Modality's inventive interface would serve people who only used two fingers to type—indeed, it almost encourages limiting the number of fingers involved to no more than two.

Once one becomes habituated to the Modality interface, it becomes harder and harder to understand why we persist in having dozens of individual physical keys as the default means of inputting text into our composing spaces. A screen occupying the space of a conventional button keyboard could present composers with a traditional QWERTY keyboard layout, a Dvorak keyboard, the Modality interface, or any of dozens of other possible configurations. Modality demonstrates that a touchscreen interface would have considerable potential for widespread adoption, especially because it does not require ten actively engaged fingers. This will only become viable if people could forego their lingering attachment to the physical feedback they receive when a plastic key is depressed. But this is an attachment that is likely generational.

We are teetering on the edge of change. In 2016 and again in late 2018, the Chinese computer company Lenovo introduced low-end laptop/tablet blends with *no keyboard at all* and an e-ink touchscreen surface sitting in the space where a keyboard would be expected. The most recent of these, the YOGA A12 can deliver an approximation of the traditional QWERTY keyboard on the e-ink touchscreen, but it also is set up to capture handwriting via a magnetized panel that can sit under any sheet of paper. With proper programming, this same touchscreen could be repurposed to accommodate any of a number of text-input programs, and QWERTY typing would take its place as one among *dozens* of ways (along with handwriting and speech) that ideas move from the mind of the composer into a machine and, then, instantaneously, into cloud-based storage.

People whose first experience with typing as a form of textual input via smartphones will not be as attached to either the physical sensation of "tapping" words with their fingers or the sounds of typing. Indeed, one can easily envision a future circumstance where because of the touchscreen interface, there will be occasional complaints that someone using a *laptop* with conventional keys is typing "too loudly."

While some people are demonstrably nostalgic for the specifics of the typewriter as a technology, most of us don't really care that much how an individual chooses to input words into a composing machine. The notion that QWERTY is distinctively better than its near-peers is absurd. It is simply the keyboard that "stuck"—initially developed because of the limitations of existing technology. It has persisted beyond the natural lifespan of that technology through sheer force of habit. By contrast, one of the greatest characteristics of digital tools is their degree of flexibility. They can, by turns, be pretty much anything. There is no need, going forward, for QWERTY to persist, except as a virtual keyboard space, which would allow those habituated to QWERTY to continue with their preferred approaches. Adding in a sonic cue to indicate when a key has been struck is, for contemporary hardware designers, child's play. Literally. There are children now alive who could easily manage this programming challenge.

The larger question is when and where ought we make efforts to push free of that which we have become habituated to, and when should we allow conventions to remain conventions? Moving our composing spaces from the physical to the virtual is a first step in unleashing the latent potential of the tools now in many of our hands.

The possibility of a flexible interface, offering multiple input options, sitting in the space where the keyboard has resided raises important questions about how and whether the supposed "discipline" of typing enhanced the lives of those who became skilled at QWERTY's conventions. It has long been suggested that using one's own hands to fill white rectangles with alphanumeric characters *builds* writerly skills. This argument has persisted even though several writers who would be considered "canonical" by most English departments were—at points in their careers—either unwilling to write by their own hands or simply preferred not to do so. For much of his career, John Milton was blind and dictated his poetry to stenographers. Milton's works after "On His Blindness" (circa 1655), including *Paradise Lost* (1667), were all dictated. Milton *never saw* the words of his most expansive and celebrated work on a page, and his hands were uninvolved in the composition. Fyodor Dostoevsky dictated his novels to a stenographer who became his wife—Anna Grigorievna (and, given the closeness of their relationship, it is likely Grigorievna ended up influencing aspects of Dostoevsky's work). Henry James, after becoming arthritic in his early fifties, dictated *The Turn of the Screw*, *The Wings of the Dove*, and *The Ambassadors*, among other books. There has been considerable energy devoted to the perceived differences between oral and written composition, but in these (and other) cases, celebrated, indeed *towering* examples of the writer's art, were not, in the conventional sense, *written*. These works, were, rather, spoken aloud and captured by others' hands. So, while the means by which imagined words become letters is *not* entirely neutral, we ought not assume with absolute confidence that we will be able to distinguish among compositions composed in one way and not the other. And while Milton, Dostoyevsky, and James depended on amanuenses, it is quite likely that composers facing similar challenges might turn not to people, but to relatively affordable pocket-sized computers, if they wished to make use of a machine that could record their words and render them into text.

It is notable that within this chapter, which positions itself as an examination of technological interfaces that might initially be understood as relatively neutral in their pursuit of greater efficiency, this is the second point where, for varying reasons, we have considered cases of writers who were disproportionately men speaking or dictating words to others of lower status (secretaries and amanuenses) who were disproportionately women. It is also striking that over the course of the twentieth century the words "typewriter" and "computer" might have been understood to refer to either a machine *or a person*, usually a woman, who performed the labor of computation or rendering unfinished prose into "finished" typescript. In her 1998 book, *How We Became Posthuman: Virtual Bodies in Cybernetics, Literature, and Informatics*, N. Katherine Hayles reconstructs the daily lived experience of Janet Freed, who was, in a very real sense, *the interface* between participants in the Macy Conferences on Cybernetics in the mid-twentieth century and the audiences who would ultimately read their influential work:

> "Take a letter, Miss Freed," he says. Miss Freed comes in. She gets a lovely smile. The man speaks, and she writes on her stenography pad (or perhaps on her stenography typewriter). The man leaves. He has a plane to catch, a meeting to attend. When he returns, the letter is on his desk, awaiting his signature. From his point of view, what has happened? He speaks, giving commands or dictating words, and things happen. A woman comes in, marks are inscribed onto paper, letters appear, conferences are arranged, books are published. Taken out of context, his words fly, by themselves, into books. The full burden of the labor that makes these things happen is for him only an abstraction, a resource diverted from other possible uses, because he is not the one performing the labor. (82–83)

Hayles rightly observes the degree to which the labor here described was *physical* as well as intellectual labor.

> On a level beyond words, beyond theories and equations, in her body and her arms and her fingers and her aching back, Janet Freed knows that information is never disembodied, that messages don't flow by themselves, and that epistemology isn't a word floating through the thin, thin air until it is connected up with incorporating practices. (83)

It is this aggregation of practices that are represented, in virtual form, in the desktop interfaces that persist to this day. While superficially neutral, the iconic files, folders, and wastebaskets point toward suites of responsibilities that were positioned as low status "women's work." To the degree that these interfaces are now being supplanted by app-driven interfaces, and other alternative approaches to composition and production, we are taking slow steps toward a more level playing field.

Reputable figures suggest that of the 5.3 billion people over the age of fifteen in the world, roughly five billion of them have smartphones. Notwithstanding an ongoing digital divide with respect to computers and tablets, *most of the planet* now has on their persons, throughout the day, a computer significantly more powerful than practically *every* desktop personal computer released prior to the turn of the millennium. Higher-end releases have specs that would make them competitive with many of the desktops from the first decade of the twenty-first century. Further, an *immense* amount of writing takes place on these machines every day. Most of it is meant to be ephemeral, *even though most of it is logged and preserved in cloud storage from the moment of composition*. Thus, *serious* writing (at least in terms of volume) is being produced on machines that are, typically, not understood as serious writing machines.

The practical implication of this is that more of the five billion people than have been welcomed by QWERTY and its international equivalents on smartphones will be typing on a machine that will also routinely demonstrate its increasing capacity to render speech into text. To the extent that typing remains a barrier for some composers, many will hop right past tapping works and just talk, and thereby participating more fully in the cultural conversations that have been contained by fingertip-centered modes of textual production. Whether universities and other text-intensive cultural spaces are prepared for this dramatic expansion in the levels of participation in cultural conversations remains to be seen.

What will be notable about writers' shift to verbal interfaces will be the degree to which their speech will be disciplined by the requirements of the interface. The slow, relatively enunciated speech that has become the means by which people access Siri, Alexa, and similar verbal assistants will necessarily be extended into the first widely-adopted speech recognition interface. This, of course, underscores something about *all* interfaces. The foundational presumption behind any interface is that a certain kind of user will be composing, and in this case that user will likely be presumed to be able to mobilize a formal, enunciated mode of speech. While practically all current composing machines offer writers the opportunity to simply record speech (in the form of something like a voice memo) how and whether that speech will be effectively rendered into functional prose swings heavily on whether the writer will be able to meet the speech recognition program at *least* halfway, and the power of the implied model for disciplining how one *ought* to speak will be profound.

Writing will also reflect speech conventions with more and more precision. SMS texting often superficially resembles speech, many composers of text messages gravitating toward speech patterns in their messages. This is reinforced by the degree to which SMS apps typically invoke the "speech bubble" conventions common in comics. Further, because social cues were not available in the first generation of text messages, composers began hacking punctuation symbols to provide some "facial" and gestural cues for their readers. As time passed, it became clear that actual graphics could do more than hacked punctuation to convey shades of meaning that could not be delivered by the alphabet alone. It is common now for a smartphone to include access to close to four thousand emojis, many of which have both surface and stealth meanings. Entire conversations have transpired in emojis alone. Yet, in academic circles, it is quite possible to have conversations about writing that *never* touch on typography or visuals even though the composer's access to sophisticated tools for managing typefaces and visual information are perhaps the most important aspects of the digital writing tools developed prior to widespread adoption of the Internet. With some elegant coding, the developers of Microsoft Word and MacWrite offered composers opportunities to move away from preparing typescripts that would then be manipulated on their behalf by editors and designers. It should go without saying that not all composers in the 1990s were prepared to take full advantage of these opportunities. But almost two generations later, almost all beginning writers approach the act of composition with considerable skills with respect to typography and visuals. And the feedback loop between the creativity of composers and the creativity of hardware and software designers is already placing remarkable opportunities in our hands.

The smudged surfaces of today's touchscreen tablet computers testify to contemporary composers being "hands on" in ways that previous generations of computer were not. The keyboard, mouse, and trackpad were—for decades—the dominant means of transmitting ideas from composer to screen. But touchscreen tablets encourage modes of textual production that in some ways recall fingerpainting. While on an intellectual level, composers using touchscreens to write notes with their fingertips understand that they are using an interface, the experience is one of "writing" into a surface. Over and above the experience of fingertip and stylus note-taking and sketching, the current base model iPads offer startlingly effective speech recognition systems and—of course—virtual keyboards. Once text is onscreen, fingertips "pinch and zoom" text and manipulate it more directly than in any prior computer interface. For composers of my generation and older, these modes of interaction with text often feel cumbersome. Most in these demographics are too habituated to the keyboard to function efficiently without it. But this will almost certainly not be the case for a generation for whom touchscreen tablet computing is their foundational experience with digital technologies.

For the generations being introduced to writing on expressly social machines like iPads, Chromebooks, and other touchscreen devices, the Romantic construction of authorship that frames writing as solitary will seem at least quaint, and possibly downright bizarre. Typewriters were alphabet machines. Even the presence of SMS messaging by itself radically alters a composer's perception of writing space. Elements of literate culture still have a lot invested in the notion of writing as a journey deep into the self . . . a process of silencing the world in pursuit of something presumably authentic that is framed as lying *within* writers. But not all writers thrive in sensory deprivation, much less social deprivation.

Fictional or poetic texts might benefit from the composer's descent into contemplative silence, but academic writing has long been understood as a conversation, primarily with one's predecessors. The genre of the literature review exists in no small part to ensure that today's composers have had the benefit of surveying the already known territory and thus being nudged toward *terra incognita*. But the work of academic writing is accretive and incremental. Academia is thus ill-equipped to orient itself to the speed with which ideas are now able to travel. Thus, national conversations traveling at tweet-speed only occasionally benefit from the expertise of leading academics. The publication timelines of traditional academic presses feel increasingly archaic, with most leading print journals being published on a *quarterly* basis.

Yet, despite profound shifts in the technologies at hand, the preferred conventions of written composition have remained largely intact for over a century. To the extent that the future holds a moment that will be identified as a decisive breaking point between "how we used to write" and "how we write now" this moment will not be felt in real time. The distinctions will never be a sharply defined as the moment a baby stops crawling and starts walking. Both the World Wide Web and the smartphone were perceived as incremental shifts in communication technologies—until they weren't.

Because computers as composing tools are inherently social, they depend on critical mass. Their potential as points of connection among composers is only realizable when enough people are on a shared platform, with a baseline understanding of the shared tools and practices that work within the new communicative space. This is the point where our experience of the technology turns from McLuhan's famed rear-view mirror and begins to look forward.

When we think of McLuhan we often also intuitively think of the distinctive visual style that Quentin Fiore and Jerome Agel developed for some of McLuhan's most popular works, characterized by high-contrast photographic images and austere white-on-black Helvetica typography. I argue here that we think of too few composers in this way. Having a distinctive visual look and feel is a mark of baseline competence for so many aspects of contemporary communication, yet these skills are too often bracketed from writing as if the look and feel of words on pages (real or virtual) are peripheral to the embedded meaning of the words themselves. If this argument suddenly were to flip to COMIC SANS, with all of the cultural coding embedded in a contemporary reading of this particular typeface, well then, readers would do well to question the seriousness of this argument, would they not?

One of the central ironies of our current circumstance is that many composers are tunneling through a graphically rich OS to get to composing spaces where visuals are at least on the back burner and sometimes not considered at all. Indeed, people are profiting from products that argue that the graphic richness of contemporary computers is at odds with serious writing. The increasingly social orientation of digital composing tools has prompted a cottage industry in applications that strip away the capabilities of digital media in order to present composing spaces that consist of unformatted words. One popular example of this type of interface is offered by Cold Turkey Writer. Cold Turkey Writer offers no formatting, no options, nothing but a blank space for text. The name "Cold Turkey Writer" is notable. It suggests that its users are suffering from a form of addiction. The addiction metaphor is too often applied to digital media. It tends to ignore the possibility that the metaphoric "drugs" in this parallel are often sites of human connection. If the reason a person is "always on her laptop" is that she is exchanging journal entries with the members of her online breast cancer support group, then most reasonable people would endorse this as a meaningful use of time.

The "internet addiction" metaphor is grounded in a nostalgic framing of the pre-computer world as one in which relatively limited access to the production of "professional-looking" texts facilitated what is positioned as a superior literate culture. This implied argument is grounded in aggressive forgetting of just what people did with their free time prior to the advent of the Internet. For example, while it is not uncommon in my neighborhood park to hear someone grousing about twenty-first century parents being too distracted by their smartphones, the playgrounds of the 1970s were not idyllic spaces filled with parents engaging non-stop with their children. In my experience, after the kids got pushed on the swingset and pointed toward the monkey bars, adults turned to literature and their literary diet consisted of Jacqueline Susanne, Robert Ludlum, *The National Enquirer*, and local daily newspapers (and as an aside, most of the parents were smoking). Somehow a pocket of cultural critics has persuaded themselves that the Internet is standing between people and their baseline desire to read Proust. One especially tiresome example of this is Sven Birkerts, whose *Gutenberg Elegies* was a rallying cry for those who had persuaded themselves that a literate culture that mattered would evaporate with the codex book sometime before the turn of the millennium. As pointed out earlier, people in 2020 read voraciously and wrote copiously.

Again, the goal should be isolating the specific activities that are central to a perception of literate culture worth maintaining and then asking whether the advent and popularity of digital media actually offers opportunities for the expansion of those activities. In their 2000 book *Remediation*, Jay Bolter and Richard Grusin argue that one of the most striking things about digital media is its capacity to incorporate and reinvigorate almost all previous analog media. The foundational premise of the digital humanities movement is that research with digital tools will reinvigorate humanities disciplines that are in need of a broader connection with larger audiences. Over the course of the last few decades, scholars in the humanities have, variously, positioned digital media as both destroyers and saviors of the humanites. Of course, they are neither. There are new tools, offering new and distinctive opportunities. But the core of intellectual life will, in the near term, remain more constant than not.

In many cases, what internetworked digital tools have offered to composers is a palpable shift from options that have functioned like binary off-on switches to dials. This is ironic, given that everything in digital spaces is built upon binary code, but nonetheless, from the perspective of the composer, there are numerous examples of dials replacing switches. Publication used to be a straightforward switch. Either a text had enough apparent gravitas or quality that it helped it navigate its way through all the various locks attached to the publication process or it did not. Because print depended on expenditures of labor, resources, and space, many aspiring authors never made it past even the first editorial assessment, much less all the way to being published in something bound. Contemporary composers, by contrast self-select for all manner of "publications." Further, social media offers numerous opportunities to weigh and rebalance their relationships as composers with specific audiences. For example, we all now collectively understand Twitter and tweets to be both public and published, and something placed into Twitter's ecology is widely understood as something that the composer has chosen to make public and thus reportable and also something for which the composer is generally held accountable (with occasional exceptions for youthful indiscretions). Facebook, by contrast, is a space where most people choose some level of privacy controls. Thus, a Facebook

141

post is fairly understood as "among friends" and—even if newsworthy—re-publication of a semi-private Facebook post would be a violation of norms that have evolved around the platform.

While neither Facebook nor Twitter is an appropriate space for sustained argument, each is also an incursion into publication—in the sense of composers selectively making their texts public. The presence of relatively low-stakes opt-in social media spaces mean that the opportunity to publish ideas is more widely distributed than ever before. Add to this opt-in publishing platforms like *Medium*, which is based on a streamlined revenue-sharing model with people who offer their writing on the platform, and we begin to understand that publication is becoming more about the act of making words public than it is about participation in a publishing ecosystem. Publication, which had been a firewall of sorts, demarcating the line between authors and non-authors, is now a highly permeable boundary, with millions of people self-publishing (albeit in very low-stakes ways) every day. This is a space where the off-on switch of publication has given way to a dial of publication scaling from Twitter to the thousands of pages (and counting!) of George R.R. Martin's *A Song of Ice and Fire* series.

Part of the challenge we now face is that the dials are only sometimes readily available to some composers some of the time. While almost all composers readily understand that posts typed in social media spaces are *not private*, many composers demonstrably struggle with both understanding just how public their posts are and how to get their hands on the dials that might be used to increase or decrease the degree of public access to their writings. Sites like Facebook and Twitter routinely suggest that control is in their users' hands, while quietly being aware that their business models and revenue streams depend heavily on posts that generate—if not fiery controversy—something on the order of buzz. In the case of these two businesses, the possibility of relatively private writing is maintained largely in the interests of making the sites remain magnetic enough that writers do not migrate to other writing spaces. That said, the sites overtly structure their systems toward public symbolic acts.

The academic embrace of digital tools among scholars of writing, is, in part, driven by an awareness that digital tools have the *potential* to rebalance the scales. To the degree that authorship has remained an exclusive enclave within the broader orbit of writing, the advent of more flexible, adaptable, and fluid writing spaces would, at first blush, appear to offer opportunities for a broader range of voices to be heard, both within and outside the academy. It remains to be seen how expansive our definitions of writing will become. What is clear, though, is that the ways human ideas arc toward alphanumeric expression will vary greatly from what is currently at hand. This ought to be celebrated. The limited interfaces of typewriters offered far too narrow windows. A computer desktop pointing back toward white rectangles to be filled via QWERTY is obviously not a one-size-fits-all interface. Further, it has no inherent cognitive merit.

The desktop metaphor that has, until recently, surrounded the default writing spaces of the digital era (as opposed to our internetworked era) perpetuated the site of stratified and sexist structures of textual production. One of the better qualities of tablet and smartphone interfaces is the degree to which they place more neutral backdrops for the work of writing into people's hands. Even more promisingly they are tools that, by design, welcome textual production through typing, touch, and speech. For too many years, our interfaces have constrained our opportunities and our conceptualization of the possibilities of internetworked writing. The comparative flexibility and variety of interfaces in current writing spaces has the potential to free more people to reach for the clouds.

7 On "Surrender to the Digital Revolution": Nostalgic Rhetorics and the *New York Times*

It is not often that I can pinpoint the exact moment one of my academic projects started, but in this case—I can. This project started at 7:13 a.m. on Friday, September 25, 2015, when I read "So Long to E-Books" as the headline for a letter by novelist Anne Bernays to *The New York Times*. Aside from the obligatory "Re:" Bernays's letter reads in full:

> It took me three books' worth to realize that reading a book off a plastic tablet is a pain. The "pages" often turn back or forward by themselves. A tablet has no personality; a real book is almost a living thing.
>
> I guess that a lot of people feel the same way. This is heartening news. (Bernays par. 1–2)

In this concise-yet-expansive expression of distaste, Bernays somehow persuades herself that the inert pages of a codex book are more like a "living thing" than the sometimes animated, sometimes *literally moving* pages of a multimedia ebook. The letter ends with Bernays presuming that others share her distaste for tablet-based reading and concludes: "this is heartening news." At the time I read the headline, I had already embarked on this project, with ebooks being squarely in the mix because they are one of the most developed examples of internetworked writing delivered via cloud-based servers. I knew damn well ebooks weren't going anywhere anytime soon. But the *Times*'s editors' selection of Bernays' letter and the embedded judgement in the headline the editors composed for Bernays' letter raised questions for me about how the *Times* addressed ebooks within its pages. The rhetorical positioning here, in which the presumed audience is expected to share the composer's valuation of print and distaste for the digital felt all too familiar—and not just in the *Times*'s letters pages.

Bernays' letter was written in response to a September 22, 2015, *Times* article by Alexandra Alter titled "The Plot Twist: E-Book Sales Slip and Print is Far From Dead" (Alter, "The Plot Twist"). The headline pursues a common strategy in the *Times*'s discussions of ebooks—namely framing ebooks as a competitor to print in some sort of zero-sum game. This is, of course, at odds with our collective awareness of the many reasons why people buy ebook readers. It is likely the case that ebooks capture a significant number of book readers who are not especially interested in print texts—or not able to comfortably read print books because of, for example, failing vision. The headline is roughly reflective of Alter's framing throughout this article, which repeatedly suggests that ebooks have lost ground in a sort of "contest" between digital and print book platforms.

This Alter article is especially suspect because it relies heavily on thin data from a single source: The Association of American Publishers. The AAP is not an especially reliable source. The AAP is a trade organization made up of 1,200 members, but significantly, it encompasses the "Big 5" publishers: Holtzbrinck/Macmillan; Hachette; HarperCollins; Penguin Random House; and Simon & Schuster. Even more significantly, it does not include Amazon. So, when AAP offers up sales data, it is excluding perhaps the largest sales channel for books in the United States (though Amazon is cagey about its data). Further, AAP has an adversarial relationship with Amazon, as the Big 5 publishers were locked in a long legal dispute with Amazon over the pricing of ebooks, with the AAP objecting to Amazon using books as a "loss leader" and discounting best-sellers well below the prices of their print counterparts. The AAP won this battle, and the impact on ebook pricing was predictable. The first five months of 2015 happen to coincide with the Big 5 having achieved a $1.20 per copy price increase for ebooks sold on Amazon's Kindle platform relative to April of 2015. Industry observers responding to a subsequent similar story about a supposed "eBook decline" in *Publisher's Weekly* were quick to point out that the failure to include Amazon combined with the price increase effected by the Big 5 Publishers were likely contributors to the purported decline in ebook sales. I'll note in passing that *Publisher's Weekly* has a robust comments section the likes of which is not found in the more manicured spaces of the *Times* online.

To be fair, buried late in Alexandra Alter's article about "E-Book sales slipping" and "print being far from dead" is a faint acknowledgement that there was a likely relationship between the hike in prices and the decline in ebook sales. Indeed, the 8.4 percent improvement in paperback sales, which had been priced "several dollars cheaper than their digital counterparts," seems to just about counter-balance the ten percent drop in ebook sales reported by the AAP. But given that Amazon is cagey about sales data, we really need more information than what Alter and the *Times* offer here. Alter's article is notably thin on data (offering no tables or graphs) and in paragraph form, the data embedded in the argument is often hard to parse:

> Now, there are signs that some e-book adopters are returning to print, or becoming hybrid readers, who juggle devices and paper. E-book sales fell by 10 percent in the first five months of this year, according to the Association of American Publishers, which collects data from nearly 1,200 publishers. Digital books accounted last year for around 20 percent of the market, roughly the same as they did a few years ago.

> E-books' declining popularity may signal that publishing, while not immune to technological upheaval, will weather the tidal wave of digital technology better than other forms of media, like music and television. (Alter, "The Plot Twist")

The first paragraph appears to imply that the 10 percent slump in sales in the Spring of 2015 meant that sales of ebooks had fallen to sixteen percent of overall sales from a twenty percent of the market level that had maintained throughout 2014 and that they had previously reached back in 2012 or so ("a few years ago"). The subsequent paragraph opens by presenting "E-Books' declining popularity" as a matter of fact, based, as far as I can tell, solely on the AAP assessment. This is a highly questionable claim. The Pew Research Center has been polling about ebook *readership*—rather than sales—for years, and given the degree to which awareness of library lending of ebooks is a near constant topic in the Tech Q&A sections of *The New York Times*, we do well to consider whether readership rates (according to Pew polls) parallel the "eBooks slip" in the *Times* headline. The answer is *not really*. A month after the *Times* published the September article and letter addressing Spring 2015's purported sales "slip," The Pew Research Center published a report titled, "Slightly fewer Americans are reading print books, survey finds" (Perrin). This report, drawn from a roughly annual poll that was administered in March and April of 2015 documented a seven percent drop in book readership in *all* media relative to 2011. In alignment with this, the report recorded its first dip in ebook readership ever, of *one* percent, relative to a *four* percent drop in print readership. Indeed, for whatever reason, the 2015 Pew polls reported slight declines in print, ebook, and audiobook consumption relative to 2014. But relative to 2011, when Pew's polling started, ebook readership was *up* ten percent and print readership was *down* seven percent.

After surveying this reporting, *The Observer* offered a stinging rebuke to the *Times* calling out the *Times* by name for its continuing to report on a "slip" in ebook sales that is based on only a partial assessment of the market. In Brady Dale's 2017 article tellingly titled "Despite What You Heard, The E-Book Market Never Stopped Growing," *The Observer* reported on the development of non-traditional publishing opportunities on Amazon's Kindle platform that were not reported by the AAP. The *Observer* article outlines the findings of a source that attempted to scrape Amazon's data and thereby arrived at a four percent annual growth rate in ebook sales in 2016 relative to 2015 and, thereby, describes the e-Book market as never having declined (Dale). The *Observer*'s direct challenge to the *Times*'s reporting on ebooks illustrates the degree to which—by relying upon the Association of American

Publishers—the *Times* is accepting and promoting a skewed view of the market for ebooks from an organization that views ebooks as competing with—rather than complementing—its core products. Excluding Amazon's (admittedly hard-to-extract) sales from overall print and ebook sales is akin to attempting to discuss TV sales while excluding Best Buy, or prescription medication sales without including Walgreen's (and further, accepting as gospel figures on these sales from a consortium led by Wal-Mart and Target, both of whom compete directly with Best Buy and Walgreen's).

My frustration with *The New York Times*'s engagement with ebooks is driven not only by my sense that the *Times* relies on questionable data, but also my determination that the *Times*, in its editorial content, is demonstrably generally biased against the digital. This bias seems apparent everywhere in the text of the paper except for the *Times*'s often-incredible multimedia projects. As a regular reader of the *Times*, I have arrived at the conclusion that the *Times* has, for years, demonstrated apparent biases toward print and against digital texts. This may seem obvious, given that the paper has a century-and-a-half investment in optimizing its practices for print delivery, but I also see this as problematic, especially if the *Times* continues its substantial hold on defining and delimiting what literate life in the US is all about. The *Times*, after all, has a book review section that is one of the leading participants in national conversations about what people should read, and is also the arbiter of the *New York Times* best seller lists, among the most prominent lists of their type in the United States. So, if—as I suspected when I read the September 2015 articles—the *Times* has settled into a bias toward print, that bias influences how our national engagement with internetworked digital texts plays out in United States culture.

Reflecting on the prominent placement of Bernays's letter, and then on Alter's heavy reliance on a source that pointedly excluded Amazon's substantial share of the ebook market, I began to wonder whether I, as a *Times* reader, was being pulled into a proxy battle that reflected the larger tensions between the *Times* as a leading representative of traditional print journalism and Amazon, a notable disruptor of traditional print *everything*. Further, the time period in which the *Times* repeatedly and pointedly dismissed the category of one of Amazon's signature products, the Kindle ebook reader, was also a time when Amazon founder Jeff Bezos had purchased *The Washington Post*, pouring money into one of the few newspapers capable of challenging *The New York Times*'s standing as national paper of record. One can envision the *Times*'s internal frustrations over the rise of ebooks, paired with Amazon's reticence with respect to sharing sales figures, compromising the accuracy of its bestseller lists. Corporations like Amazon are often described, at least initially, as "disruptors," and to the extent that this description fits the

Amazon of the first decade or so of the twenty-first century, many of its disruptions were directed, whether intentionally or not, at the ways the *Times*, as a very traditional media organization, had organized its business. In the pages that follow, I'll be addressing why this contest between corporate giants is not merely a subject for business textbooks. Indeed, these companies are, indirectly, fighting over control over how people will engage with and perceive internetworked texts. And ebook platforms, as one of the most affordable entry points for people engaging with internetworked texts, end up being a significant space for framing how these interactions with internetworked media will unfold.

A broader look at available data illustrates the degree to which the *Times*'s gravitational pull is distorting our perception of the ways people read. Alter's 2016 article based on the AAP's report from that year is titled "We're Buying Paperbacks, Audiobooks and Coloring Books—but Not E-Books" trumpets a spike in paperback sales and a supposed decline in ebook sales (once again, Amazon is not included here). The opening three words are an all-caps shout at the *Times*'s readers: "PAPER IS BACK." This same article documents a *nine* point spike in reading of purchased books on smartphones, rather than e-readers. Alter's article also notes that "only" thirteen percent of eighteen- to twenty-four-year-olds "primarily" read ebooks compared with thirty percent of fifty-five- to sixty-four-year-olds. (Alter, "We're Buying Paperbacks, Audiobooks and Coloring Books—but Not E-Books"). One obvious explanation for this is the likelihood that older readers were more likely to be able to afford dedicated e-readers when that was the dominant platform for ebooks and further, that older eyes were more likely to prompt a preference for the ability to change type sizes while reading. The Pew Research Center's report from the same year constitutes a direct challenge to Alter's spotlighting of the small subsets of readers who express a "primary" reading format. The Pew Report shows that young people (18–29 in their survey) simply outread *everyone else*, with eighty percent having read a book in any format in the past twelve months, seventy-two percent having read a print book, and thirty-five percent having read an ebook. In each of these categories, eighteen- to twenty-nine-year-olds were seven percent above average. Pew's closest parallel to the 55–64 demographic Alter cites is a 50–64 tranche that breaks down as follows: seventy percent read a book in any format, sixty-four percent read a print book, and twenty-four percent read an ebook. All these are lower than average. The emphasis on a preferred primary format in Alter's article obscures the larger truth of 2016: *young people were outreading their elders and doing so across a range of formats in a range of media.* They read books on paper *and* on their phones *and* in their tablets *and* via their headphones.

Alter's article carried within it misrepresentations of statistical data to underscore a submerged narrative in which print was winning a "battle" with digital media for primacy. On the *Times*'s opinion pages, this narrative was right at the surface. Timothy Egan begins a May 2019 opinion page argument for the continuing currency of the printed book, tellingly titled "The Comeback of the Century," by claiming that contemporary readers have pointedly returned to "a spine, a unique scent, crisp pages and a typeface that may date to Shakespeare's day." Egan then offers an extended discussion of Michelle Obama's memoir, *Becoming*, which he positions as an exemplary print text. That Obama's book has sold ten million copies leads Egan to the following pronouncements:

> Storytelling, Steve Jobs may have forgotten, will never die. And the best format for grand and sweeping narratives remains one of the oldest and most durable.

> But also, at a time when more than a third of the people in the United States and Britain say their cellphones are having a negative effect on their health and well-being, a clunky old printed book is a welcome antidote. (Egan par. 11–12)

Steve Jobs had been deceased for *eight years* at the time Egan wrote these words. A cursory examination of Jobs's life suggests that storytelling mattered to him. David Zax's memorial essay after Jobs's death was titled, simply, "Steve Jobs, Storyteller." Jobs is being held up by Egan as an iconic advocate for the digital, and further, as a straw man articulating a position that few people, regardless of their preferred media, would ever hold or voice publicly. Further, Egan's staging of a contest between *cellphones* and printed books, with cellphones positioned as unhealthy and printed books positioned as curative is a disingenuous framing the various media formats for long-form reading.

In Egan's eyes, the sale of ten million copies of Michelle Obama's memoir reestablishes print as "the best format for grand and sweeping narratives" like Obama's. But that ten million copy sales figure was across *all* formats, including, notably, audiobooks and ebooks, as well as print books. Egan overlooks the possibility that the strong sales of Obama's audiobook (it was then at the top of audiobook and CD audio best-seller lists) might be because audio is, for many, the "best format," especially for those who might be interested in hearing Obama's words *in her own voice*, with her specific intonations. Further, some of those ebook sales were certainly to people who opted to read Obama's memoir on their smartphones while commuting on trains or buses. Egan's ten million copies sold includes an untold number of texts (audio and digital) that lack spines, unique scents, crisp pages, and Shakespearean typefaces. Does Egan really wish to dismiss the experiences of those who have connected with *Becoming* in media other than his personally preferred printed books? Is it too much to ask that he (and we) simply celebrate readers' substantial ongoing engagement with texts they find compelling, regardless of their preferred media?

Having witnessed what appeared to be a pattern of bias against ebooks within the pages of the *Times*, I set out to discover how and whether the *Times* as a whole presents articles with discernable bias for or against ebooks relative to print, and whether this has changed over time. I reviewed the ten most "relevant" articles on ebooks over the first twenty years *The New York Times* addressed ebooks (from 1998–2018). I performed a single coder content analysis followed by a second wave of rhetorical analysis, but the content analysis phase was compromised by the variability of the *Times*'s "Relevance" sort function. Put simply, the "relevant" results are highly variable, and visibly change from day to day even if one is looking well into the past (when the question of relevance should be settled once and for all). While I was able to establish a corpus of 167 arguably relevant texts (with a cap of ten per year) for most of the years involved, these articles may not ultimately be much more than a random sample of the articles mentioning ebooks in a given year. Further, there were a few years where there were—according to the *Times*'s own search engine—fewer than ten articles addressing ebooks to draw from. This is in part due to a period in the early 2000s where e-Reader development stalled.

With the limitations of this sample acknowledged, I read all the articles in this corpus and attempted to get a sense of whether bias towards or against ebooks was apparent. In my assessment, 111 of the 167 articles I encountered were either neutral or effectively balanced in assessments of pros and cons of ebooks. But also, 96 of the 167 or fifty-seven percent of the articles directly benchmarked ebooks against print. Thus, if the *Times* is addressing ebooks, it is likelier than not that the *Times* is doing so with print as a benchmark (this trend has tapered slightly in recent years, as might be expected with the increasing normalization of ebooks).

Of the seventeen articles from 2012–2017 with a detectable bias, only one offered a significant positive assessment of ebooks that was not counterbalanced by significant negatives. Significantly, that occurred in an interview with Francis Ford Coppola (who, by his own account, likes using an ereader for reading at night and likes being able to collect his highlighted passages). As an interview, this sidestepped the default *New York Times* editorial processes. While I looked at fifty of the 429 total articles from this five-year period (with 290 of these falling in 2012 and 2013) this was more than ten percent of the ebooks articles the *Times* published during that stretch, and given that my methods also revealed significant positive stretches (with

1998 – 2000 being pretty much sunshine, lollipops, and rainbows on the ebook front) I feel confident saying that the *Times* was, in the years in question, presenting an increasingly negative stance toward ebooks relative to print and further, was inclined to promote shaky data that reinforced this negativity. But why?

My answer is that the *Times* is engaged in a rhetoric of nostalgia.

In an article written for a cultural studies journal that, nevertheless, has a lot to say about rhetoric, British scholar and critic Stuart Tannock identifies three key elements of nostalgic rhetoric:

- The positing of what Tannock labels a "pre-lapsarian world";
- The identification of a point of division or catastrophe; and
- The framing of the present as somehow lacking and post-lapsarian, thereby prompting a longing for the past.

These three elements show up again and again in the *Times*'s Opinion pages and also essays within the Sunday *Times* book review section. For example, Mohsin Hamid and Anna Holmes's essay, which is labeled "How Do E-Books Change the Reading Experience," is not so much about tracing changes, but rather about framing the current moment as a dystopian cyborgian "jacked-in age." It contains every element of Tannock's nostalgic rhetoric and creates a clear "us" and them dynamic between those who will leave the powered exoskeletons in the closet in pursuit of something more human, and those with built-in cranial processors who, in an expression of their compromised humanity, scan *Brave New World* on a Kindle.

In a letter selected by the *Times*'s editors and bearing their chosen title, "A Digital Unbeliever," Ira Sohn hits all of the elements of Tannock's formula, identifying himself as an "old believer" as opposed to those who "converted to the new religion of digital life." Sohn also identifies the "cut" point as "the digital nightmare that was inflicted on us!" Note the presumptuousness of this "us" in which *Times* readers are constructed as people who share "that 'ol time religion" and are not living in the post-lapsarian world of lateness, inefficiency, rudeness, and degradation of the English language. (As an aside, I really appreciate that the online version of this letter features no less than five icons for possible digital interactions with this text).

Nostalgic rhetorics are not merely a rallying point for the current *Times* readers. They are also the basis for a print-centered literate culture that the *Times* is overtly seeking to perpetuate. In an excerpt from "The Learning Network" an educational arm of the *Times* in which students are encouraged to read articles like "The Plot Twist: E-Book Sales Slump and Print is Far From Dead" (which is the jumping off point here), the canard of "eBooks declining popularity" is repeated and then students are asked the following:

- Are paper books better than ebooks?
- Do [print books] offer a richer, more satisfying reading experience because you can physically hold them and turn the page?
- Are [print books] better because they are free from technical problems like low battery power and glitches?
- Do print books carry more emotional and sentimental value because you can touch the and see them on the shelf?
- Or, is the story not over yet — and e-books will still take the place of paper books in the long run?

The story *is* not over yet, but readers of the *Times* would do well to be wary about whether this august newspaper will be able to fairly report on the story as it unfolds. The first question neatly conveys the preferred answer. The sequencing is chronological, but the question should at least be something like: "Which makes for a better reading experience, paper books, or ebooks?" The next three questions are all examples of leading the witness. The final question maintains the specious presentation of a contest between media forms, without acknowledging the very real possibility that they might complement one another. And one last point, this page closes with an invitation for students to leave comments, as is common with this genre. While students weighed in on parallel pages, not a single comment appears to have been offered here. Perhaps the students who read this—despite all the time they supposedly spend drifting on their devices—know a rigged game when they see one. The *Times* bears a disproportionate impact on the literary life of the United States. This pattern of dismissal has real consequences for how we understand digital media more broadly.

We must question what we are being offered in exchange for holding the line against digital texts and valorizing print. To the extent that we are being offered a nostalgic celebration of an Eisenhower-era construction of literate culture, replete with sexism and an elitist rejection of supposed lowbrow culture, we should refuse the offer.

The *Times*'s implicit bias against ebooks was especially apparent in Alter's August, 2019 article that announced Matt Salinger's decision, as heir to J. D. Salinger's estate, to allow ebook editions of the four books J. D. Salinger published while he was alive: *The Catcher in the Rye* (1951); *Nine Stories* (1953); *Franny and Zooey* (1961); and *Raise High the Roof Beam, Carpenters and Seymour: An Introduction* (1963). Rhetorical analysis, focusing on word choices and the placement of ideas within the articles reveals the degree to which the *Times* emphasizes the negative when ebooks are the topic at hand.

From the very first paragraph of "J.D. Salinger, E-Book Holdout, Joins the Digital Revolution," Alter's writing suggests that Salinger's resistance to electronic formats is something that ought to be celebrated. Alter

153

writes: "Even as publishers and consumers adopted e-books and digital au-dio, Salinger's books remained defiantly offline, a consequence of the writ-er's distaste for computers and technology." While it is possible to read "de-fiance" here as "intransigence" that is not where Alter is headed. In the sec-ond paragraph, J. D. Salinger's son is introduced as follows: "Matt Salin-ger, who helps run the J. D. Salinger Literary Trust and is a vigilant guard-ian of his father's legacy and privacy." Much later in the article, Matt Salin-ger's prior claim to fame is acknowledged in strikingly neutral language: "A film producer and actor who played Captain America in a 1990 action film that was never released in US theaters, Mr. Salinger, 59, is to some degree an unlikely representative for a reclusive literary icon." Matt Salinger's sole starring vehicle made slightly over ten thousand dollar budget against a ten million dollar budget in the immediate wake of Tim Burton's re-booting of the Batman film franchise in 1989. He is presented by the *Times* as a "vigilant guardian" without clear acknowledgment that the film in which he played a "vigilant guardian" is an infamous cinematic failure. The third, one-sen-tence paragraph merits quotation in full:

> This week, in the first step of a broader revival that could reshape the world's understanding of Salinger and his writing, Little, Brown is publishing digital editions of his four books, making him perhaps the last 20th-century literary icon to surrender to the digital revolution. (Alter par. 4)

This presentation is striking for its presumption of the continuing rele-vance of Salinger's work, and for phrasing that does not fully acknowledge that J. D. Salinger is no more. The phrasing: "perhaps the last literary icon to surrender to the digital revolution" positions Salinger, who died in 2010, as a "last literary giant standing." While, in the United States, we might be expected to celebrate revolutions, Alter's article underscores the apparent virtuousness of the late J. D. Salinger's "standing" in opposition to the sup-posed digital revolution.

Matt Salinger is presented as also under siege, from people who are presented as unsavory:

> He now has to fend off people his father called "wanters"—fans and journalists who hounded Salinger for an interview, an autograph, a photo, another book. These days, the wanters come to the author's son, seeking permission for film adaptations, plays, Salinger tote bags. (Mr. Salinger said he is firmly opposed to screen adaptations and nixed the tote-bag idea.) (Alter par. 13)

Note that there is a significant distinction between the fans the elder Salinger labeled "wanters" and the people bringing *business* proposals to Matt Salinger. While these offers may be unwelcome, they are easily differentiated from the relatively one-way interactions with "fans and journalists." Note further that *Alter is a journalist*. She is thus in the class of "fans and journalists" derided by J. D. Salinger and also *by her own prose* unless she distinguishes herself from being a "wanter" by not wanting an interview, autograph, photo, or another book. This sentence underscores how declassé it is within this construction of literate culture to even approach a writer whose work one appreciates, or express a wish to connect with that person in a material way or, worse, to suggest that one might enjoy reading more of that person's writing. Indeed, by this point, Alter's article is shaping up as a primer on how one behaves appropriately in response to a famous author's determination to radically distance himself from his audience. We can observe, in passing, that there is probably no more surefire recipe for an explosion of "wanters" than self-imposed removal from both writing and interaction with the press.

A later paragraph, describing Matt Salinger's ongoing preparation of some of his father's unpublished work, celebrates *both* Salingers as painstaking adherents to the old ways:

> Matt Salinger has been preparing the unreleased work for publication since 2012. He sometimes found himself getting lost in the files, entranced by his father's voice. "Everything's a rabbit hole," he said. Creating digital files has been daunting, he said, because he has not been able to find reliable optical-recognition software to convert the handwritten pages into electronic text, so he types the material himself. (Alter par. 19)

J. D. Salinger's manuscripts are handwritten, and thus defy ready reduction to digital form. Thus, Matt Salinger has spent eight years (and counting) preparing manuscripts. Examples of Salinger's handwriting make clear, whether by man or machine, the work of conversion will prove challenging. The scales are rebalanced slightly by Alter's fleeting characterization of the Salinger estate as "among the most stubborn holdouts against digitization" but by the following paragraph J. D. Salinger is again presented as not merely resistant to digital media, but apparently disgusted by it: "Matt Salinger resisted requests to issue e-books for years, knowing his father's aversion to the internet. He once tried to explain Facebook to him and remembers he was 'horrified' by the notion of digital oversharing." Later in the same text, J. D. Salinger is again mobilized as a principled advocate for the purity of the reading experience: "[Matt Salinger] has also explored the possibility of releasing audiobook editions but said his father abhorred the idea of his books being performed or interpreted in any way in another medium." (Alter par. 25)

While Alter presents the Salingers as the avatars of an urbane, literary life being haphazardly ravaged by digital media, it is hard to read this portrait of the Salinger family without becoming as least somewhat uncomfortable with J. D. Salinger's apparent attachment to control. Control was a recurrent theme throughout Salinger's life, with one manifestation being his well-earned reputation as one of the most litigious writers in history. The 1987 case *Salinger v. Random House* revolved around Salinger's objection to a biographer having gained access to letters Salinger had written to friends and including elements of the letters in the context of a scholarly biography. Significantly, Salinger successfully objected to the biographer *paraphrasing* passages in the letters, resulting in one of the most restrictive copyright decisions on record and effectively killing the biography. A 2009 copyright case revolved around Salinger's objections to a novel by Fredrik Colting titled *60 Years Later: Coming Through the Rye* that featured a septuagenarian version of Holden Caulfield escaping from a nursing home. Salinger succeeded in suppressing publication of Colting's book in the United States.

Any discussion of J. D. Salinger and control should also acknowledge the significant negative consequences of his pursuit of a relationship with Joyce Maynard when she was eighteen and he was fifty-three. Writing in the wake of the #metoo movement—a movement facilitated by inter-networked social media—Maynard wrote of her experiences with Salinger, ironically enough, in *The New York Times* in an article with a title that centers Salinger, "Was She J.D. Salinger's Predator or His Prey?" and indicts Maynard with either of the listed alternatives. Maynard writes:

> In the spring of 1972, following the publication in The Times Magazine of an essay of mine accompanied by a particularly guileless photograph of me (bluejeans, scruffy hair, no makeup), I had received a letter from J.D. Salinger in which he offered his admiration, friendship, mentorship and spiritual guidance—and, in subsequent letters and phone calls, urged me to leave college, come live with him (have babies, collaborate on plays we would perform together in London's West End) and be (I truly believed this) his partner forever.
>
> I gave up my scholarship and dropped out of Yale, cut off communication with my friends and moved (with a suitcase of miniskirts and record albums I was forbidden to play) back to my home state of New Hampshire to be with him. Seven months later, during a trip we'd taken to Florida, with words as devastating as they had once been

captivating and entrancing, he put two $50 bills in my hand and in-
structed me to return to New Hampshire, clear my things out of his
house and disappear. (par. 4–5)

Maynard had written a 1998 autobiography in which she addressed J. D. Salinger's treatment of her at length, but she observes that the #metoo movement has not made her feel vindicated for having told her story: "it does not
appear that enlightenment concerning the abuses of men in power extends
retroactively to women who chose to speak long ago, and were shamed and
humiliated for doing so" (Maynard). In light of Maynard's account, Salinger's famed self-recusal from the public eye and from the conventional interactions of literary celebrity may well have been driven by a wish to limit
public attention to notably questionable aspects of his personal life. The
reclusiveness for which Salinger was lionized as expressing a purist's refusal
to "play the game" may have been nothing more than strategic self-protec-
tion. Further, though it may seem somewhat invasive to surface these aspects
of Salinger's private life, when his abuse of power and excessive, controlling
treatment of Maynard end up rhyming with iron-fisted management of his
texts and his persona, it is reasonable to ask whether *this* is the literary lion
the *Times* should both celebrate and defend.

Maynard's account invites us all to revisit the degree to which J. D.
Salinger has been celebrated for his protectionist approach his own writings and his insistence that they be limited to the medium in which they
were originally presented, namely paper books. While it is tempting to default to "he wrote them, so why doesn't he get to decide?" the other side of
the equation is the public's own serial purchases of literally millions of copies of his writings, especially *Catcher in the Rye*. At what point is Holden Caulfield's narrative, or, the character more generally, bought and paid for? At
what point does he become part of the shared cultural property of the people who have paid market rates to read Salinger's novel for almost seventy
years? Sixty-five million copies have been sold. Why is Salinger celebrated
for offering minimal access to his texts and his own reflections on the composition, meaning, or impact of those texts?

Constructing Salinger as a high-minded holdout against an unwelcome digital revolution dovetails with *The New York Times*'s long history of promoting print at the expense of the digital. In a sense, this is to be expected.
Few institutions have a greater ongoing investment in the particular affordances of print than the *Times*. It is one of a handful of papers maintaining a
national distribution network. When the *Times* addresses ebooks, in particular, its writers tend toward flat dismissal and celebrations of the codex print
book as emblematic of a literate culture that ought to be preserved. Miss-

ing from this conversation is an apparent awareness that this specific literate culture has not always *worked* for everyone.

E-readers like the Kindle allow their users to tweak letter sizes and the colors of the text to better accommodate the needs of readers who have not always been well served by the standardized (and limited) character of print texts. One obvious implication of this is that readers with limited vision due to age or other deviations from typical visual capacities are able to use e-readers to comfortably engage with written texts. Further, readers with dyslexia are greatly helped by the flexibility of e-readers as a reading space.

My middle sister was diagnosed with dyslexia as a child. She remains a voracious reader despite having to work half again as hard as most people to process the letters in front of her. In 2016, Kindle devices moved to offer OpenDyslexic as a font choice. Developed by Abbie Gonzalez, Open Dyslexic is a font that increases the readability of texts for dyslexic readers by gradually expanding the width of characters from top to bottom, and making other subtle tweaks to character shapes, thereby decreasing the likelihood that similar characters like b, d, p, and q will be mistaken for one another. Gonzalez offers OpenDyslexic on a pay-what-you wish basis at his website. I invite us to pause to reflect for a moment on a United States culture that celebrated J. D. Salinger for his relentlessly protectionist stance toward his own words and has not yet lionized Abbie Gonzalez for developing a way to make written words more available to the estimated twenty percent of people in the United States who must contend with some degree of dyslexia every day.

If the experience of reading is at all compromised by digital delivery, what *are* the texts that suffer from their presentation in digital forms, and by how much? There is precious little empirical data to support the notion that the experience of reading *A Midsummer Night's Dream* on a Kobo ereader is significantly worse (or better) than reading it in an inexpensive Dover Thrift Edition. It is intuitively clear that if the choice is between having students read the play in digital format (where public domain editions are all but free) or them not reading it at all (because print books, however modestly presented, *cost*), then having them read is probably better than not. And it is by no means clear that twenty-first century students' reading experiences are compromised by engaging with texts on e-readers. More than a decade of research exists countering ambient claims that reading via screens was or is somehow cognitively compromised relative to print reading. In a 2011 study comparing comprehension and retention among students who used e-readers with those who read print, the authors concluded that, for the college students of that moment, e-readers (in this case the admittedly "clunky" Nook) were a viable alternative:

> Overall, whether reading from a text or an eReader, students recalled the same number of idea units from the text, regardless of what mode of reading they used. Likewise, on all but the first Quick Write, there were no discernable differences in the complexity of student responses. (Schugar, Schugar, and Penny, 183)

A 2019 study comparing the reading experiences of young readers (average age of twenty-four) using the relatively refined KindleDX interface arrives at a similar place, concluding: "most of the measures we used to assess the text comprehension did not show any differences between print- and e-book" (Mangen, Olivier, and Velay par. 34). The exception to the generally parallel outcomes was a plot reconstruction task in which students using e-readers did not perform as well as students using print in reconstructing the sequence of events in a fictional narrative. The researchers speculate that this may be due to the comparative lack of fixity in e-book text spaces and the lack of visible page numbers in some interfaces. These examples suggest that the widely perceived "gap" between the cognitive experience of reading print and e-books is unlikely to withstand strict scrutiny. Further, because these studies' participants were college-age students and younger adults, it is likely that increasing practice and comfort with screen reading is minimizing the degree to which e-reader spaces are viewed as disrupting, rather than complementing a "normal" reading experience.

It is likely that one of the greatest drivers of perceived differences in the experience of reading on screens relative to print reading is the degree to which *tablets* and *smartphones* also function as spaces for other potentially distracting functions. While the high-definition screens of contemporary smartphones are, in many ways, ideal reading spaces (portable, lightweight, high-resolution, flexible type sizes, available color) their positioning within an interface that is structured to deliver text messages, social media updates, and news notifications makes them poor candidates for those who wish to have the experience of being "transported" by text. This is, perhaps, why there is, at present, a continuing market for dedicated monochromatic e-readers that are pitched as mimicking the look and feel of codex books. The Norwegian study, employing the KindleDX, managed to deliver essentially level outcomes, probably because the KindleDX was successful in approximating the codex reading experience. But we might choose to look forward, with anticipation, to the moment when composers are freed to take full advantage of the latest multimedia potential within most color e-readers.

While I am not immune to the charms of a well-crafted codex and have purchased my fair share of coffee-table *objets d'art* in book form, the simmering potential of this moment is now clear. The technologies now delivering text offer tremendous untapped opportunities for composers. Further, more digital texts ultimately implies more access for more people. Given the choice between celebrating the delights of literacy and literate cultures and celebrating the media form that housed those activities, I suggest that we benefit from focusing on *people*, their activities, and at least the potential for wider and more affordable distribution of textual information.

Because the codex (and the accumulated shelves and stacks of codices) have become iconic as representations of commitments to literate culture, and further, because of the ephemerality of digital texts, there is resistance to the notion that the very same activities once housed in codices might also live in the relatively ephemeral spaces of internetworked digital media. This attachment to the codex as medium is at the heart of the "credibility bookcase" phenomenon during the Coronavirus pandemic of 2020, in which a manicured bookcase became the Zoom background *du jour* for a certain stripe of television-ready expert. Amanda Hess's May 2020 essay on the phenomenon for *The New York Times* finds Hess, in an unusual stance for the paper, casting a gimlet eye toward the phenomenon:

> The credibility bookcase, with its towering, idiosyncratic array of worn volumes, is itself an affectation. The expert could choose to speak in front of his art prints or his television or his blank white walls, but he chooses to be framed by his books. It is the most insidious of aesthetic trends: one that masquerades as pure intellectual exercise.
>
> It is remarkable how quickly the bookcase has become obligatory, how easily it has been integrated into the brittle aesthetic rules of authority. The appearance of the credibility bookcase suggests that the levers of expertise and professionalism are operating normally, even though they are very much not. (par. 9–10)

The current wave of nostalgia for the specifics of the print codex book is not necessarily misplaced, so long as there is a recognition that not all books were ever worthy of these attachments. Airport and beach fiction paperback books, with their almost-translucent greyish paper served a distinct purpose—getting the latest Tom Clancy, Stephen King, or Nora Roberts tome into the hands of eager readers. With rare exceptions—little time or energy was put into the look and feel of the book cover, expect to make the book feel "on brand" relative to the previous books from the same writer. The spines of these books were easily broken, the pages readily curled. If, after an international flight or a trip to the shore the book was much the worse for wear, so be it. Such books, even in perfect condition, generally border on worthless on the used book market.

When the codex print book was, in effect, the only game in town, it was easy to mistake the medium's limitations for virtues. Many contemporary arguments about how to write and how writing should be are grounded in maintaining the generally monochromatic and regimented spaces of what Jay Bolter labeled "The Late Age of Print." Notwithstanding Bolter's implied timeline, I remain persuaded that print will not "go" anywhere so much as it will be reenvisioned and recalibrated. Print remains the ideal space for certain types of projects and certain types of arguments. The coffee table book is just one example of the kinds of books we can easily envision persisting indefinitely in the absence of a wholesale transformation of the communicative landscape, and here I am envisioning something on the order of a *Mad-Max*-style dystopia where a daily fight for resources precludes any time for reading or reflection. Print remains unparalleled as a delivery medium for photography (at least as photography now is understood). To the extent that two dimensions, extremely high resolution, and color are involved, print remains—and will remain—the go-to. Yet, most print texts only occasionally take advantage of this opportunity. But not all books merit the kinds of nostalgia stirred up by phrasing like "The Late Age of Print."

When nostalgia for the book is voiced, it rarely ever is for the kinds of books that had spiral or plastic bindings that were designed to allow the text to lay flat, with both pages facing up. That said, we all understand that for certain texts (technical manuals and style handbooks are obvious examples) the ability to serve up two pages while a reader's hands might be otherwise occupied is a virtue. But that same binding feels inappropriate for, say *The Complete Works of Shakespeare* even though the plays of Shakespeare are, in one sense, scripts that actors might appreciate having in a flat format. But the codex spine has become a marker of value, or seriousness of purpose, and thus one can search in vain for the spiral-bound Shakespeare.

The United States's capacity for nostalgia is remarkable. The crude, blocky video games of my youth are now an aesthetic touchpoint, with "8-bit" signifying a certain innocence and perhaps misplaced enthusiasm for what might be possible within such a limited palette. There is clearly an ongoing market for people wishing to play videogames that reflect the aesthetics of the Atari 2600, though I am here to say definitely—despite my having worn a blister into the crease of my thumb while playing the joystick-based Atari 2600 version of *Space Invaders—these games weren't very good*. Yet, a thriving subculture is organized around the preservation of this specific aesthetic and this very crude and limited gameplay, with new "homebrew" games being released for this now forty-plus-year-old platform. While these games are clearly a source of joy for a certain kind of gamer, few of them would argue that these games are superior to contemporary games (with "more enjoyable" distinguished from "better").

Yet, it remains quite common for people to signal their own connection to literary life by expressing contempt for digitally delivered texts. Codex books—alongside snap mousetraps and vinyl records—remain one of the few technologies widely seen as optimal despite a more general arc toward refinement and improvement in technologies. The books filling contemporary bookstore shelves are generally not the kinds of texts that prompt print nostalgia. We only rarely see luxuriously marbled page ends, leather covers, engravings, or any of the more filigreed elements of the bookmaker's art. And nor should we. For print to continue to draw people into neighborhood and independent bookstores and away from online booksellers, books must be affordable more often than not. But when print is achieving little more than alphanumeric delivery, it might just as well be digital.

The impulse to critique the ebook when it might be the answer to a domestic couple's long-standing incompatibly over the ambient irritations of a booklight or might be capable of delivering text scaled to the limited or failing eyesight of a dedicated reader seems grounded in a lack of attention to the possibility that one's own preferences might be *preferences* and not an index of one's erudition or cultural status.

Because we have the capacity to place texts into clouds, and recover them at our convenience, we now can ask which texts *should* be rendered into print and which iterations of print will appropriately serve the content at hand. Once the digital default is established, print's profile may parallel that of vinyl records (and this is not a bad outcome, by any stretch). Most buyers of vinyl are now seeking artefacts that announce themselves as the by-products of "extra" effort with respect to design, craft, and materials. In a world where almost-infinite jukeboxes like Spotify can be had for a month for the price of 1/4 of a single vinyl LP, the vinyl LP has moved from central delivery medium to *objet d'art*. Many young people who listen to most of their music via streaming services can intuitively identify a subset of records whose qualities point them toward a preference for physical ownership.

Having seen this dynamic play out in parallel ways in the media for music, television, and motion pictures, in all of which there has been an observable shift from primary delivery media to crafted/archival editions, we can foresee a time where we will rebalance which kinds of texts will inhabit print and digital media. And certain kinds of texts can and should find their preferred home in digital spaces. A preference for hearing Michelle Obama read her words aloud, as opposed to engaging with print is at least reasonable, and for visually impaired readers, borders on necessary. Further, readers who opt to engage with Obama's memoir with the highlights of others made visible, as a kind of guide to the spaces where others have found significance or value, are not somehow having a deeply compromised reading experience. Indeed, such readers might well appreciate the insights of others, and by their own accounts have a better reading experience in internetworked reading/writing spaces.

If the cloud delivers readers the equivalent of inexpensive paperbacks, and further, delivers them in ways where readers can—at their discretion—choose to engage with the composer's words or choose to engage with the crowdsourced highlights for that task, we do well to respond to the *New York Times* and other purveyors of print nostalgia by asking, pointedly, *what of significance has been lost*?

The cloud is, surely, a heavily corporate space, and we do well to be wary of all the ways an interaction between composer and reader can morph into data. But when one considers the ways it is possible for the one-step-above ephemeral texts to incorporate color and visuals without prompting significant additional costs, or to embed texts in a cultural conversation that is made visible through highlights and shared annotations, then we do well to ask whether these baby steps into the possibilities of cloud-based spaces might be a moment that prompts nostalgia sometime in the future.

```
e:!0,value
m));return t}},f.n
e);return t}},f.n
r,i;i.slice();for(var a=0;a<i.
n,f,i=r[0],l=r[1],a=r[2],c=0,s=
prototype.hasOwnProperty.call(l,n
l=t[i];0!==o[l]&&(n=!1)}n&&(u.spli
(r){if(n[r])return n[r].exports;var t=
exports,f),t.l=!0,t.exports}f.m=e,f.c=
(e,r,{enumerable:!0,get:t})},f.r=
Object.defineProperty(e,Symbol.toS
(value:!0})},f.t=function(e,r){if(1&r&&(e
return e:var t=Object.create(null);if(f.
value:e}),2&r&&"string"!=typeof e)for(v
function(e){var r=e&&e._esMod
t},f.n=function(e,r){return Obj
r),r),f.o=function(e,r){return Obj
webpackJsonp=window.webpackJsonp||[],l=i.
webpackJsonp=window.webpackJsonp||[];!function(e){
var p=l;t()}([]);!function(e){
r(i[a]);var p=l;t()}([]),o[f]=
)f=i[c],o[f]&&s.push(o[f][0]),o[f]=
c++)for(p&&p(r);s.length;)s.shift()();
for(var t=u[r],n=!0,i=1;i<t
r++){for(var t=u[r],n={},o={1
r++)){for(var t=u[r],n={},o={1
[a]))return e}var n={},o={1
t[0])))}return e}
};return e[r].call(e.
defineProperty(e,
ngTag&&Obj
Module
```

8 Keywords for Writing in the Clouds

In this chapter, I will take three passes at explaining a set of ten keywords that have risen to the surface of the previous chapters' discussions of what writing in the clouds means in this moment. In the first pass, I will offer the ten as a visual group. I'll then revisit each keyword in turn, offering brief explanations of the signature aspects of each. In the final pass, the "reflections" sections for each keyword, I will offer vignettes, observations, and speculations about the paths we have taken to this moment and where we might be headed from here.

Ten Keywords for Writing in the Clouds

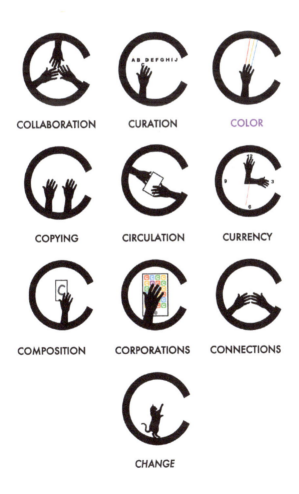

COLLABORATION   CURATION   COLOR

COPYING   CIRCULATION   CURRENCY

COMPOSITION   CORPORATIONS   CONNECTIONS

CHANGE

I imagine some looking at the above aggregation will have a response along the lines of "keywords? Looks more like 'C' words . . ." and if I were observing such a grouping, I would be wary with respect to the possible shoehorning involved to make them appear so tidy. As it turns out, all these words, or their cognates, appear frequently in the pages surrounding this chapter. As this list took shape, the real challenge was not maintaining the potential mnemonic value of having words starting with the same letter. Rather, making sure that these concepts were distinct enough from one another felt challenging. As I move to brief explanations of these keywords, the reader will note numerous points of intersection and overlap. That said, I stand by this list as a bounded set of significant touchpoints that will help guide our steps as we navigate the intersections of writing practices and internetworked writing tools.

The Keywords in Brief

COLLABORATION—The spaces of internetworked writing are many degrees more collaborative than the writing spaces of the past half millennium. This is a time for composers to consider how and whether their writing might benefit from coordination and cooperation with their fellow writers.

CURATION—The deluge of written work at this moment invites a broader investment in the curation skills that organize and frame our understandings of existing works. Further, a revised understanding of the rhetorical canon of arrangement as a pathway toward invention offers opportunities to realize functionally new works by way of curation and recombination of extant works.

COLOR—The widespread adoption of internetworked digital media is prompting increased reliance on color as a marker of meaning. This is in part due to the relatively low investments required to produce color compositions relative to print. It is also due to the need to differentiate ideas and concepts from one another in the compact reading spaces offered on smartphones.

167

COPYING—Opportunities for curation and recombination are often facilitated by the degree to which digital tools facilitate near-frictionless copying. This presents an opportunity to consider ways in which cloud-based spaces might facilitate derivative works that productively build on works that could be more readily at hand than they now are. These opportunities swing on whether copyright laws are adapted to the shifting meanings of what copies are and how they might move through culture.

CIRCULATION—Because of their ready reproducibility, cloud-based compositions have the potential to move through culture in something approaching real time. With each step from the digital, to the networked digital, to the internetworked digital, the reach of any given text has expanded exponentially.

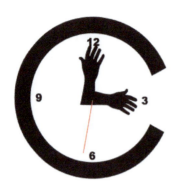

CURRENCY—A bias toward novelty is potentially one of the more worrisome aspects of cloud-based writing. The steady drumbeat of new writings, some of them directly responsive to existing writing in an almost conversational sense presents a challenge to the more sustained genres of written composition. That said, the clouds also offer platforms where even arcane and challenging works can be brought into conversation with contemporary conversations and critiques.

COMPOSITION—Increasingly, cloud-based spaces invite writers to craft multimedia and multimodal texts. When we wish to observe a distinction between the production of alphanumeric characters and the production of texts that navigate multiple media and/or modes, the embedded layers of meaning in "composer" and "composition" offer intuitive pathways to understanding the ways writing is now expanding and taking advantages of the opportunities found in internetworked writing spaces.

CORPORATIONS—Cloud spaces overwhelmingly depend on the resources of major multinational corporations. Composing in cloud-based spaces, therefore, necessarily implies a measure of compromise, whether in the form of invasions of personal privacy or in blurring the question of how and whether composers own and control the by-products of their labor. Corporations do not build cloud spaces without the expectation of profit. We do well to ask how we end up paying.

168

CONNECTIONS (and **DISCONNECTIONS**)—The initial promise of the Internet was that it would offer new ways for people to connect. This promise depends on access to high-speed broadband internet that is not yet fully available and affordable. It further depends on access to hardware, as the look and feel of the Internet available within laptops and desktops increasingly diverges from the Internet found in phone and tablet interfaces. When connecting, we need to consider the limits of our reach.

169

CHANGE—The implicit "lockdown" prompted by the technological limitations of print as a medium are giving way to the relatively uncertain and malleable spaces of internetworked digital communication. We approach texts with a baseline awareness of their comparative instability. The fixity associated with something having gone to press is now challenged by the floating awareness that composers might choose to revise a cloud-based text at any moment.

COLLABORATION: Reflections

One frustrating marker of how slowly academia responds to broader social movements is the publication date of Lise Ede and Andrea Lunsford's *Singular Texts/Plural Authors*, issued by Southern Illinois University Press in 1990. While co-authorship has long been common in many disciplines (especially the so-called "hard" sciences), Lunsford and Ede's book speaks to the degree to which collaboration was actively discouraged in many academic humanities disciplines. Ede and Lunsford, drawing on decades of feminist scholarship, and with knowing eyes cast toward the potential of both computers and the then-novel and largely non-public Internet, argue powerfully for a change in how collaboration should be understood and valued within the academy. While that argument is *still* unfolding among tenure and promotion committees, the opportunities for collaboration in Internet spaces are many and will inevitably reshape how we relate to writing as a practice.

When working within Google Docs, composers engage with a much simpler, more streamlined interface. That said, one of the most striking aspects of Google Docs is the degree to which it has clearly been designed from the ground up to facilitate collaboration. One of the most jarring moments I have experienced as a composer in the recent past was watching as a parade of "anonymous animal" icons popped onto the menu, each representing an unnamed viewer and potential collaborator/editor on a widely shared document within my university. Eventually the zoological parade crept from right to left to the point where the "animals" obscured my view of the Google Docs menus. And the names of the animals were themselves distracting! Anonymous Alligator and Anonymous Badger were supplanted by Anonymous Chupacabra and Anonymous Dingo. Eventually, I reached Anonymous Nyan Cat, named after a famous meme featuring a cat with a Pop-Tart for a torso. In this first iteration, Google's interface designers had valued collaboration so highly that the entire menu system was potentially visually secondary to the presence of other composers. And the at-times whimsical naming of anonymous collaborators further suggested that collaboration was a potentially fun alternative to the way we had been composing written texts to that point.

The Google Docs interface speaks to the prospect of collaboration being understood as one that brightens the experience of writing. The quirky animal names would be out of step with, for example, a family gathering online to collectively write an obituary for a loved one. It is also telling that crowdsourced lists of anonymous animal names witnessed within Google Docs typically rise to over seventy distinct names, suggesting that Google's interface designers viewed the possibility of simultaneous composition of a single text by literally dozens of contributors was a top-level priority in their design processes.

Google Docs exemplifies a significant shift in the construction of writing tools, responding to the implications of always-on high-speed internet connections for the practice of writing. Within academia, where there are routine calls for subcommittees to jointly compose documents or reports, Google Docs has been widely adopted. That said, it is less than fifteen years old as I write, and it is fair to say that composers are only now beginning to understand the new horizon of possibilities available to them. Writing *was* a lonely job for most of the twentieth century. By the end of the twenty-first, this might well seem like a quaint and dated characterization.

CURATION: Reflections

The sheer volume of textual production in the twenty-first century places a premium on the skillsets associated with effective curation. Simply put, there's too damn much stuff being produced today to ever hope for perfect archives. That's probably a good thing, too.

While geeks across America still mourn the dark days when a parent threw out their collections of gaming cards or comic books, not *all* those purges involved a pristine *Magic: The Gathering* Black Lotus card or a mint condition copy of *Amazing Fantasy* #15 (for the non-geeks reading, that's the first appearance of Spider-Man, which would now fetch in excess of $1,500,000 at auction . . . but I digress). Much of the disposal of disposable popular culture is . . . shall we say . . . *deserved*. The parents who threw out heaps of pop culture detritus also threw out a lot of copies of comics like *Hong Kong Phooey*, an adaptation of a ridiculous and racist Saturday morning cartoon series of the mid 1970s. We might all benefit from forgetting that *Hong Kong Phooey* ever happened, though I've ironically just extended its cultural lifespan, however briefly. The point here is that while it is always tempting—especially within academic circles—to try and preserve *everything*, we can't and we don't.

My own university's library system is bursting at the seams. Its print holdings exceed its storage capacity. Tough decisions are made all the time. Nor is it possible—even with remarkable advances in technology—to capture everything transpiring via Internet. One surprising challenge I've faced as an internet researcher is the difficulty involved in securing even a portion of Twitter's Tweetstream. This is in part due to Twitter's own reluctance to offer access to the "full firehose" of Tweets. But this is also in part due to the potentially overwhelming nature of the task. It is a matter of settled historical fact that Twitter played a significant role in the "Arab Spring" of 2011. Clearly, Tweets from this period record a political movement happening in real time and merit both scholarly attention and historical preservation. Yet, the task of even base levels of curation would test human limits. One researcher, University of North Carolina professor Dean Freelon, used Twitter keyword searches to amass a corpus of over 7,500,000 numerical tweet IDs and matching user IDs from seven countries, most of which dated from January through March of 2011. Freelon made this roadmap to the tweets available for a time at his personal website, dfreelon.org. Freelon acknowledged the collection process was compromised *both* by Twitter's API query restrictions and the limits of the tweet collection tool, TwapperKeeper. After laying out the raw numbers of tweets involved, Freelon effectively warns against attempting to work with the data unless one brings a substantial skillset to the task:

These data will be all but useless to anyone without at least a basic understanding of all of the following:

- APIs and how to retrieve data from them,
- a programming language like PHP or Python,
- and a relational database system such as MySQL.

And even with this knowledge, recreating the full data sets would still take months of 24/7 automated querying given Twitter's API limits. (par. 6)

Thus, one of the most significant moments of social activism via social media is imperfectly archived, on an ad hoc basis, by a researcher whose site offers repeated warnings that it may prove extremely difficult to gain access to the dataset. The title for his 2012 blog post neatly encapsulates the reality of the situation: "Arab Spring Twitter data now available (sort of)." Even worse, a follow-on post from 2017 features another researcher attempting to work with the dataset only to report that ninety-seven percent of the tweets from the country he sampled (Algeria) appear to have been deleted.

Inevitably, paring processes of varying precision and quality will be brought to bear on archives like these, and inevitably, *these paring processes will be imperfect*. While paring processes generally are targeting *Hong Kong Phooeys*, the occasional *Amazing Fantasy* will sometimes be lost. Composers of primarily alphanumeric compositions in our current moment develop their projects with an awareness that their writings, however ephemeral they may seem, are candidates for preservation and archiving simply because the cloud-based storehouses are so capacious that there is often not a lot of motivation to trash *anything*. That said, without regular maintenance and care, which is to say without *curation*, even incredibly significant upwellings of text-based political and social communication will drift away, and human memory will have to suffice when data is no longer available.

 ## COLOR: Reflections

Of the many speculative arguments I offer within this text, the one about which I feel most confident is this: black and white texts will announce themselves as having likely been composed prior to the second quarter of the twenty-first Century every bit as much as black and white movies and TV shows announce themselves as likely having been produced prior to the mid 1960s.

To underscore my argument, I'll briefly revisit the gradual movement toward color in cinema and televisual media. Color was recognized as having special value in cinema almost from the inception of the medium. Cinema pioneer George Méliès invested an incredible amount of time and energy to have the individual frames of his 1902 film *Le Voyage Dans La Lune* hand-tinted to delight the audience with full spectrum color. But this massive investment was not possible for most films, and from an aesthetic standpoint, one could very well argue that Alfred Hitchcock's 1940 black-and-white film *Rebecca*, with Academy Award-winning cinematography by George S. Barnes, is a greater visual success than the over-the-top technicolor spectacles of 1939, which included, notably, *Gone With the Wind* and *The Wizard of Oz*. For more than thirty years after color production was commonplace, black-and-white production remained popular. With the exception of *Spartacus*, Stanley Kubrick's early films featured rich black-and-white cinematography. 1968's *Night of the Living Dead* serves as an example of a production that was filmed in black-and-white for both aesthetic and financial reasons (black-and-white film stock was less expensive than color). 1973's *Paper Moon* and 1974's *Young Frankenstein* serve as early examples of the use of black-and-white cinematography to enact nostalgic nods to the cinematic conventions of earlier times.

Throughout the 1960s, cinematic aesthetics wavered between black-and-white and color, but the secondary market for motion pictures, television, was an overwhelmingly black and white medium until 1965, with 1966 marking the United States' major networks' first all-color broadcast seasons. Even so, the networks' broadcasting of color content was only part of the equation. The presence of color content did not prompt consumers to immediately rush out and purchase new televisions, and some stubbornly refused to pay a premium for color content.

My hope is that the parallels to the ways we now consume textual content are obvious. While the monitors for *computers* quickly moved from monochromatic to color screens, thereby facilitating an internet culture in which color is a common indicator of navigation options, significance, or mood, the delivery systems for long form prose, ebook readers, have *not* consistently followed suit. Indeed, an entire class of ebook readers is proudly and pointedly monochromatic, including Amazon's Kindle's e-readers and Kobo's entire line of e-readers. In fact, after briefly labeling its LCD Fire line of tablets "Kindle Fire" Amazon has retroactively pried the two brands apart, with Kindle now referring only to monochromatic e-readers

This bias toward monochromatic screens in a world where smartphone and tablet screens are all insistently and vibrantly colorful suggests that a significant portion of the population is at least habituated to and very likely *prefers* monochromatic screen spaces for long-form prose reading. Color e-ink technology has the potential to change this equation, by minimizing the eyestrain associated with color LCD screens, but whether it is this specific technology or its successor that makes the experience of reading color texts as comfortable and as energy efficient as the current generation of monochromatic ereaders, we can anticipate that color will eventually move from being perceived as an extra to the default in the ereader space. In the short term, this will mean ereaders will be able to reproduce the lavish color plates found in early editions of L. Frank Baum's *Wizard of Oz*.

The next step, and it is one that I eagerly anticipate, is the moment when contemporary composers begin to exploit the new possibilities afforded to them by the presence of platforms that are color by default.

Throughout this book, I have selectively used color to underscore my arguments. While there is no moment so dramatic as Dorothy's first steps into Munchkinland—in the 1939 film adaptation of Baum's book that I remember seeing for the first time, sadly, on my family's black-and-white television, which is to say not really seeing it *at all*—there are small moments, throughout this text where, if you happen to be reading it in a black-and-white medium, you will have missed the full import of my arguments. This is true despite the substantial support and creativity of my editors and Parlor Press. After all, *you may have chosen* to read this book on a monochromatic ereader. But please know that I chose to compose in color, because there were shadings of meaning that I hoped would be available to most readers.

COPYING: Reflections

One significant consequence of "always on" high-speed internet connectivity is the radical compression in the perceived distance between texts. Further, despite increasingly restrictive interpretations of copyright laws, most of the books, films, and music recordings that have had even momentary popularity are available online . . . one way or another. This, in turn, is prompting new modes of invention that leverage the proximity and presence of others' texts. I would expect no one to be startled to learn that many of the texts quoted herein were cut-and-pasted from available electronic versions of the works I knew I wished to cite. While I would briefly entertain an argument that I might have internalized something embedded within each quote by painstakingly retyping the words on my own keyboard, I also probably would have introduced errors that have been sidestepped by my incorporation of "the thing itself" into my own text.

One extension of copying becoming a baseline skill for writers is that any artefact reduced to digital form is—by default—subject to remixing and mashing-up. While content providers have worked to develop firewalls that at least make it somewhat difficult for others to excerpt, cut, copy, paste, remix, and mash, they are engaging in a colossal and neverending game of "whack-a-mole." The efforts expended to assert copyright in response to most remix projects far exceeds the likely monetary reward for doing so. And doing so opens a content provider to significant negative publicity. Additionally, twenty-first century composers should at least consider whether and how to position themselves relative to the likelihood that their work—if at all popular—will be incorporated into future works.

Because this project was delivered in 2021, it participates in lingering print conventions with respect to how it engages with other texts. It follows a conventional academic citation system. The pointers to others' works, by way of which a diligent critical reader might determine whether I had taken another writer out of context, are stockpiled in citations at the back of this volume. And every time I add another traditional citation, part of me asks, *why is this not a link*? The answer, frustratingly enough, is a body of law that was initially presented as "an act for the encouragement of learning": United States copyright law. Most of what has been published is available in one archive or another. Project Gutenberg was an early effort to place as many public domain texts as possible online. To this, we can now add the commercial efforts of Amazon to render the books that it sells into searchable electronic forms, and the Google Books project that blends the by-products of scanning major university libraries with an increasingly expansive archive of digital texts. But because Amazon and Google's collections are embedded within their larger commercial projects, they are limited to offering "previews" and excerpts of the texts that are now housed in full on their servers. It would be better if we could all come to an agreement on the circumstances under which the public might see some or all these pages without paying for the privilege.

I lean to the copyleft, but not so far that I would strip composers of texts of their ownership rights in deference to public access, *even if* those rights are routinely bargained away to publishers in the context of a dramatic power imbalance. That said, because our works so often incorporate and depend upon others works, I would like to see the advent of streamlined copyright laws that—through a combination of collective cataloging, mechanical licenses, micropayments, and limited access passes—would allow us all to take full advantage of internetworking our texts. In a previous chapter, I invited readers to consider Richard Lanham's distinction between looking at and looking through the surface of a text. If we were to truly internetwork our collective libraries, clicking on that passage would lead directly to a vetted copy of Lanham's work, and the reader could look at (or through) the surrounding two pages before and after the quote to gain a broader sense of the context for the small section of Lanham that was copied into this text. *At present, there is no technological impediment to this*. There is, however, a legal obstacle. Our copyright laws are directed at presumably scarce print copies, and not at the culture of copying and pasting that now facilitates our building upon the works of our predecessors.

US copyright laws need to better align with the practical implications of a culture that copies *all the time* and has found ways to build distinctive and worthy works from the incorporation of the remarkable archive that is scattered throughout the Internet.

 CIRCULATION: Reflections

I wish to start this discussion of circulation by revisiting one of the simplest forms of internetworked writing: a meme. A meme is, typically, an invitation to blend image and text as a form of play within a set of overt or implied constraints. For example, the overarching "rule" of LOLCATs memes is that cat speech is either a childish or pidgin form of English, albeit with a soupçon of feline contempt for humanity. One subset of LOLCATs memes takes the format "I'm in/on your [X], [verb]ing your [Y]." This structure, presumably drawing on the feline penchant to materialize in unexpected spaces, offers participants a chance to manifest cleverness within the sharply constrained creative space defined by the implied rules of the meme. It is with this structure in mind that my former student, Clancy Ratliff—now Professor of English at the University of Louisiana Lafayette—developed her own LOLCAT meme, posting it to the online photo-sharing site, flickr, with a Creative Commons license, and with the title "My first lolcat" on May 3, 2007.

About a decade later, Ratliff posted to social media that she was surprised to learn that her image was now *the* exemplary image for the LOLCAT meme genre on Wikipedia. It remains there to this day. I might be envious of this achievement.

We can likely reconstruct the steps that led to Ratliff's meme arriving within Wikipedia. In August of 2016, a Wikipedia editor determines (rightly, in my opinion) that the image then on the site did a poor job of reflecting the distinctive misspellings common to the genre. The editor then, in all likelihood, gravitated to flickr owing to the site's commitment to foregrounding whether particular photos were offered with Creative Commons licenses that would allow them to be reused without compensation. I

Fig. 8.1: Clancy Ratliff's lolcat meme, via Wikipedia

guessed at the likely license preferences the editor would have used, and sure enough, Ratliff's meme popped up four rows deep, clearly announcing itself as one of the better executed contributions to the site. This unexpected journey of Ratliff's meme from her desktop to the pages of Wikipedia is illustrative of the degree to which internetworked writing has the capacity to travel beyond the scope of the composer's imaginings. These travels exceed the capacity of print to surprise us, in part because digital texts are—in many cases—built from the ground up to facilitate their participation in digital ecologies of circulation and exchange.

Now Clancy's meme is in our Wikipedia, exemplifying the LOL-CAT meme format. And thereby, it has traveled as fully and as far as its composer ever might have imagine. By so doing, this modest meme is illustrative of internetworked circulation patterns of that simply did not exist in the fairly recent past.

CURRENCY: Reflections

Because networked digital texts typically developed to function in an ongoing "present" moment, their composers do not always take the time to fully note the time and circumstance of a text's composition. While blogs and news sites *do* tend to maintain reasonably solid time and date markers for texts composed within their structures, these structures also suppress past texts in deference to present texts. In many cases on-site archiving has been subject to redesigns and relocations that make past texts difficult—if not impossible—to access.

Viral and memetic compositions have become iconic representations of twenty-first century internetworked digital communication. While composers can sometimes aim for viral outcomes, the memetic is up to the audience, who ultimately determines whether a given piece of cultural text is worthy of adaptation, transformation, and parody. As such, the memetic is a direct descendant of Aristotle's claim that the audience "determines a speech's end and object." How and whether composers successfully connect with their audiences is a question now processed at remarkable speeds and with remarkable reach (sometimes truly global). A meme exists to prompt the next riff on the "rules" established by the meme. As such, each variation on the structure of an existing meme is a way of doinking a metaphoric balloon aloft. Each iteration of a meme with significant popular uptake keeps it hovering in a rolling present, with many hands working to sustain is as a site for further interaction.

Print offered the daily newspaper, sometimes with morning and evening editions, as the peak of its orientation toward compositions that reflected the present moment. Television brought us closer still to composed texts responding to events as they unspooled live on our screens. Internetworked writing offers an all-but-instant site for compositions responding to events as they happen. I have, for many years, hosted a virtual "Oscar Party" online, delighting in my guests' critiques of windy speeches as they unfolded, or their well-crafted takedowns of the cutesy scripted patter that award presenters are obliged to read. At its best, the guests build off one anothers' witticisms, leading to an escalating hilarity that seems calibrated to the overblown spectacle of Hollywood celebrating itself. But as a resident of Minneapolis, I was also witness to another variant of this dynamic in the immediate wake of George Floyd's murder.

George Floyd died in May, 2020 after multiple members of the Minneapolis Police Department knelt on his body for roughly nine minutes, with Officer Derek Chauvin kneeling on Floyd's neck for most of that time. The killing—one of too many recent cases of unarmed Black Americans dying at the hands of police officers—was unflinchingly filmed by a brave young woman and circulated on social media, triggering a wave of protests in the Twin Cities and throughout the world. The protests escalated over a series of three days, and one of the most nimble news organizations covering the escalating confrontations between protestors and police was a left-leaning self-described "alternative media" collective named Unicorn

Riot. Because Unicorn Riot was sometimes operating with smartphones as cameras, it was able to quickly move into spaces that larger media outlets had trouble reaching. I found Unicorn Riot's coverage within Facebook, and this resulted in Unicorn Riot's sometimes hitchy video being paired with a panel of live real-time commentary from those watching the coverage. At times some were critical of Unicorn Riot's reporters, or technical difficulties, but others would defend them. In lulls, the Facebook live stream associated with Unicorn Riot became a space where viewers began discussing what might constitute effective action in response to police violence.

The Internet's bias toward the *now* is both a strength and a weakness, but in this specific case, viewers united by a sense of outrage and grief began forging a micro-community directed at shaping effective interventions over the near term. As such, the unlikely union of a strongly leftist media collective and the largest, most monopolistic social media corporation in the United States blended together to create a realtime community discussion space that contemplated what meaningful interventions in a developing story could and should be.

179

In these fitful and fierce moments, I saw a glimmer of hope for the future of similar moments. The Internet was offering channels for people who were shocked by what they were seeing, but hoped to be able to be part of building toward better days. Internetworked writing is one of the ways we will grapple with these moments in the future, and my hope is that we will continue to develop skills and mores that help us work constructively in internetworked writing spaces.

COMPOSITION: Reflections

I have long argued that the term *writing* has become so tethered to the production of alphanumeric characters within white rectangles—real or virtual—that it no longer encompasses the full range of writing practices that people pursue, especially the writing in internetworked digital spaces. The tendency to dismiss styles of writing that are facilitated by writing technologies has a long history, with one of the most entertaining being Truman Capote's tart dismissal of the Beat writers: "That's not writing; that's just typewriting." Significant shifts in writing technologies have often produced moments of wariness regarding the writing strategies facilitated by those tools. To a writer enculturated in the strategies and rhythms of longhand, the prospect of Jack Kerouac, likely loaded up with Benzedrine, typing one hundred words per minute on a 120-foot scroll so as not to "break his flow" seems like a direct violation of the serious writer's obligations: to contemplate, to reflect, *to revise*.

I have, over the past twenty years observed a parallel dynamic whenever a digital composition—however serious-minded—incorporates multimedia elements that are actually quite easy to incorporate into internetworked texts or slideshows. The term used to describe these elements of the text is often "bells and whistles."

Those who object that "composer" is as tethered to musical composition as "writer" is tethered to the production of alphanumeric characters have a good point. They're likely correct. *And that's fine.* I argue for *composer* and *composition* as alternatives to *writer* and *writing* precisely because they invite consideration of musical composition as a baseline model for what it means to invent. Further, the cultural capital associated with those we call composers pushes back the institutional framing of composition as a first-year course and not as a set of practices that are developed and maintained throughout a lifetime.

In musical terms, a composer is understood to be more than a musician and more even than a songwriter. A composer is generally thought of as a person who understands music to such a degree that they can score the simultaneous voicings of multiple instruments in order to produce a desired effect. These might range from simple chords to expansive, dissonant orchestral attacks. *This is a great starting point for discussing the composing techniques of internetworked writers.*

Composers of digital writings routinely consider how best to combine alphanumeric characters, images, and typographic treatments to achieve their communicative or rhetorical goals. Internetworked writing adds to these choices the potential incorporation of existing works from most previous popular media forms (cinema or TV clips, found audio, music, animation). Further, internetworked writers consider whether their own works incorporate motion or spatial dimensionality. My hope is that *composer* supplants *writer* as the favored term for makers of the kinds of complex texts facilitated by internetworked writing. In addition to the invocation of musical composition as a metaphoric model, the use of composer also has the effect of minimizing the apparent gap between *writers* and *authors* that is too often maintained by gatekeepers in our culture. A beginning writer may question whether they have what it takes to become an author, but effective instruction in internetworked writing can make damn well sure that they settle into becoming a *composer*.

CORPORATIONS: Reflections

The framing of distant servers as clouds represents a remarkable instance of rhetorical sleight of hand. The positioning of the composition spaces of the twenty-first century as comparable to free-floating natural ephemera neatly sidesteps the kinds of questions that would immediately arise if people equated the cloud with, for instance, the three top purveyors of cloud services: Amazon, Microsoft, and Google. Further, the cloud isn't free-floating or ephemeral at all. It is a vast network of wires, servers, antennae, satellites, and other stuff fashioned from metals and plastic. The servers, in particular, generate considerable heat and need to be cooled. Thus, the composing spaces we sometimes describe by gesturing vaguely toward the heavens, are, in fact terrestrial, and sometimes subterranean. Further, these clouds are not participants in the natural environment, but disruptors of it, that must be counterbalanced with the kinds of green computing initiatives that are presented as markers of corporate responsibility.

At present, more than half of the global cloud infrastructure is controlled by two Seattle-area companies (Amazon and Microsoft). Adding Google alone pushes this number very close to two-thirds of the global cloud infrastructure, meaning that the Pacific coast of the United States is home to the corporate owners and decision-makers for an immense amount of collective activity. Outside of their cloud initiatives, these three companies have very different business models. Amazon sells goods, Microsoft sells software and operating systems, and Google sells user data that allows advertisers and sellers to target their marketing initiatives. Nevertheless, they all have settled into business models that involve warehousing ideas. In many cases, these storage spaces feel *free* to users, but they all are structured in ways that point toward goods, software and operating systems, and the aggregation of increasingly precise uder data.

Those old enough to have experienced the sometimes utopian and liberatory rhetorics associated with the "dot edu" era of the Internet will likely recall the degree to which it was once possible to see the Internet as the space where academic and theoretical challenges to corporate ownership and the propertization of ideas would finally be realized. The ready reproducibility of compositions, paired with the efficiency and reach of peer-to-peer networks seemed poised to open doors to almost-perfect libraries of . . . well, pretty much everything. John Perry Barlow's 1994 *Wired* essay, "The Economy of Ideas," remains one of the best encapsulations of the aspirations of this moment:

> [W]e are sailing into the future on a sinking ship.
>
> This vessel, the accumulated canon of copyright and patent law, was developed to convey forms and methods of expression entirely different from the vaporous cargo it is now being asked to carry. It is leaking as much from within as from without.

181

Legal efforts to keep the old boat floating are taking three forms: a frenzy of deck chair rearrangement, stern warnings to the passengers that if she goes down, they will face harsh criminal penalties, and serene, glassy-eyed denial.

Intellectual property law cannot be patched, retrofitted, or expanded to contain digitized expression any more than real estate law might be revised to cover the allocation of broadcasting spectrum (which, in fact, rather resembles what is being attempted here). We will need to develop an entirely new set of methods as befits this entirely new set of circumstances. (par. 6)

While Barlow has been proven largely right about the limits of strategies like digital rights management (DRM) that cannot fully keep a motivated copyright scofflaw from trolling the darkweb for a free copy of a desired scrap of media, this has not led to a wholesale recalibration of authorship and ownership within United States culture.

The Internet once seemed on the verge of eliminating all of the corporate "middlemen" who have, historically, taken too great a share of ownership and compensation from the people composing various kinds of texts. In some cases, consumers have successfully used the presence of perfect digital copies as leverage. The experience of Napster as a test case for the construction of a near-perfect library of popular music has prompted a wave of reasonably affordable subscription music services that offer remarkable aggregations of almost everything one might ask for. While these services address consumer demands, they are not yet adequately compensating the composers whose work they are reselling, and in this they resemble the traditional physical record business far more than they ought to.

In the case of traditional written texts, it was, in the wake of the rise of the public Internet, momentarily possible to dream of more direct channels for distribution, and further, a rebalancing of copyright that was not centered around repositioning text as chattel and momentarily repositioning composers as owners for the purpose of securing that chattel. While the sale and control of written work has grown more challenging and more complicated, the remarkable corporate countermove has been to rebalance the equation by quietly moving into ownership of the spaces where written work now unfolds. Thus, though the structure of our writing tools invites us all to understand "authorship" as a socially connected phenomenon and one that does not necessarily imply full ownership of one's written work, the increasing corporate ownership of cloud spaces is ensuring that composers and audiences are never quite able to connect with one another without participating in larger corporate structures.

CONNECTIONS (and DISCONNECTIONS):
Reflections

One night in 1998, I was on the campus of Pennsylvania State University, taking a pause from a very late-night dissertation writing session and trying to refresh my collection of biker movie soundtrack music. I had arrived at a personal preference for this microgenre because the songs tended to be wordless and . . . *driving*, the perfect backdrop for a tired writer in the final push. I also felt a measure of justification in downloading this music. The soundtracks to movies like *The Wild Angels* and *The Glory Stompers* were out of print. I already owned some on LP, always purchased used. They were not available on compact disc, or on any other format. To the extent that downloading MP3s violated the owners' copyrights, it was not leading to a reduction in revenue. These records were all-but-abandoned within the music industry of that time. On this particular night, as I scrolled through a particularly rich trove of tracks using one of the crude pre-Napster peer-to-peer clients, I was startled when a chat window popped up and the curator of the trove engaged me directly. Over the next few exchanges, it became clear that he was really hoping to find someone who enjoyed chatting about biker movie soundtracks as much as he did. At 2:45 a.m.

183

This moment still resonates with me because while I was up late because I was writing and had stumbled onto a repository of MP3 files of a musical subgenre that seemed to help me work, the curator was apparently up because he was lonely, and because he was looking out for people who shared a very narrow and specific musical interest. The curator kindly pointed me towards other deep pockets of similar music and respected my stated need to return to writing about latent theories of authorship within the works of Hélène Cixous, rather than join him in a discussion of stereo panning in the works of Davie Allan and the Arrows.

In this, the Internet of 1998, the occasions where two possible biker movie soundtrack enthusiasts were on the Internet at the same moment were so rare that the curator took the risk and reached out. I had no awareness of his geography, his timezone, or even absolute certainty that he was a he, but in that moment I felt distance collapse in a way that felt new to me. The context is important here. The Internet, to that point in my life, had functioned primarily as a content repository. It was not an especially well-indexed repository, either. This story unfolds a year prior to Google's public debut in 1999. As a graduate student, I had developed substantial research skills, and I was able to port those skills to the relatively new task of finding content via the Internet. To the extent that I connected with others, it was typically planned and structured, with an experimental graduate seminar taught online being the most prominent example. This experience had not prepared me for the possibility that my online activities might spark an unexpected conversation in much the same way that a considertation of a record at a used record store might prompt a neighboring crate-digger to weigh in on the merits of the performer of the record.

I'm sure many long-term users of the Internet can point to parallel moments—where the potential for connectivity announced itself as at least as important as the aggregation of content—before or after my personal epiphany in 1998. For those who began using the Internet after generations of social media placed all-but-real-time conversational connections at the center of their structures, I imagine it is hard to grasp the feel of this internet-of-content, most of which was delivered in the absence of conversational connection.

A sense of this phase of the Internet's development resurfaces whenever one experiences a lack of available bandwidth. The all-but-real-time conversational character of social media and of the collective composition and revision of documents in spaces like Google Docs absolutely depends on the participants' collective access to high-speed internet connections. And, it must be noted, this is *not* a given for many people. Even within the United States, profound disparities with respect to access to high-speed Internet remain.

As of this writing, the Biden administration is emphasizing rural broadband as part of its infrastructure initiatives. This superficially seems like a reasonable point of emphasis. A *New York Times* article by Eduardo Porter titled "A Rural-Urban Broadband Divide, But Not the One You Think Of" reports that eighty-six percent of urban households have broadband, relative to only eighty-one percent of rural households. The other side of this statistic, though, is that there are currently 13.6 urban housholds without broadband relative to 4.6 rural households in a parallel circumstance. As Porter reports, Joi Chaney, of the National Urban League testified before the House Appropriations Committee in ways that raised questions about how and whether the proposed investments in rural broadband contributed to racial disparities within the United States:

> We . . . have to be careful not to fall into the old traps of aggressively solving for one community's problem—a community that is racially diverse but predominantly white—while relying on hope and market principles to solve for another community's problem — a community that is also racially diverse but disproportionately composed of people of color and those earning lower incomes. (qtd. in Porter, par. 7)

Porter's article goes on to underscore that the greatest obstacle to broadband usage is typically not access to physical connection points, but affordability. Porter's article, falling as it does at the end of over a year in which the pandemic prompted physical schools to close, is a jarring indictment of the unrealized promises of the Internet as envisioned in the 1990s. *The preferred delivery mechanisms (live video) for most of the public schools in the United States from March of 2020 through June of 2021 were not available or affordable for the children in roughly 1/5th to 1/7th of the country.*

As a practical matter, the conversational connections that sometimes form the basis or backdrop for written compositions are disproportionately distributed throughout the United States. This is true despite an awareness, dating back to the 1990s, that connection might be at least as important as content. To the extent that the current infrastructure does not serve a huge swathe of the United States' population, we have not connected with one another to the degree we *need* to so that we can face the challenges of our collective future.

CHANGE: Reflections

I am fortunate enough to teach a class titled "Rhetoric, Technology, and the Internet" at the University of Minnesota-Twin Cities, and I have done so for many years. Over the past two decades I have had the privilege of observing how students are engaging with the Internet as the Internet itself has grown and evolved. I have also benefitted from the wisdom of these students as they have proven to be early adopters of most of the internet-phenomena-of-the-moment over the years. In the mid 2000s I recall leading an undergraduate class through the key terms at the heart of my colleague Laura J. Gurak's 2001 book *Cyberliteracy: Navigating the Internet With Awareness*: speed, reach, anonymity, and interactivity. I then asked the class to break into small groups and challenged each group to come up with a fifth term that might stand alongside Gurak's chosen four. One group offered *change* as a term, spotlighting the degree to which the Internet as they experienced it was constantly in flux. Indeed, at that moment in internet history, the phenomenon of "link rot"—in which sites established with the best of intentions were abandoned leaving broken links all over the World Wide Web—was a substantial part of the experience of navigating the Internet. Additionally, the students were speaking to their own frustration as the content of the sites they were visiting proved malleable, sometimes changing overnight without notice. The class appeared persuaded by this small group's arguments that *change* was a significant element of their experience of the Internet.

But then a second group volunteered that they had arrived at a very nearly opposite proposed keyword. Their chosen word was *permanence*. This group's argument was that their early forays onto the Internet were often preserved whether they wished for them to be or not. This conversation occurred prior to the Web 2.0 era and the widespread popularity of large social media platforms. That said, the Internet Archive was out there and in some cases these students were able to use it to dredge up mortifying missteps that would have been voluntarily hurled into the memory hole if at all possible.

The subsequent classwide debate over whether the Internet was more characterized by permanence or change was exactly the kind of conversation instructors hope to prompt. With wit and numerous illustrative examples, the students challenged one another, until time grew short and we agreed to settle on: *permachangeability*. By this, I believe we meant a kind of mutable permanence, in which any given page was always subject to change, but the presence of the page and the changes to it were also likely to be a matter of record.

But over time, I have come to see change as encapsulating so much of the experience of writing in the clouds. Web texts are—by default—subject to the preferences of the reader. Once a text is delivered within a browser, much of the careful attention to structure by the web developer can by destabilized by resizing, tweaks to the look and feel of the fonts. Ebooks are similarly subject to reader whims. Composers preparing texts for internet-worked electronic spaces must constantly struggle with the tension between delivering texts "as envisioned" and delivering texts that are amenable to others' preferences.

The Internet also feels more tenuous to me than it did at the time we had this discussion. When viewed as an archive, the Internet as a whole seems rich and expansive . . . but this richness is often owing to the effort and goodwill of small groups or even lone enthusiasts. There are often no succession plans associated with resources that are used by specialized scholars and thinkers daily. Further, the Internet is always in the process of re-development. Resources that seem cutting-edge can look dated within the space of a half-decade. Resources that were once arguably legal (like Napster) can disappear overnight.

The Internet as an archive is fragile . . . depending heavily on committed composers, commercial viability, and the recalibration of our laws. Twenty-first century composers thus face the challenges of not only being conscious of where we are, but also where we might be in the near future.

Conclusion: Clouds, from Both Sides Now

One of the more common challenges directed at scholars addressing writing technologies is that their understanding of shifts in these technologies tilts too strongly toward either a revolutionary understanding of those technologies or an evolutionary understanding. A large portion of Elizabeth Eisenstein's career has been devoted to arguing for (as in the title of her best-known book) "the printing press as an agent of change." This argument exposed Eisenstein to charges of technological determinism (deriving from her overt positioning of technology as an agent) but also considerable pushback against the superficially not-so-startling claim that moveable type was—within the context of Europe—a revolutionary technology. Eisenstein was repeatedly challenged for describing the advent of moveable-type printing as (in one of her chapter titles) "an unacknowledged revolution."

In a 2002 *American Historical Review* article titled "An Unacknowledged Revolution Revisited," Eisenstein reviews some of the major challenges to her claim, all of which argue that an *evolutionary* understanding of the impact of the printing press is to be preferred to a *revolutionary* understanding. Significant to Eisenstein among these challenges is Paul Saenger's suggestion that the practice of silent reading, which Eisenstein ascribes to the post-type era, actually predated Gutenberg, and a series of studies that documented "how manuscript book dealers anticipated the commercial practices of later printers and how the hand copying of books persisted long after printers had set to work" (87). These arguments were directed at Eisenstein even after she deferentially described the advent of print as a "long revolution," thereby creating a borderline oxymoron when the concept of revolution is mapped against its use in political contexts. All of which raises the question, if a significant body of scholars rebel at describing *Gutenberg* as revolutionary, just *what* could possibly clear the hurdle? In the years since Eisenstein, the siren songs of revolution have proven irresistible to many scholars surveying shifts in writing technologies and practices.

Yet, in *The Printing Press as an Agent of Change*, Elizabeth Eisenstein arrives at a paragraph in which she clearly tries to have revolution both ways:

> Statements about literacy rates during the fourteenth and early fifteenth centuries are likely to be . . . vague. . . . In the absence of hard data, plausible arguments may be developed to support sharply divergent opinions and there is no way of settling the inevitable conflict between revolutionary and evolutionary models of change. Thus one may envisage a relatively swift "educational revolution" in the six-

teenth century, in which case, the effects produced by printing will loom large; or, one may instead describe a "long revolution" which unfolds so slowly that these effects are completely flattened out. (Eisenstein 61)

Eisenstein's reframing of "revolution" in this paragraph alerts us to the possibility that in the context of technologies of writing and literary, "revolution" just *can't* mean what it means elsewhere. This alerts us that those of us living through the advent of the Internet should probably approach our own "long revolution" with an openness to the possibilities of substantial reinvention of writing practices to take advantage of the opportunities that are latent within the tools we now use for written composition.

Dennis Baron's 2009 book *A Better Pencil* is another of many texts lurking in the DNA of this book that overtly invokes revolution as a metaphor for its core argument. From a 2020 perspective, it is tempting to want to go back in time to revise its subtitle: *Readers, Writers, and the Digital Revolution*. Indeed, "digital revolution" is the foundation for Baron's smart argument that digital writing technologies are far more than "a better pencil." This argument obliges Baron to flatten differences between this "revolution" and its supposed predecessors. Baron writes:

> [I]n many ways the printing press did for literacy what earlier manuscript revolutions had also done: it created new means and opportunities for textual transmission; it both reinforced and threatened established ways of meaning; and it stimulated disruptions in the social, political, and economic realms.
>
> Computers too achieved their initial impact by allowing writers to produce familiar documents, but they also claim our attention, and a place in our reading and writing, by disrupting the older ways of doing things textually. (xiii)

Yet, this "disruption" is taking soooooo long. For all the new genres facilitated by digital media, the dedicated writing applications found within digital technologies project a remarkably narrow construction of what it means to write into the present and future. As illustrated in the preceding pages, many of the programs and apps facilitating writing in 2021 still generally resemble Microsoft Word's interface, initially developed in 1987 as a response to a similar interface for MacWrite. MacWrite shipped with the 1984 Apple Macintosh but was hamstrung by space limitations on the disk housing the program that capped documents at about *eight* pages (Kirschenbaum xiv). While my project acknowledges that practices of internetworked writing are distinctive in many senses, these practices are also marked by how much of the past they carry forward. One cannot overlook the degree to which the most collaborative and connected of the most adopted internetworked writing applications, Google Docs, has maintained a thirty-year old interface as the framework for how we might now write together.

Engaging with this interface must be so jarring for the teenagers writing their first scholarly projects of any length. The computer or tablet they are using as, in effect, a "better typewriter" has been their gateway to other worlds (of warcraft and otherwise). It is the space where Beyoncé videos have dropped unexpectedly in the dark of night. It is the home of TikTok videos that taught them the latest dance, or vegan recipes intertwined with a side dish of emotional support. It is the space for zombie movies and another pass through "Idiocracy" on Hulu. It is where spreadsheets crunch numbers and slideshows give points more power. It is the home of both "Woman Yells at a Cat" and "Doge." It is the space of *all* the virtual things, flexible, and fluid, and facilitating entirely new genres of creative expression. Yet, the word processing interface is very nearly as stable as the QWERTY keyboard. Possibilities swirl around the tools we are using to write much as we have written for the past century.

Evolution and revolution have become the available metaphoric shorthand for, on the one hand, steady and incremental change and sudden, dramatic (and thrilling) upsettings of most if not all of the available apple carts. The scope and range of writing, media, and textual circulation practices is so expansive that a scholar or critic will be able to find copious evidence for claims on either side of this apparent binary. The parable of the blind men and the elephant is instructive in this case. Without any one of us able to see the whole "elephant" of writing and textual circulation practices, it falls to some of us to argue (rightly) that an elephant is like a pillar, to others to argue (rightly) that it is like a rope, and to still others that it is sharp and pointed. The shifts in writing and textual circulation practices are evolutionary *and* revolutionary (at least) and much depends upon which part of the elephant your hand has found.

All of which is to say, in the current moment, evolution/revolution contests should no longer be a high priority. Aspects of contemporary writing technologies are clearly evolutionary in nature, with typewriter-mimicking elements of Microsoft Word serving as substantial everyday evidence. But the distinct and unprecedented nature of some writing spaces—with Twitter's aggressively portable 140-character real-time text-driven ecology being a striking example—argues for the revolutionary character of at least *some* applications of internetworked writing tools. Importantly, internetworked writing is not any *one* thing. Depending on the audiences sought, the builders of contemporary writing tools might choose to empha-

191

size aspects of novelty *or* familiarity. The pitch might be *either* "this tool helps you compose in the ways you're already used to (but faster or better)" *or* "this tool can help you do things unimaginable with non-digital tools."

At the heart of the needed next steps are a dramatic expansion in our understandings of what counts as "writing." My home department, the Department of Writing Studies at the University of Minnesota, was founded in 2007, drawing together faculty from across disciplines who specialized in rhetoric, technical communication, and composition studies. In the conversations the faculty shared surrounding the formation of the department, we arrived at a brief mission statement, which appears to this day on our website: "We explore all aspects of written communication, preparing students for a world where writing is not only textual, but also digital, visual, social, and networked." The final four terms point towards aspects of written communication that have not always been in the foreground. The experience we are now sharing—of internetworked writing facilitated by cloud-based spaces—pulls all these aspects of writing toward the surface.

Understanding writing as digital, visual, social, and (inter)networked implies an expanded understanding of when and where writing is happening. This starts with not casually dismissing any of the platforms that people use for everyday ephemeral writing as somehow beneath consideration as writing tools. While a smartwatch like the Apple Watch might facilitate textual production by means of speech, once speech is rendered as text, we have writing on our hands (or wrists). While smartphones are still weighted heavily toward consumption, rather than production, of others' writings, they are—despite their small form factors—computers that are exponentially more powerful than the arguably game-changing Apple Macintosh of 1984. Indeed, the processors of current smartphones are often more powerful than those in laptops and desktops from less than a decade ago. By the time we consider tablets, we are engaging some of the most flexible writing tools in the history of humankind. Strikingly, most tablets already facilitate swift toggling between typing and "freehand" notetaking and drawing.

That our collective creativity can be made available to one another in—effectively—real time is one of the more miraculous developments in media history. This is by no means unprecedented. Both the telegraph and the telephone signaled first a desire and then a capacity for real-time communication. But contemporary digital tools make writing in its broadest sense available in what is practically real time, thereby facilitating collaboration at speeds and on scales that have never been experienced to this degree. The hitch in this landscape of opportunity remains images. They still cost. They are still processor-intensive and increase the likelihood that what the composer sees and what the reader sees will diverge. But, as the preceding pages have shown, text and image have overlapping histories, and the degrees to which they participate in written composition are the by-products of specific technological affordances and audience preferences that have ebbed and flowed over time. Still, the tendency to default to an evolutionary/revolutionary binary is hard to shake.

The work of the late evolutionary biologist Stephen Jay Gould offers one possible pathway out of the evolution/revolution binary. Gould's theory of *punctuated equilibria* argues that evolutionary development need not be steady and regular. Indeed, Gould argues, there are moments when the relatively stable states are disrupted (that's the "punctuation") and in these times, evolutionary development—typically understood as steady and incremental and in character—is instead explosively fast. In these times, species appear and transform, at rates that defy the initial understandings of Darwin's evolution by means of natural selection. Gould's paradigmatic example of punctuated equilibrium, the Cambrian explosion, is a period in which the "gradualism" long associated with Darwinian evolution is simply at odds with what the fossil record shows. As Gould explains in his 1990 book *Wonderful Life: The Burgess Shale and the Nature of History*:

193

> Modern multicellular animals make their first uncontested appearance in the fossil record some 570 million years ago—and with a bang, not a protracted crescendo. This "Cambrian explosion" marks the advent (at least into direct evidence) of virtually all major groups of modern animals—and all within the miniscule span, geologically speaking, of a few million years. (23–4)

This sounds revolutionary, both in spirit and in scope, but a later section in *Wonderful Life* is titled "A Quiet Revolution" and finds Gould reflecting on the variety and complexity of what are later *come to be described* as revolutions:

> Some transformations are overt and heroic; others are quiet and uneventful in their unfolding, but no less significant in their outcome. Karl Marx, in a famous statement, compared his social revolution to an old mole burrowing busily beneath the ground, invisible for long periods, but undermining traditional order so thoroughly that a later emergence into light precipitates a sudden overturn. But intellectual transformations often remain under the surface. They ooze and diffuse into scientific consciousness, and people may slowly move from one pole to another, having never heard the call to arms. (79)

Thus, moments of punctuated equilibrium are neither purely evolutionary nor purely revolutionary. Indeed, Gould argues, they are "normal" events within the broad sweep of history. As such, they offer an invitation to understanding natural selection as either an evolutionary tortoise or a revolutionary hare. When equilibria are punctuated, this does not mean that all the "rules" of conventional evolutionary development have been temporarily suspended. It would be more accurate to say that a "fast forward" button has been hit and that eons of development have been compressed. Gould's "quiet revolution" parallels Eisenstein's "long" and "unacknowledged" revolution. In each case, we can recognize a period of dramatic transformation, which leads to the explosive arrival of new life forms or new media forms, but both of these moments can appear to move slowly or unfold over a long period of time depending on how one keeps score. With the complexity of Gould's framework in mind, we might describe the era in which the Internet became a public phenomenon as a moment of punctuation, and the intervening (almost) three decades as an explosion, of sorts. But we also must grapple with the degree to which so much of our experience of these decades is shaped by the accumulated inertia surrounding what writing is and does. My sense is that we do well to work our way out of the evolution/revolution binary and commence a search for metaphoric models that are more aligned with the experiences of our current moment. So, if inter-networked writing is neither mostly evolutionary nor mostly revolutionary, then how are we to understand it?

One alternative worthy of consideration becomes available when we drop a letter or two from "evolution" and "revolution"—which are too often positioned as poles even though they need not be. A neighboring word, *volution*, and its associated array of meanings offers valuable perspective on how we might choose to occupy a third space without the embedded limitations of evolution and revolution as frames. The *Oxford English Dictionary* offers three related definitions for volution: (1) "a rolling or revolving movement"; (2) "a spiral turn or twist; a coil or convolution"; and (3) "a whorl of a spiral shell." The *American Heritage Dictionary* also offers "one of the whorls of a spiral gastropod shell" as an available meaning.

Spiral gastropod shells, like those of a snail or nautilus, are often said to be exemplars of the Fibonacci sequence—an orderly mathematical progression that is the basis for the "golden spiral"—though in the case of individual gastropods growth is *not* necessarily so very orderly. But the whorl of a nautilus shell, whether or not it adheres to the golden spiral, is exemplary of a growth pattern that is, on the one hand, marked by continual expansion (at least until the nautilus expires), but also *at the same time* greatly determined (and indeed limited by) the growth that occurred in the immediately preceding chamber, and indeed *all* the preceding chambers dating back to the birth of the nautilus. Importantly, this is *not* an argument for oscillation between the axes of evolution and revolution. Rather it is an argument for understanding progressive growth and dramatic expansion as *simultaneous* and *interconnected* patterns of development.

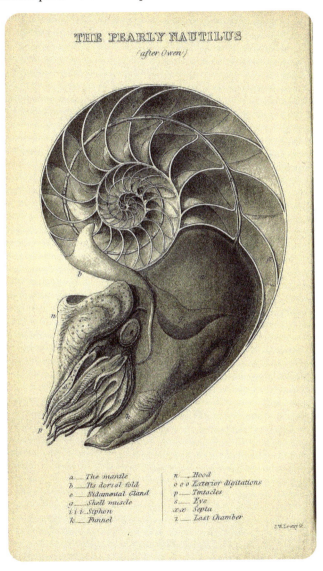

Figure C.1: Volution as expressed in a nautilus shell from S. P. Woodward, A. N. Waterhouse, and Joseph Wilson Lowry's 1880 A Manual of the Mollusca, via Wikimedia Commons.

The nautilus's shell serves an iconic representation of how certain modes of growth depend heavily upon the shape and scope of previous years' growth patterns. A volutionary model also limits our thinking if we process its "golden ratio" as the necessary model for how our understandings of writing develop in response to our adoptions of new writing tools. The regular geometric progression of the nautilus shell is, at times, at odds with the practical reality of our lived experience. There are moments of punctuated equilibria, when growth or a response to a changed environment seals off past chamber/homes with startling speed. There is also the embedded challenge of trying to identify these moments as they unfold. Those who have lived through the past forty years can point to a number of apparently transformative moments in our experience of written communication that later felt incremental or anticipatory.

One advantage to embracing the nautilus's volutionary development pattern as a metaphoric frame for our experience of shifts in composing technology is the opportunity this frame offers to embrace the possibility of moments of closure *that remain connected to the present*. "Volutionary" is not yet in dictionaries, but it speaks to a growth pattern that is expansive and transformative while remaining physically linked to and shaped by past growth cycles. As the nautilus grows, it seals off the space it formerly inhabited by creating a septum, each of which is pierced in the middle by a duct. The space between two adjacent septa is known, in what feels like a remarkable coincidence, as a *camera*.

In our day-to-day lives, cameras are (or were) devices (or now, a combination of hardware and apps) we use to record our present moments for future reflection. They are collectors of our future past. With the press of a button, we create an additional contribution to our archives. Humans' cameras are, strikingly, one of the spaces where past, present, and future blur. We record so that our future selves might remember. But the nautilus's camerae offer a different kind of closure. When the nautilus generates a septum, that is a moment marking—in a sense—the nautilus having grown in ways that mean it no longer fits in its existing "home." The nautilus is decisively closing off its ability to live in that space, even as that space is actively shaping its next home.

When discussing digital technologies from the very recent past, we are now able to recognize septa. There are practices that dominate literate ecologies that are now effectively closed off. Consider, for example, the phenomenon of the digital disc-based multimedia encyclopedia. From 1993 until 2009, Microsoft was producing annual updates to an expansive multimedia encyclopedia, primarily delivered on CD-ROMs and later on DVD.

Encarta was, for many of these years, the best known and most recognized digital iteration of the encyclopedia form.

And it's *gone*.

Microsoft's digital and multimedia *Encarta* encyclopedia, rightly hailed in 1993 as a landmark achievement in the history of human knowledge, was delivered on shiny silvery discs that now reside in landfills. And the landfill layer that houses *Encarta* is only a few layers above the layers that house once-prized copies of *The World Book Encyclopedia* that sat at garage sales until they, too, were abandoned. The encyclopedia as a genre is one of the spaces where it is possible to observe the degree to which digital technologies—and then internetworked digital technologies—*did* sometimes supplant their immediate print predecessors. While a generation of bookish youngsters may never know the thrill of discovering the transparent, layered pages of the *World Book* that walked readers through the specifics of various bodily systems (nervous, digestive, reproductive) they ought not be pitied for missing out on this experience. Nor should we mourn Microsoft's decision to stop producing editions of *Encarta* in 2009. The cloud, with its biases toward the visual, multimedia, and the multimodal, has the potential to offer consumers of the encyclopedia genre so much more. The perceived need for an annually updated commercial product occupying the encyclopedia niche gave way to the constantly and relentlessly updated *Wikipedia*, which offers collective efficiency (and occasional—and usually momentary—inaccuracy) for the price of whatever it costs you to access to the World Wide Web. This is not to say that *Wikipedia* is necessarily better than *Encarta* (or the *World Book*). Despite the opportunities presented by cloud spaces, *Wikipedia*'s pages tend toward static, print heavy pages where *Encarta* developed rich motion graphics (for its time), and both *Encarta* and its print predecessors made massive investments in aggregating experts to write their core content.

We are now both *within* a space defined by *Encarta* having set the tone for online encyclopedias, and *beyond* that space, where the boundedness of the CD-ROM format seems altogether quaint. A septum stands between us and products like *Encarta*. *Encarta*'s time is definitively over. The game of constructing and circulating encyclopedias changed decisively and definitively. But our present moment is still informed by the kinds of intellectual and developmental work that produced *Encarta* in the first place, and further, by the entire history of the encyclopedia as a genre.

A *volutionary* stance toward understanding writing and writing technologies implies an acceptance of the *simultaneity* of change and constancy in writing technologies and writing practices. Writing technologies will, inevitably, seek to meet their audiences where they are. They will incorporate the familiar in order to bridge to the possible.

197

At its core, writing has remained remarkably constant. The human need for self-expression is profound, and its rough parameters have been established and largely stabilized for centuries. There are, however, distinctive patterns of written communication that at least *felt* distinctive and novel at specific points in our shared history. For example, novelistic writing is no more than one thousand years old. The earliest candidate for a novel, Murasaki Shikibu's *Tale of the Genji*, was completed in 1021 AD. The degree to which *Tale of the Genji* satisfies the generic requirements for what we now understand to be a novel is debatable, but by the 1605 publication of Miguel Cervantes' *El ingenioso hidalgo Don Quijote de la Mancha*, most scholars agree that we have a new chamber on our hands, and a point of demarcation between the time before the novel and a post-novel landscape of possibility. That we are not always sure what to *name* these new genres at the point when they arise does not minimize our capacity to identify decisive breaking points in writing practices.

In some cases, we can infer that the advent of specific technologies served as a driver for the development of specific writing practices. We have only had print technologies for about six hundred years. Journalism (on a roughly contemporary model) arose roughly a half-century after the advent of print. While we can point to millennias worth of historians using writing to sift through the events of the past—even the recent past—in order to wrangle some meaning from these events, the notion of timely reportage of the *previous day's events* visibly arose at a relatively recent and specific point in time and has persisted to the present while expanding throughout a range or writing-associated media. The development of a specific mode of writing like journalistic writing carries with it the development and accretion of techniques, practices, and styles appropriate to the task at hand, so much so that a reader with even a basic education can distinguish historical writing from journalistic writing even though, in a broad sense, they are both types of writing directed at making the past available to future readers.

The challenge of the current moment is that the septa that arguably might mark the closing of one chamber to open the next have been arriving so quickly. The first e-mail messages recognizable as such (by which I mean those bearing the now-familiar "@" sign as the break between name and "address") date from 1971, and e-mail represents a striking disruption of the then-extant conventions for correspondence. SMS Messaging, the basis for contemporary text messages, dates back to 1992, but this genre of writing has proven a profound intervention into daily and even familial life. Text messaging's graphic traveling partner, the emoji, dates back to a specific type of Japanese mobile phone in 1997. Surely, we must recognize a breaking point between the times where text and image were strictly compartmentalized in messaging and a current moment where it is not uncommon for significant and complex concepts to be rendered entirely in emojis, with perhaps one high-water mark being an emoji-only retelling of *Les Miserables*.

The ready availability and portability of images and the degree to which composing machines now accommodate images, are one of the most distinctive aspects of twenty-first century writing. A generation of composers has become habituated to the ready availability of symbols (with emoji being the most available example) with both overt and conventional meanings. This generation has become at least comfortable with the use of images, and in many cases, has demonstrated remarkable creativity. One small step beyond the mashing together of emojis to construct sentences, of sorts, is the range of play we see among composers of memes. While the genres of memes have grown complex enough to merit sustained study, many of the more popular genres consist of 1–2 rectangular images with the textual content all-but-blasted at the reader in a tweaked version of the IMPACT typeface. The conventions of the genre are intuitive and simple, but the crafting of a combination of text and image is challenging enough that it has become conventional wisdom that one cannot craft a meme, so much as one "seeds" a meme that a larger crowd then selects as a site for revision, expansion, and play.

With this toggling between words and images being conventional within the spaces where even beginning writers practice their composing skills and strategies, it is becoming increasingly clear that twenty-first century composers are particularly adept with respect to whether and how they incorporate images into their more formal compositions. By the time students reach high school they are intuiting when a screenshot might be worth the picture's historic benchmark of "a thousand words" and opting not to write (in the traditional sense) when they can show. Further, students' nimbleness in navigating relationships between texts and images is reinforced by their engagement with slideware like PowerPoint, Keynote, or Google Slides. While all these platforms have their limitations and flaws, they all also offer composers the opportunity to do fine-grained positioning of images in relation to text.

Those of us fortunate to be teaching at this time are seeing glimmers of possibility as images creep from the margins toward the centers of scholarly communication. Wordy descriptions of visual or mixed textual/visual content are being dispensed with, in favor of simply letting readers *see* what is under analysis or critique. Even so, the conventions of scholarly writing are responding too slowly to the opportunities now at hand. It is commonly the case that scholarly publication structures and guidelines insist upon the separation of texts and images. At the most extreme end of this spectrum are approaches that encourage composers to park images in appendices, which implies that images *disrupt* rather than complement textual content. This same message of the visual-as-disruptor is also conveyed by labeling systems that present visual content as "figures" and require captions explaining the role of the image within the larger body of the text. A review of the images presented in this text will reveal that while *most* are "figures" a few are not.

"Figures" have always battled against the limitations of available text technologies. My invocations of the nautilus and The Golden Ratio have mnemonic associations with the ionic columns that happen to be found on many campuses at colleges and universities. In attempting to locate a royalty-free image that would serve to reinforce the visual connection among these natural, conceptual, and architectural examples of volution I located, within *Wikipedia*, an elegant page that consolidated nine separate figures. In this case, the insistent need to label these and maintain their participation in the numeric progression of figures within the text stands at odds with the more pronounced need embedded in this page: to *label* the subtly distinct subtypes of ionic columns and help readers differentiate among them. The text that walks the reader through these distinctions, though it *could* have fit within this space, is segregated from "the image space" in order to stay with its alphanumeric companions in "the text space." It is not only the loveliness of this image that marks it as belonging to a past we no longer inhabit. It is also the limited ways in which text and image are understood to relate to one another.

The "figure" is a settled convention within academia, and indeed for certain kinds of writing, especially those which toggle back and forth between text and data displays, this careful labeling of each image as it arises makes all the sense in the world. But these conventions seem remarkably stilted and stodgy when contemporary composers are readily able to construct compositions in which the relationships between texts and images are—if not straightforward—obvious and intuitive. We must remind ourselves that sophisticated compositions involving texts and images are not merely emblematic of the twenty-first century, they were also central to the rise of print magazine in the late nineteenth and early twentieth centuries. Further, the use of sophisticated blends of text and image to pursue serious arguments has been significantly present within humanities since at least the 1967 publication of Marshall McLuhan and Quentin Fiore's collaboration *The Medium is the Massage: An Inventory of Effects.*

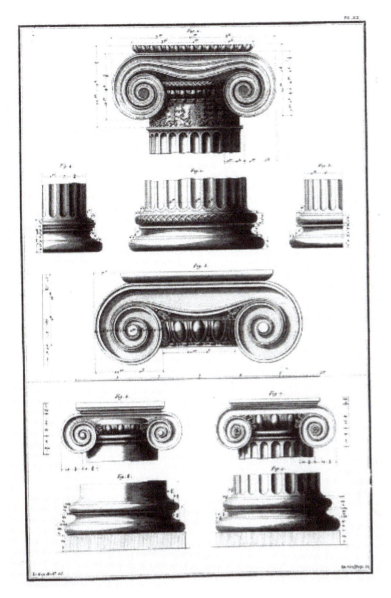

Figure C.2: A figure full of figures, but lacking crucial (con)textual information, from Julien David le Roy's 1758 Les Ruines des plus beaux monuments de le Gréce.

McLuhan and Fiore's book gleefully upends then-extant publishing conventions with textual content varying from few to no words on some pages and longer blocks of fairly traditional scholarly prose on others. All this textual content is set against stark, high-contrast black-and-white images in compositions that were written by McLuhan and then designed by Fiore. A third, initially uncredited, collaborator, Jerome Agel, gathered visual illustrations that, in his estimations, corresponded to McLuhan's written text. *The Medium is the Massage*, then, is the by-product of collaborators who serially undertook the tasks of writing (McLuhan), curation (Agel), and design (Fiore). In the generations since, McLuhan, Fiore, and Agel worked to disrupt the look and feel of conventional scholarly arguments; their distinctive areas of specialization have all become spaces where developing composers typically have accumulated at least *some* skills with the very best contemporary composers routinely demonstrating their talents for writing, curation, and design, *but not necessarily in that order*. Indeed, one of the remarkable aspects of contemporary composers is that because they often have strong skills in all these areas, it becomes increasingly difficult to unravel what once seemed so distinct. Contemporary composers are often writing *and* curating and *designing* all at once. The collaboration that was once spread across three people is often now simply an expression of accumulated skills for contemporary composers. They often *can* handle it all.

This concentration of skills within individual composers is complemented by the multiplier effect that kicks in whenever such composers are able to gather within virtual spaces that facilitate collaboration. To cite one obvious example, the Google Drive suite of applications is effectively indifferent with respect to the number of composers/collaborators within a given document or project. As far as a Google Doc is concerned, nine composers are as welcome as one. The only real cap on such collaborations is the cognitive dissonance of the visual chatter that arises in the Google Docs interface when multiple composers are working simultaneously.

We should pause here to acknowledge that it is somewhat of a miracle that such collaborations occur at all. To make such collaborations work, a group of composers identifies a cloud-based space, which exists, in practical terms, in a floating number of server farms distributed across the globe. To the extent that the composers have high-speed internet connections (and not everyone does), their changes to a shared document are all-but-instantaneous. This experience is distinctive from all modes of writing to this point in human history. And it is remarkable how quickly it has become a "natural" mode of composing texts.

This astonishing moment in the history of writing, where the pool of potential real-time collaborators extends, at least theoretically, to *all* the people who have available high-speed connections, is one whose implications we will only be able to fully grasp over time. But our experience thus far tells us that writing in clouds is different in ways that *will make* a differ-

202

ence. The challenge at hand is how long it will take us to see all the opportunities now at hand.

I am perhaps *too* partial to Marshall McLuhan's observation that when we face new technologies, we often do so while looking in the rearview mirror. I presented McLuhan's words earlier in this text. I used the same quote as an epigraph for my first book. But every time I have referenced this metaphor in print (as opposed to within a slideshow presentation) I have been embarrassed that the quotation felt incomplete. I intuitively knew that the proper way to quote this was as presented in *The Medium is the Massage: An Inventory of Effects*. The book was, after all, a collaboration. The "effect" is a by-product of the collaboration between McLuhan, designer Quentin Fiore, and curator Jerome Agel. And in a twenty-first century context, it should be quoted in full:

The past went that-a-way. When faced with a totally new situation, we tend always to attach ourselves to the objects, to the flavor of the most recent past.

We look at the present through a rear-view mirror. We march backwards into the future. Suburbia lives imaginatively in Bonanza-land.

(McLuhan, Fiore, and Agel, 74–75)

And yes, while I am looking back at this image to look forward, I am also noting the ease with which I was able to readily locate a specific, remembered pair of pages from a favorite text online, to cut and paste them into my own text, and to research and confirm the collaborative processes that led to their existence in the first place. In the midst of exploding the possibilities of the codex book as a medium, McLuhan, Fiore, and Agel invited us to march (or drive) forward into the future. Writing in the clouds, as so many of us now do as almost second nature, is a further invitation for us to refocus our attention from the rear-view mirror to how much open road lies ahead.

Postscript: The End of "Viral" Writing

While my arguments to this point have encouraged exercising care and caution before we definitively state that "this [novel technology] *destroys* that [established cultural practice]," this project is dedicated to articulating the ways changes in cultural practice accumulate and shape our interactions with writing technologies. As this project drew to a close, it was striking how much my experience of composing it had been informed by the experience of the global pandemic of 2020–21. I began this project writing primarily in my comfortable second story loft office space, looking out onto a deck where my late-night writing was once disrupted by a standing raccoon, tapping demandingly on the sliding glass door as if he were a household pet we had forgotten to let in earlier in the evening. I then moved into a basement office, next to our clothes dryer and our HVAC unit, having ceded the upstairs office space so that my wife and daughters could use the upstairs spaces as we sheltered at home while maintaining virtual presences at workplaces and schools during the COVID-19 outbreak. I moved to a standing desk wedged into the living room, and then concluded this project while writing sitting at our dining room table, often accompanied (or interrupted) by a rambunctious juvenile rescue dog who joined our family in the midst of a very dark year. When the basement became thermally uncomfortable, my wife rightly pointed out that I might as well use the living room—even though it would be visually awkward—because no one would be coming over to visit for months. While framing this book's arguments that writing is more social and connected than it has ever been, I have migrated from relatively low-traffic spaces in our home to the most high-traffic space we have, except for our kitchen. The Coronavirus has kicked me and my laptop around our house, and I am deeply aware that this is *nothing* compared to what others have endured as the virus continues to prey on the people of an exhausted nation. In all these spaces, the act of writing *felt* roughly the same, even as I moved from spaces of isolation to spaces marked by the passings and presence of others. But I was able to move through these spaces because my writing technology was compact enough to "fit" into all these spaces. And yes, that was and is certainly true of a writer's notebook. But my laptop is also my bookshelf, my stack of articles, my mailbox, my office, my meeting room, my classroom, and my research library. It is fair to observe that the site of composition is now the site of more human interaction—more human connections—than ever before. Human connections, of course, are not an unalloyed positive.

I now find myself realizing that we are on the verge of a significant change in how we conceptualize the types of writing that we have, to this point, called *viral*. It is clear that, for all who are at least teenage in 2021, the experience of these times will prevent us from ever using the word viral without the primary association being one of overwhelming sadness and loss. Children who learned to "shelter in place" after their playgrounds were closed will, no doubt, be less inclined to describe a benign scrap of internet fluff in terms that will reverberate with the policy failures and tragedies of the coming months.

The viral metaphor grew out of Richard Dawkins' notion of the meme, a concept Dawkins developed well before the Internet had any popular traction. Dawkins' initial construction of the meme as an "idea, behavior, or usage that spread from person to person within a culture" is embedded in Dawkins' critique of religion, with the *idea* of God being one of Dawkins' favorite examples of a meme. Dawkins' rejection of religious doctrine makes clear that the "spread" embedded in the initial definition is meant to have negative epidemiological resonances. While rejecting some of the ways internet cultures had adapted the concept of the meme, in a 2013 interview with *Wired*'s Olivia Solon, Dawkins accepted the accuracy of the virus metaphor:

How do you feel about your word meme being reappropriated by the internet?

The meaning is not that far away from the original. It's anything that goes viral. In the original introduction to the word meme in the last chapter of *The Selfish Gene*, I did actually use the metaphor of a virus. So when anybody talks about something going viral on the internet, that is exactly what a meme is and it looks as though the word has been appropriated for a subset of that. (Solon par. 8)

But in a world where the associations with the word viral are pervasively and insistently dark, even when describing scraps of culture that are often meant to deliver light, what new metaphors might we seek for—especially—those microgenres of blended texts and images meant to live on the virtual corkboards and refrigerator doors of our cloud-based spaces?

To the extent that these genres have, in the recent past, been deployed as blasts of intentional misinformation, the word viral might well seem apt. Many who watched the 2016 and 2020 United States elections have good reason to wonder about the degree to which voters were swayed by intentional deceptions couched in Facebook-ready formats. But, while *viral* might capture an aspect of the danger such efforts present to a body politic, the term has not yet accrued the focus and power of "fake news" as a means by which to challenge and ultimately dismiss suspect content.

Further, the part of *viral* that has always seemed off is the degree to which it obscures the obvious desire of composers to share ideas, however small, however fleeting, with one another. The makers of the "woman yells at a cat" meme are not trafficking in sickness. If anything, they are making intellectual snack food, the functional equivalent of popcorn. While the nutritional value of these efforts is suspect, life is sometimes better with a little butter, and a little salt. Indeed, in this context, it is somewhat disappointing that the term *cookie* already had a settled internet association before the terms *meme* and *viral* were ported to describe the memetic internet content we consume so freely.

The concepts of the memetic and viral seem so deeply intertwined that it is difficult to envision one without the other. That said, the association of the meme, the iconic representation of twenty-first-century internetworked, cloud-based writing becomes associated with the viral primarily through Dawkins' characterization of religion as a "thought virus." In the absence of the viral metaphor, the memetic could and should map more directly onto Dawkins' own baseline genetic metaphor, and this, with its internal positives and negatives, is a better place for the metaphor to reside. Genes circulate and propagate in *so many* ways. In addition to the obvious pathways of animal sexual reproduction are the rich possibilities of germination and pollination. A small fraction of the memes I have observed have, I concede, felt like viruses in their movement and in their impact. But many more have felt like genes, or like pollen, or like jackrabbits sprinting through a crowded shopping mall for no damn reason.

When a small idea catches hold of imaginations, and then many hands invest time and energy to distribute that idea, each contributing to the preservation, alteration, expansion, and survival of that idea, we *could* describe that as a(n) (e)volutionary moment. To reinforce an obvious point, metaphors matter, and if the overarching metaphoric model for the transmission of compositions via the Internet is grounded in illness, this inevitably will shape people's understandings of their interactions with one another in the internet as a media space.

We must push back against the presentation of the virus as the baseline metaphoric frame by which we describe rhetorically apt compositions that circulate quickly and expansively within internetworked spaces. This is not to suggest that every composition that succeeds in reaching a broad audience is commendable. All the people likely to read this book have lived through the consequences of corrupt and deceptive (but undeniably effective) communication via the Internet. However frustrating the day-to-day low-water marks of human expression might be, the impulse to compose in order to connect with an audience, if anchored by good will, ought not be framed as a manifestation of disease. Indeed, at many points in human history, that very impulse has been part of the cure. This is why, generation after generation we not only write about writing—how it looks and feels to us in our respective moments—it is also why, generation after generation, we write. It is why we will continue to write. Whether on pages, keyboards, tablets, touchscreens, or in clouds, or in spaces we cannot yet imagine, we will use words as a means of reaching out to one another, connecting, and, ultimately, understanding who we are.

Works Cited

Abamu, Jenny. "Google's Education Suite Is Still Free, But New Add-Ons for Administrators Come With a Fee—EdSurge News." *EdSurge*, 23 Jan. 2018, bit.ly/3HMOy6P.

Alter, Alexandra. "J. D. Salinger, E-Book Holdout, Joins the Digital Revolution." *New York Times*, 11 Aug. 2019, sec. Books, https://nyti.ms/3nLGmKb.

—. "The Plot Twist: E-Book Sales Slip, and Print Is Far From Dead." *New York Times*, 22 Sept. 2015, sec. Business, https://nyti.ms/3l3wOZq.

—. "We're Buying Paperbacks, Audiobooks and Coloring Books—but Not E-Books." *New York Times*, 26 May 2016, sec. Books, https://nyti.ms/30PP7uj.

Amazon.com. "Self Publishing | Amazon Kindle Direct Publishing," https://amzn.to/3DNSm3w.

Aristotle. *On Rhetoric: A Theory of Civic Discourse*. Translated by George A. Kennedy, Oxford UP, 2007.

Asimov, Isaac. *I, Asimov: A Memoir*. Random House, 2009.

Banks, Adam J. *Race, Rhetoric, and Technology: Searching for Higher Ground*. Routledge, 2005.

Barlow, John Perry. "The Economy of Ideas." *Wired*, 1 Mar. 1994, https://bit.ly/3DNrZe5.

Baron, Dennis. *A Better Pencil: Readers, Writers, and the Digital Revolution*. Oxford UP, 2009.

Berger, Michele Tracy, and Kathleen Guidroz, eds. *The Intersectional Approach: Transforming the Academy through Race, Class, and Gender*. U of North Carolina P, 2010.

Bernays, Anne. "Opinion | So Long to E-Books." *New York Times*, 25 Sept. 2015, sec. Opinion, https://nyti.ms/3DMY9Gp.

Berners-Lee, Tim, and Mark Fischetti. *Weaving the Web: The Original Design and Ultimative Destiny of the World Wide Web by Its Inventor*. HarperBusiness, 2011.

Birkerts, Sven. *The Gutenberg Elegies: The Fate of Reading in an Electronic Age*. Fawcett Columbine, 1995.

Blum, Andrew. *Tubes: A Journey to the Center of the Internet*. Harper Collins, 2012. Kindle.

Bolter, J. David. *Writing Space: The Computer, Hypertext, and the History of Writing*. Erlbaum, 1991.

Bolter, J. David, and Richard Grusin. *Remediation: Understanding New Media*. MIT P, 1999.

Brooke, Collin Gifford. *Lingua Fracta: Toward a Rhetoric of New Media*. Hampton P, 2009.

Bufete, Tercius. "The High Cost of Wasted Printer Ink." Consumer Reports, 17 Aug. 2018, https://bit.ly/30Tzm4U.

Dale, Brady. "Despite What You Heard, The E-Book Market Never Stopped Growing." *Observer* (blog), 18 Jan. 2017, https://bit.ly/3FIiI7D.

Diels, Hermann, and Rosamond Kent Sprague. *The Older Sophists: A Complete Translation by Several Hands of the Fragments in Die Fragmente Der Vorsokratiker, Edited by Diels–Kranz. With a New Edition of Antiphon and of Euthydemus*. Hackett, 2001.

Ede, Lisa S., and Andrea A. Lunsford. *Singular Texts/Plural Authors: Perspectives on Collaborative Writing*. SIU P, 1992.

Egan, Timothy. "Opinion | The Comeback of the Century (Published 2019)." *New York Times*, 24 May 2019, sec. Opinion, https://nyti.ms/30VPZNC.

Eisenstein, Elizabeth L. "An Unacknowledged Revolution Revisited." *The American Historical Review*, vol. 107, no. 1, 1 Feb. 2002, pp. 87–105. doi.org/10.1086/ahr/107.1.87.

—. *The Printing Press as an Agent of Change: Communications and Cultural Transformations in Early-Modern Europe*. Cambridge UP, 1980.

—. *The Printing Revolution in Early Modern Europe*. 2nd ed., Cambridge UP, 2012.

Fitzpatrick, Kathleen. *Planned Obsolescence: Publishing, Technology, and the Future of the Academy*. NYU P, 2011.

Flusser, Vilém. *Does Writing Have a Future?* U of Minnesota P, 2011.

Foucault, Michel. *Aesthetics, Method, and Epistemology: Essential Works of Foucault 1954–1984*, 2nd ed., edited by James D. Faubion, Penguin, 2019.

Freelon, Dean. "Arab Spring Twitter Data Now Available (Sort Of)." *Dean Freelon, Ph.D*, https://bit.ly/30PPHbt.

Google. "Go Google: Google Drive—YouTube." 24 Apr. 2012, https://bit.ly/3cIekcs.

Gorgias. "Encomium of Helen." Tranlated by George Kennedy in *The Rhetorical Tradition: Readings from Classical Times to the Present*, edited by Patricia Bizzell and Bruce Herzberg, Bedford/St. Martin's, 1990.

Gould, Stephen Jay. *Wonderful Life: The Burgess Shale and the Nature of History*. W. W. Norton & Company, 1990.

Grimes, Adrienne. "Women and Typewriters Are Not Inseparable." *Medium*, 23 Jan. 2019, https://bit.ly/3r1gQmp.

Gurak, Laura J. *Cyberliteracy: Navigating the Internet with Awareness*. Yale UP, 2008.

Haas, Christina. *Writing Technology: Studies on the Materiality of Literacy*. Routledge, 2013.

Hachman, Mark. "Apple's Skeuomorphic Designs: On the Way Out?" *PC-MAG*, 1 Nov. 2012, https://bit.ly/3oOJf4x.

Hafner, Katie. "U.S. Is Lagging Behind Europe In Short Messaging Services." *New York Times*, 7 Dec. 2000, sec. Technology, https://nyti.ms/3CMfJZS.

Hamid, Mohsin, and Anna Holmes. "How Do E-Books Change the Reading Experience? (Published 2013)." *New York Times*, 31 Dec. 2013, sec. Books, https://nyti.ms/3nMNMwR.

Hayles, N. Katherine. *How We Became Posthuman: Virtual Bodies in Cybernetics, Literature, and Informatics*. ACLS Humanities E-Book. U of Chicago P, 1999.

Hess, Amanda. "The 'Credibility Bookcase' Is the Quarantine's Hottest Accessory." *New York Times*, 1 May 2020, sec. Arts, https://nyti.ms/3r4nyYB.

Hoffelder, Nate. "Kindle Update v5.7.2 Adds Open Dyslexic Font, New Home Page (Screenshots)." *The Digital Reader* (blog), 2 Feb. 2016, the-digital- https://bit.ly/3l3AbzB.

Hu, Tung-Hui. *A Prehistory of the Cloud*. MIT Press, 2015.

Johnson-Eilola, Johndan. *Datacloud: Toward a New Theory of Online Work*. Hampton P, 2005.

Kember, Janis Jefferies and Sarah. *Whose Book Is It Anyway? A View From Elsewhere on Publishing, Copyright and Creativity*. Open Book Publishers, 2019, doi.org/10.11647/OBP.0159.

Kennedy, Krista. *Textual Curation: Authorship, Agency, and Technology in Wikipedia and Chambers's Cyclopædia*. U of South Carolina P, 2016. Kindle.

Kirschenbaum, Matthew G. *Track Changes: A Literary History of Word Processing*, The Belknap Press of Harvard UP, 2015.

Kostic, Zona, Nathan Weeks, Johann Philipp Dreessen, Jelena Dowey, and Jeff Baglioni. "BookVIS: Enhancing Browsing Experiences in Bookstores and Libraries." *SIGGRAPH Asia 2019 Posters*, pp. 1–2. Brisbane QLD Australia: ACM, 2019, doi.org/10.1145/3355056.3364594.

Lanham, Richard A. *The Economics of Attention: Style and Substance in the Age of Information*. U of Chicago P, 2006.

Lauer, Janice M. *Invention in Rhetoric and Composition*. Parlor P, 2004.

LeFevre, Karen Burke. *Invention as a Social Act*. SIU Press, 1987.

Levy, David M. *Scrolling Forward: Making Sense of Documents in the Digital Age*. Simon and Schuster, 2012.

Lunsford, Andrea A., and Lisa Ede. *Singular Texts/Plural Authors: Perspectives on Collaborative Writing*. SIU P, 1992.

Lyons, Kate, and agencies. "Notre Dame Fire: Macron Promises to Rebuild Cathedral within Five Years." *The Guardian*, 17 Apr. 2019, sec. World News, https://bit.ly/3xiuAdw.

Mahler, Jonathan. "The Invisible Hand Behind Harper Lee's 'To Kill a Mockingbird' (Published 2015)." *New York Times*, 12 July 2015, sec. Books, https://nyti.ms/30Vy3uJ.

Mailloux, Steven. *Reception Histories: Rhetoric, Pragmatism, and American Cultural Politics.* Cornell UP, 1998.

Mangen, Anne, Gérard Olivier, and Jean-Luc Velay. "Comparing Comprehension of a Long Text Read in Print Book and on Kindle: Where in the Text and When in the Story?" *Frontiers in Psychology*, vol. 10, 2019, doi.org/10.3389/fpsyg.2019.00038.

—. "Comparing Comprehension of a Long Text Read in Print Book and on Kindle: Where in the Text and When in the Story?" *Frontiers in Psychology*, vol. 10, 2019, doi.org/10.3389/fpsyg.2019.00038.

Markoff, John. "Why Can't We Compute in the Cloud?" *Bits Blog* (blog), 24 Aug. 2007, https://nyti.ms/3xhKNzC.

—. "Why Can't We Compute in the Cloud? Part 2." *Bits Blog* (blog), 24 Aug. 2007, https://nyti.ms/3cIpoGw.

Mason, Andrew. "Beat Doctor: Tom Moulton and His Extended Disco Remix Forever Changed Dance Music." *Wax Poetics* (blog), 28 June 2013, https://bit.ly/3HM1BUd.

Maynard, Joyce. "Was She J. D. Salinger's Predator or His Prey?" *New York Times*, 5 Sept. 2018, sec. Books, https://nyti.ms/3cJVi5e.

McCorkle, Ben. *Rhetorical Delivery as Technological Discourse: A Cross-Historical Study.* SIU Press, 2012.

McLuhan, Marshall, and Quentin Fiore. *The Medium Is the Massage: An Inventory of Effects.* Gingko Press, 2001.

Mod, Craig. "Books in the Age of the IPad." Mar. 2010 https://bit.ly/32hSxpN. https://bit.ly/3xqnQKM.

—. "Post Artifact Books and Publishing." Journal. *@craigmod*, June 2011. .

Moore, Christopher. "Signed First Editions of Sacre Bleu." https://bit.ly/30S5O82.

Ngak, Chenda. "CERN Reactivates First Web Page for 20th Anniversary." CBS News, 30 Apr. 2013, https://cbsn.ws/3nJjriM.

Norman, Don. *The Design of Everyday Things: Revised and Expanded Edition.* Basic Books, 2013.

Perrin, Andrew. "One-in-Five Americans Now Listen to Audiobooks." Pew Research Center, 25 Sept. 2019, https://pewrsr.ch/3HNsyXI.

—. "Slightly Fewer Americans Are Reading Print Books, New Survey Finds." Pew Research Center, 19 Oct. 2015, https://pewrsr.ch/3HRoUsC.

Phillipp, and shevyrolet. "Woman Yelling at a Cat." *Know Your Meme*, https://bit.ly/30SMyQ8. Accessed 2 Dec. 2020.

Phillips, Whitney, and Ryan M. Milner. *The Ambivalent Internet: Mischief, Oddity, and Antagonism Online*. John Wiley & Sons, 2018.

Porter, Eduardo. "A Rural-Urban Broadband Divide, but Not the One You Think Of." *New York Times*, 1 June 2021, sec. Business, https://nyti.ms/3l6cF50.

Porter, James E. *Rhetorical Ethics and Internetworked Writing*. Greenwood Publishing Group, 1998.

Quandahl, Ellen. "Aristotle's Rhetoric: Reinterpreting Invention." *Rhetoric Review*, vol. 4, no. 2, 1986, pp. 128–37.

Quintilian. *Institutio Oratoria*. Translated by H. E. Butler, Harvard UP, Later Printed ed., 1980.

Rawnsley, Richard. "Motivations for the Development of Writing Technology." *On the Blunt Edge: Technology in Composition's History and Pedagogy*, pp. 30–51, Parlor P, 2012.

"Rhetorica Ad Herennium—Cicero." *Cicero*, vol. 1. Translated by Harry Caplan, Loeb, 1954.

Sauerberg, Lars Ole. "The Gutenberg Parenthesis—Print, Book and Cognition." *Orbis Litterarum*, vol. 64, no. 2, 2009, pp. 79–80, doi.org/10.1111/j.1600-0730.2009.00962.x.

Schugar, Jordan T, Heather Schugar, and Christian Penny. "A Nook or a Book? Comparing College Students' Reading Comprehension Levels, Critical Reading, and Study Skills." *International Journal of Technology in Teaching and Learning*, vol. 7, no. 2, p. 19, 2011. https://bit.ly/3nLT8IP.

Shea, Andrea. "Jack Kerouac's Famous Scroll, 'On the Road' Again." *NPR.org*, 5 July 2007, https://n.pr/3xk3lix.

Sheff, David. "Crank It Up." *Wired*, 1 Aug. 2000, https://bit.ly/3DN7K09.

Shifman, Limor. *Memes in Digital Culture*. MIT Press, 2014. Kindle.

Singerman, Howard. "Art Journal at Fifty." *Art Journal Open* (blog), 1 Feb. 2011, https://bit.ly/3kZeNLN.

Sohn, Ira. "Opinion | A Digital Unbeliever." *New York Times*, 23 Nov. 2017, sec. Opinion, https://nyti.ms/30X0259.

Solon, Olivia. "Richard Dawkins on the Internet's Hijacking of the Word 'Meme.'" *Wired UK*, 20 June 2013, https://bit.ly/30WJfiO.

Stone, Brad. "Amazon Erases Orwell Books From Kindle." *New York Times*, 17 July 2009, sec. Technology, https://nyti.ms/3HNrdQG.

Tannock, Stuart. "Nostalgia Critique." *Cultural Studies*, vol. 9, no. 3, 1 Oct. 1995, pp. 453–64, doi.org/10.1080/09502389500490511.

Thudt, Alice, Uta Hinrichs, and Sheelagh Carpendale. "The Bohemian Bookshelf: Supporting Serendipitous Book Discoveries through Information Visualization." *Proceedings of the 2012 ACM Annual Conference on Hu-*

man *Factors in Computing Systems—CHI '12*, 1461. Austin, Texas, USA: ACM Press, 2012, doi.org/10.1145/2207676.2208607.

Tuckel, Peter, and Harry O'Neill. "Ownership and Usage Patterns of Cell Phones: 2000 –2005," n.d.

Venkat, Girish. "Loudcloud: Early Light on Cloud Computing." *CNET*, 23 Mar. 2009, https://cnet.co/3xjwWsD.

Verhovek, Sam Howe. "Business; The Future, Through Microsoft's Glasses." *New York Times*, 25 June 2000, sec. Business, https://nyti. ms/3xpeyhZ.

Woolf, Virginia, *A Room of One's Own*, edited by Susan Gubar. Harcourt, 2005.

Writing Studies, College of Liberal Arts. "Writing Studies Department." University of Minnesota, https://bit.ly/3xkvcQo. Accessed 14 Dec. 2020.

Yale Center for Dyslexia & Creativity. "Dyslexia FAQ." Yale University. 2017. https://bit.ly/3nNfuJI. Accessed November 24, 2021.

Zax, David. "Steve Jobs, Storyteller." *MIT Technology Review,* https://bit. ly/3DNtEjP.

Zee. "Steve Jobs: The IPad Concept Came BEFORE the IPhone." *TheNextWeb*, 1 June 2010, https://bit.ly/3HLTcjD.

Index

About the Composer

John Logie is Associate Professor of Rhetoric and Director of Graduate Studies for the Rhetoric and Scientific & Technical Communication Programs for the Department of Writing Studies at the University of Minnesota-Twin Cities. His 2006 book *Peers, Pirates, and Persuasion: Rhetoric in the Peer-to-Peer Debates* addressed questions of information policy and persuasion. His scholarship has also been published in *Rhetoric Society Quarterly*, *Rhetoric Review*, *College English*, *First Monday*, *Computers and Composition*, and a number of edited volumes. These articles reflect his sustaining interest in internet studies, rhetorical invention, visual rhetoric, and challenges to the body of laws known collectively as "intellectual property."

Photograph of the composer by Lisa Miller.
Used by permission.